growing up with addiction

Also by Tian Dayton

*Emotional Sobriety: From Relationship
Trauma to Resilience and Balance*

*Trauma and Addiction: Ending the Cycle
of Pain Through Emotional Literacy*

*The ACOA Trauma Syndrome: The Impact of
Childhood Pain on Adult Relationships*

*Treating Adult Children of Relational Trauma:
85 Experiential Interventions to Heal the Inner Child
and Create Authentic Connection in the Present*

*Sociometrics: Embodied, Experiential
Processes for Relational Trauma Repair*

*The Living Stage: A Step-by-Step Guide to Psychodrama,
Sociometry and Experiential Group Therapy*

*Heartwounds: The Impact of Unresolved
Trauma and Grief on Relationships*

*Daily Affirmations for Forgiving and Moving On: Powerful
Inspiration for Personal Change and Moving On*

*Daily Affirmations for Parents: How to Nurture
Your Children and Renew Yourself*

*One Foot in Front of the Other: Daily
Affirmations for Survivors of Addiction,
Abuse, and Other Stressful Situations*

Praise for *Growing Up with Addiction*

"In *Growing Up with Addiction*, Dr. Tian Dayton compassionately gives voice to the wounded child parts and burdens carried by adult children of addiction. This book offers not just insight but deep empathy—illuminating how internal systems impacted by addiction can find pathways toward integration, resilience, and wholeness. A deeply needed contribution to both clinical and personal transformation."

RICHARD C. SCHWARTZ, PhD
founder of Internal Family Systems, author of *No Bad Parts*

"In *Growing Up with Addiction*, Tian Dayton offers a compassionate and insightful exploration of the intergenerational impact of relational trauma. By interweaving personal narrative, clinical wisdom, and embodied therapeutic practices, she creates a compelling bridge between lived experience and emerging neurobiology. Her willingness to share her own history adds rare authenticity, keeping the reader engaged on a deeply personal level. Just as importantly, her decades of clinical practice bring depth, clarity, and grounded insight to complex emotional and relational dynamics. This book serves as both an accessible introduction and a valuable resource for anyone seeking to understand—and heal—the legacy of trauma in families."

STEPHEN PORGES, PhD
creator of Polyvagal Theory, author of
The Polyvagal Theory and *Safe and Sound*

"Dr. Dayton has written the book I wish I'd had when I first began to understand how deeply childhood experiences shape us. What sets this book apart is its embodied approach; it doesn't just explain why ACAs struggle, it shows them how to rewire their nervous systems through experiential practices. As someone who trains practitioners worldwide in addressing the impact of relational trauma on our biology, I can say this is required reading for understanding the full picture of recovery, repair and reclaiming our true selves."

AIMIE APIGIAN, MD
addiction medicine physician, author of *The Biology of Trauma*

"Tian Dayton's integration of Somatic Experiencing (SE) into Relational Trauma Repair® (RTR) and psychodrama offers a powerful pathway for Adult Children of Alcoholics (ACAs) and those with complex PTSD to transform pain into embodied healing and relational repair. By blending SE's body-based trauma resolution with RTR's structured emotional processing, the body finally gets to 'speak' the unspeakable—completing the story not just in words but through movement, sensation, and presence, restoring coherence between the mind, emotions, and body. The nervous system can find safety by completing decades of unresolved survival responses, offering a tangible path to healing for those whose trauma lives not just in memory but in the body itself."

PETER LEVINE, PhD
developer of Somatic Experiencing®, author of *Waking the Tiger*

"*Growing Up with Addiction* is a validating and empowering book that offers a pathway to healing intergenerational trauma. Tian's understanding of trauma and attachment wounds, and their impact on both the individual and the family system, is only surpassed by the multitude of tools she offers the reader. This book brings the knowledge of adult children and recovery to new heights. Thank you, Tian, for continuing to be a champion for those whose lives have been affected by living in a family impacted by addictions."

CLAUDIA BLACK, PhD
PhD, author of *It Will Never Happen to Me* and *Unspoken Legacy*

"Tian Dayton's new book is absolutely one of the best. Her writing and clinical work has helped so many families; her work teaches and touches."

ROBERT J ACKERMAN, PhD
founding board member of the National Association for the Children of Alcoholics and Addiction, author of *Perfect Daughters* and *Silent Sons*

"Tian Dayton is a trusted clinician and author. To change the life of a person toward greater knowledge, meaning and joy is a gift. Tian's perspective—from her life and her ability to capture wisdom through her words—takes the reader on a journey to discovery and healing."

SHARON WEGSCHEIDER-CRUSE
founder of Onsite Workshops, author of
Another Chance and *Choicemaking*

"Dr. Tian Dayton brings a rare blend of clinical depth, lived experience, and transformative storytelling to every page of this groundbreaking book. Dr. Dayton's insights are grounded in decades of clinical practice and research, and she communicates with clarity, compassion, and practical wisdom that practitioners and readers alike can apply in real life.

"I wholeheartedly recommend this book as an essential resource for anyone dedicated to understanding and healing the impacts of trauma and addiction."

FRANCES BLACK
senator and founder of the RISE Foundation, Ireland

"Dr. Tian Dayton picked up where Janet Woititz left off in her seminal book *Adult Children of Alcoholics* that literally began the ACoA movement. Dr. Dayton makes the connection for the reader between the ACoA syndrome and post-traumatic stress disorder (PTSD) often experienced by children who grew up in addicted families long after they have left their families of origin. She answered their haunting question: 'Why am I feeling the pain from my childhood now, as an adult, when I am no longer even living at home?' Those of us who understand recovery know that no one needs to accept and live out this legacy. Take this journey with Dr. Dayton—it will change your life."

GARY SEIDLER
co-founder of Health Communications, Inc., publisher of
Adult Children of Alcoholics and *Chicken Soup for the Soul*

growing up with addiction

How Adult Children of Addicts
Can Heal Family Trauma, C-PTSD,
and Codependency

Tian Dayton, PhD

ST. MARTIN'S
ESSENTIALS
NEW YORK

Published by St. Martin's Essentials,
an imprint of St. Martin's Publishing Group

www.stmartins.com

© 2026 Tian Dayton

All rights reserved. No part of this book may be used or reproduced in any manner without written permission from the author(s) and publisher.

No AI Training: Without in any way limiting the author's and publisher's exclusive rights under copyright, any use of this publication to "train" generative artificial intelligence (AI) technologies to generate text is expressly prohibited. The author reserves all rights to license uses of this work for generative AI training and development of machine learning language models.

This book is not intended as a substitute for the medical recommendations of physicians, mental health professionals, or other health-care providers. Rather, it is intended to offer information to help the reader cooperate with physicians, mental health professionals, and health-care providers in a mutual quest for optimal well-being. We advise readers to carefully review and understand the ideas presented and to seek the advice of a qualified professional before attempting to use them.

All case studies offered in this book are composites. No story reflects any specific individual. Similarities to any real person are coincidental and unintentional.

Published 2026

Cover and jacket by Rachael Murray

Book design by Charli Barnes

Printed in the United States of America

BK07393

Cataloging-in-Publication data for this book is available from the Library of Congress.

ISBN: 978-1-64963-424-5

Ebook ISBN: 978-1-64963-425-2

To
My husband, Brandt,

and our children and grandchildren,

Marina and Jasper,
Friso and Isabelle,

Alex and Chondi,
Asha and Lila,

for all the reasons they already know.

Contents

Introduction	1
1 Understanding Your Past, Reclaiming Your Present: The Cost of Addiction and Relational Trauma to the Family System	21
2 What the Body Remembers: Why We Can't Think Ourselves Better	45
3 Attachment Patterns: Our Blueprint for Connection	64
4 Survival Roles: The Masks We Wear to Feel Safe and Connected	91
5 Guessing at Normal: Cognitive and Somatic Distortions and Biases	112
6 Triggers as Teachable Moments: A Window into Your Unconscious	142
7 Process Addictions: Why Can't I Stop Doing This?	162
8 The Healing Power of Grief: Giving Your Inner Child a Voice	184
9 A Sanctuary for Self: Building Boundaries That Honor Connection	202

10 Spiritual Transformation and Post-Traumatic Growth	225
Conclusion	248
Acknowledgments: Where It All Began	252
Notes	255
Index	263
About the Author	269

Introduction

Long before there was a name for being an adult child of an alcoholic or addict (ACA), I could feel something living inside me that I couldn't quite name. In my family, we called it "Dad's alcoholism," but it was more than that. It wasn't just that his drinking and abusive behavior had slowly changed *him*, which of course, it had; it was that his drinking had also slowly changed *us*.

As I grew up, I felt haunted by images and episodes, some that I could recall with crystal clarity and others that were indistinct and obscured. I somehow knew they belonged to my past, my family, but that didn't mean I didn't feel them intruding on my present. When these ghosts from our past got activated in one of my family members, they seemed to get activated in all of us. These ghosts knew one another. But they were ungovernable. It seemed they knew us, but we didn't really know them.

Our shared history could erupt over the most seemingly innocuous look or comment, but because none of us knew what was happening, otherwise pleasant, fun, or intimate moments could devolve in seconds. Suddenly, there might be silence, explosive anger, or manipulation as we vied for control over whose version of the truth was the real one. We couldn't examine it together because the pain we carried so quickly turned into blame and finger-pointing, hurt after hurt being rehashed as though they all happened five minutes ago, each of us guarding our particular interpretation of our mutual history as if our sanity depended upon it. But the truth is, none of us really knew for sure. It was as if the past and present were on some sort of psychic loop in all our heads. We were equally invested in bringing these ghosts to light and leaving them alone.

The problem was, they wouldn't leave us alone. This is the legacy of growing up with addiction. As children of addiction and relational trauma, we carry that legacy in our bodies and our hearts if it remains unconscious, but it doesn't stay there. It becomes the fuel pump that drives dysfunction throughout life. Today, I understand this blend of physiological, emotional, and behavioral dysregulation as part of a complex post-traumatic stress reaction. So often, as ACAs, we overfocus on one trauma to pin a lifetime of big and small hurts on. We look for *the* causative event or dramatic rupture, and in that searching, we miss the pattern of pervasive injuries resulting from the slow erosion of safety, trust, and connection. Unpacking these patterns is what this book is about.

My father was an alcoholic, and I was the child closest to him. I loved him, and most of the time, I knew how to reach him. "You're just so good with him, Tiannie. Go and see what you can do" was the general request—at first just from my mother, then eventually from everyone. So by the time I was five or so, I was the child sent in to talk my father out of leaving the house in a drunken rage, to get him to come to dinner, or to calm him down after he'd thrown a fit at the hotel front desk because he didn't like our accommodations. I'd be on the sidelines in the lobby, protected in public, but once we were all settled in our newly assigned resplendent rooms, I would do my part again to soothe Dad's mood. I had no understanding that the scotch in his hand was the real mood soother. I thought it was all me. I thought I was just "so good at my job." And when the alcohol wasn't available, I wasn't so good at it, and I worried.

At first, I was directly sent in to do this job. But eventually, I didn't need to be asked; I just knew. This assumed responsibility stayed with me throughout my life, forever tethering me to my father in ways that felt both like deep love and devotion and an unfair burden. I was the twenty-three-year-old child who stayed with him through eleven gruesome days in the ICU, as one by one his organs gave way—his lungs from smoking, his liver from drinking, his throat from esophageal cancer. I was the child who was there when he finally passed. The one who closed his eyes. The one who spoke to the doctors, picked out the casket, and said goodbye to the precious man I loved so much, a man who had killed himself by inches. And no one else seemed to think that was odd, because by then it was just my job. *He* was just my job.

All throughout those sleepless days and nights, a nursery rhyme kept looping in my head:

> Humpty Dumpty sat on a wall,
> Humpty Dumpty had a great fall.
> All the king's horses and all the king's men
> Couldn't put Humpty together again.

In some barely conscious way, I felt I had failed in my most important job: helping my father get sober.

Your story may be different, or it may be stunningly similar. It might not involve an addicted parent at all, but it very well might involve addiction in a grandparent or other family member. Maybe you grew up with a parent who suffered from mental illness or a traumatic injury. Perhaps they were emotionally unpredictable or dealing with a serious mental health issue or process addiction (like overeating, overspending, gambling, or sexual addiction) that changed your family functioning. Any of these scenarios can lead to complex post-traumatic stress disorder (cPTSD) and codependency, which is ultimately what I faced in the aftermath of my father's addiction and death. If you can relate to growing up in a family that seesawed between emotional extremes, like intense closeness alternating with feelings of emotional alienation, you'll likely recognize yourself in these pages. Because at its heart, these chapters are each about the lasting impact of childhood relational trauma, and the confusion and dysregulation it leaves behind.

I've written this book after fifty years of marriage to an adult child of an addict and forty years of working in the field of addictions. Over that time, I've come to understand—both personally and professionally—what it means to have grown up around my father's alcohol, smoking, and sexual addictions and the deep damage they inflicted on our family. I've also spent decades witnessing how addiction and dysfunction have shaped the lives of my clients and what it takes to truly break free from that legacy. Today, we have the gift of greater awareness, better research, and a rising emotional literacy that my generation was only beginning to glimpse. With more openness, language, and support available, healing can now be more direct and more compassionate. I wrote *Growing Up with Addiction* to help make your journey out of that legacy a little smoother.

cPTSD and ACAs

The most confusing part of cPTSD is the "post-" part. It suggests something is over, finished. But the truth is, the pain we experienced way back when doesn't just stay in the past. When pain isn't fully processed, it doesn't go away; it goes dormant. The impact doesn't end with time; it ripples forward, showing up in how we behave in our relationships and even the way we see ourselves. We carry it, often without knowing it, and it can erupt when we least expect it.

As adults, we may assume that just because we can tell the story of what happened, we must be healed. But trauma isn't stored like a narrative. It doesn't live in the parts of the brain that organize logic, language, and time. Instead, it gets embedded in the body—in fragments of sensation, emotion, and implicit memory, the kind of unconscious memory that is stuck in our body and nervous system, that lives beneath words and thought, shaping how we feel and react without us even realizing it.

That's why trauma shows up less in what we *remember* and more in how we *react*. It lives on as emotional and physiological dysregulation—in hypervigilance, in overreactions that feel too big or out of proportion to the situation at hand, or in underreactions that seem numb or oddly muted. Our responses don't always match the moment, but they make perfect sense to the body that still carries the residue of past hurt or harm. It shows up in how we withdraw, explode, dissociate, or go numb in situations that somehow activate our emotions that belong to the past, but are bleeding into the present.

And this is precisely the key: When these activations and overreactions take over, we leave the present because the unconscious knows no time. We're reliving a story from long ago and, without realizing it, importing and projecting our old pain onto new people and new relationships. We're responding to what *was* as if it still *is*, often accusing those in front of us of causing our activated emotions. This is how our present becomes hostage to our past without our understanding that that's what's happening. It is a post-traumatic stress reaction.

We find ourselves reenacting and recreating the past—not because we choose to, but because our nervous systems are wired to expect it. We carry forward the emotional rules and relational patterns we grew up with. We reenact what we never wanted to experience in the first place and swore we'd never repeat.

We often go searching for a single defining trauma, one event that can neatly explain our pain. But complex trauma doesn't usually work that way. It's not about one moment; it's about the accumulation of many. It's the repeated ruptures that were never repaired, the chronic stress that was never comforted, the connection that was unreliable, disorganized, or missing altogether. It's about what happened, yes, but also about what *didn't* happen. Over time, these unmet needs and unresolved wounds quietly erode our sense of safety, trust, and attunement. And that's what can make it hard to relax and feel safe in close, intimate relationships later on.

Healing begins by recognizing the patterns, not just in our thoughts, but in our bodies, our emotions, and our relationships. It starts with noticing how we adapted to what hurt us, and having the courage to unpack the confusion and pain underneath it, and creating space for something new.

But this isn't the whole story. You also have an equally—if not more—important story of resilience and thriving in spite of the odds! As an ACA, you adapted in ways that defy easy description. In households where clarity and consistency were often absent, you became fluent in ambiguity. You learned to track mood shifts that were never named and to attune to what was unsaid as much as to what was spoken out loud. You learned to trust (as well to doubt) your instincts.

You developed a capacity for empathy, not because it was consistently modeled, but because you needed it to make sense of your world. You cultivated creativity in the face of unpredictability, problem-solving in the absence of guidance, and a kind of relational artistry that allowed you to hold space for others even when you were aching yourself. You learned to find a higher level of congruency in chaos. These are not just compensations; they are capacities. Hard-won, deeply embodied, and very valuable.

What's remarkable is not only that you endured but that you loved. That you continued to seek connection, even when trust had been fractured. That you developed an internal set of ethics and kept trying to do the right thing. This speaks not to pathology but to an innate resilience shaped by the very conditions that threatened to extinguish it.

What others might call hypervigilance was, for you, a necessary refinement of perception—an early, involuntary education in human behavior. This sensitivity, born in survival, became a kind of emotional radar, a way of scanning for danger and deciphering subtext. But, like many adaptations forged in pain, this gift cuts both ways. The same sensitivity that allows you to intuit nuance when left unchecked, can cut both ways. It can make you wary or cause you to misread what's in front of you. It can lead you into reenactments, mistaking the present for the past, responding to what should be behind you but just isn't. This is where your strength risks becoming a liability.

To carry this sensitivity forward with clarity rather than with hypervigilance and distortion, you're asked to do something brave: to turn inward, to separate projection from perception, and to name what belongs to the past so that it doesn't keep shaping your present and your future. You need to learn how to work through rather than reenact frozen pain; how to face the dark clouds you carry—not through any fault of your own, but because of the way the brain and body hold onto (or, more truthfully, never fully process and release) the weight of traumatizing moments.

Because once you can do this, you become a kind of spiritual warrior. Then your very sensitivity becomes one of your greatest assets: a source of discernment, emotional depth, and truth. You are not defined by your wounds, but by your astonishing ability to grow through them and, in many cases, to offer something redemptive to the world because of them.

Making Stuff Up: Seeing Through the Eyes of Our Wounded Inner Child

Growing up around addiction often meant living in a double reality. Even as a child, you knew something was off. You sensed the undercurrents, the tension, the emotional incoherence. And yet the messages you received told you not to trust what you sensed. You were asked—directly or indirectly—to deny what you saw, mute what you felt, and carry on as if everything were fine. Often, these distortions were reinforced not just by the addicted parent but equally or sometimes more by the other adults in the home—well-meaning, perhaps, but invested in preserving a fragile sense of normalcy.

When our reality was denied as children—those many times we were left to make sense of our family's dysfunction alone because the adults around us were too busy, too stressed, too overwhelmed to explain—we made stuff up. We filled in the gaps with whatever our child mind could come up with. When we didn't understand why our parent was distant or unpredictable, we often assumed the problem was us. Many of us may have thought we were too much or not enough—too needy, too loud, too quiet, too invisible, too incompetent. Others of us may have developed a premature sense of power, believing we were the ones who could hold the family together or fix what was wrong. We idealized our ability to manage crisis and promote closeness. But beneath that, as with any idealization, were the fear and anxiety that we were in way above our heads or that the adults we depended upon might be falling apart.

And these interpretations, these distortions, these shaky identities, wormed their way into how we conduct ourselves and our relationships now. They formed the scaffolding for how we interpret love, conflict, self-worth, and safety well into adulthood and how we eventually operate in the families we create as grown-ups.

This is why learning to recognize and deconstruct those distortions in our perception is so important. We need to trace the emotional logic that made perfect sense in the midst of chaos and rewrite the script we've been living by. We need to look at our child self's coping strategies with compassion, get curious about how we adapted, and recognize how, over time, those very adaptations may have become the things that keep us stuck today. In an effort to untangle ourselves from the trauma of our childhoods and understand the many layers of our development that were impacted by growing up with addiction and dysfunction, we need to examine our attachment patterns—how they shape the way we partner, parent, work, and form friendships.

We need to understand why our cognitive distortions have such a powerful grip on how we partner and parent. We need to look at how we may be seeing our relationship struggles today through the eyes of our wounded inner child—so we can begin to grow that child up and learn to see with more adult eyes.

When we had to grow up too soon, we left parts of ourselves behind, stuck in childlike interpretations of a grown-up world. And now those parts show up in the present, confused and overwhelmed. We need to find those hurt little people inside of us, take them by the hand, and begin the deliberate and caring work of reparenting them and hence ourselves—bringing them into the present with the safety, understanding, and love they needed and deserved back then.

A Quick Note to Grandchildren of Addicts (GCoAs)

When unhealed trauma stays hidden, it often gets reenacted, leaving the next generation tangled in the very wounds their parent was trying to outrun. So if you're the child of someone who grew up with addiction, you may have been raised by a parent who didn't fully heal from their own childhood pain and emotional dysregulation, or didn't acknowledge or understand what they carried inside. Their defenses—like control, emotional distance, manipulation, or conflict avoidance—became the atmosphere of your home. Or their disowned rage was directed at you. And without context, without knowing their whole story, you may have blamed yourself for the disconnection.

Your parent may have overprotected you because they themselves felt unprotected. Instead of giving you what you truly needed, they may have offered what they longed for as a child. In trying to recreate the childhood they never had, they may have missed who you actually were. Because they were reaching to satisfy their own unresolved longings through you, the boundaries between your needs and theirs may have blurred. Your parent may have longed for closeness they never had or carried fear and anxiety they couldn't or wouldn't name. They may have made you feel like the needy or anxious one because they denied the neediness and anxiety of their own inner child. These emotions, if left unprocessed, could have easily spilled over onto you, reshaping natural parental emotions into something toxic. What looked like love could have become enmeshment. What looked like care could have become control.

Without your parent even realizing it, your normal childhood needs may have stirred something unhealed in them, leading them to feel threatened by what your presence stirred up from their past. Inherited trauma often hides not just in actions, but in nervous systems, in facial expressions, in chronic tension, in the space between words. As a child you may have felt that, wondered if you were causing it, or tried to make your ACA parent feel better.

So if you grew up feeling confused about your role in the household, whether you were overly responsible for your parent's emotions or unsure whether your needs were too much, please know this: You're not imagining things, nor are you the only one who has had this experience. It *didn't* start with you, but with awareness, it *can* end with you. Naming these patterns is the first step in breaking the cycle. By understanding the ACA parent who raised you, you can better understand yourself and cease shadowboxing with ghosts from your parent's past.

Stuck in the Story: Why You Can't Just Think Yourself Better

Growing up with addiction is like being raised in a petri dish for growing trauma symptom number one: a dysregulated nervous system. It's a fertile breeding ground for dysfunctional dynamics to take root and spread. As ACAs, when our nervous system gets activated or triggered by something in the present that activates unresolved wounds from our past, we can go from zero to ten and back again—from high intensity to complete shutdown, with no speed bumps in between. We blow right past the middle ground, as if it doesn't even exist. Our nervous system dysregulation becomes emotional and behavioral dysregulation. When this dysregulation gets activated, without even realizing it, we may try to control the world around us, imagining that if we can just get everyone and everything else to be as we need them to be, we'll settle down inside and feel okay.

Dr. Stephen Porges, the creator of polyvagal theory, offers a powerful framework for understanding why connection can sometimes provoke anxiety, especially for those who experienced relational trauma in childhood, when they were most vulnerable. He also shows us how we can begin to regulate our nervous system, relax, and feel more like ourselves in relationship.

Dr. Porges coined the term *neuroception* to describe the nervous system's silent surveillance circuitry that constantly scans our environment for signs of safety or threat, without us even realizing it. Our bodies are always quietly checking: *Am I safe? Can I relax? Or do I need to protect myself?* It's automatic, deeply wired, and often informed by our earliest experiences. For ACAs and others with early attachment wounds, this system was shaped by relationships that felt both nourishing and unpredictable—sometimes safe, sometimes not. That early wiring doesn't disappear; we carry it with us into adult relationships. So when our nervous system gets activated because it feels like it's detecting a threat, whether the threat is real or imagined, it instantly shifts into a self-protective mode, and we brace for conflict even if none is occurring.

A partner's silence, a friend's irritation, or a moment of emotional distance can trigger the unconscious pain of past rejection or abandonment. But we don't always recognize that connection. It feels like the threat of rejection is live, like a shock in the system, but really it's an old, scary, childhood ghost haunting us from within. In this way, our current relationships become the stage where old wounds get reenacted, until we begin to notice and bring these patterns into awareness.

Trauma can leave us stuck in these self-protective states—reactions that once kept us safe but now make intimacy feel risky. That's why recovery isn't just about gaining new insight; it has to include the body. Healing begins with learning to distinguish real danger from old, outdated alarms. It means tuning into our nervous system, tracing our automatic reactions, and gently questioning the distorted beliefs and fear states our wounds left behind.

It also means working with what Porges calls the "social engagement system," the part of the nervous system that allows us to feel safe enough to connect, to coregulate, and to fully participate in relationships that are mutual, meaningful, and alive.

Part of this healing involves developing mindfulness practices that train the nervous system to tolerate emotional middle ground, the space between extremes that once felt unfamiliar or even intolerable in our chaotic childhood. We felt safer shutting down or shifting into a fight, flight, freeze, or fawn state. Another part of our healing has to do with the deeper work of resolving attachment wounds and unlearning the habit of carrying our childhood pain into our current relationships. When we're able to self-regulate, stay out of inner reactivity, and help our bodies feel safe, everything shifts. We become more open, more grounded, and more able to connect—with ourself and with others. We can own, rather than project, our cognitive distortions and attachment wounds. We no longer have to shut down or control ourselves and others to feel safe. Instead, we can learn to move *through* our activated inner states. We can hold our past with gentle, honest awareness while choosing new ways of being. Then slowly, what once felt out of reach—true connection—begins to feel possible, starting with the relationship we rebuild with ourselves.

This doesn't mean we have to override our inner surveillance system; we still need it to accurately assess safety. We just become able to separate our past from our present so we can more accurately read what is going on and avoid getting stuck in old wounds.

My Work in Psychodrama and Relational Trauma Repair (RTR)

Early in my career, I attended a workshop with family therapist Sharon Wegscheider-Cruse that introduced me to both psychodrama and recovery. It changed my life and reshaped the direction of my work. Through her teaching, I not only began my own recovery journey but received training in family sculpting as developed by Virginia Satir, an approach I used for several years in my work. As Sharon brought this work into the addictions field, practitioners recognized that psychodrama had a deeply healing effect for addicts and family members. This was before trauma theory had been introduced into the mental health field. But intuitively those of us in the addiction field understood psychodrama's remarkable power to heal what ailed us.

Through embodied sculpturing we all experienced the profound relief of being able to clearly see the systems we'd grown up in so we could talk to, rather than about, those in our past who'd left us with words unspoken and feelings unfelt. Sharon created healing retreats using sculpturing and psychodrama that were filled with tears, joy, reconnection with self and community, and ignited new direction. However, in translating sculpturing into the program development I was doing for long-term treatment, I realized I needed to expand my skill set and create processes that were more open-ended and varied so that healing could be titrated over time.

When I encountered psychiatrist J. L. Moreno's full triadic system of psychodrama, sociometry, and group psychotherapy at a conference in New York City, with its elegant use of techniques like doubling and role reversal, I felt I had found the missing keys. That moment was a revelation. The structure was brilliant, the execution was seamless, and the theoretical grounding was both coherent and comprehensive. It seemed to fill in everything that had been missing in experiential therapy. The depth of the method and the techniques it offered were nothing short of stunning, and integrating them within the powerful healing community of addiction treatment and twelve-step programs created a healing synergy that supported my own clinical work. Zerka, Moreno's wife, co-created what we know today as psychodrama. It was at this juncture that she became an inspiration, my mentor, and friend.

These techniques allowed me to slow the process down, and include small, focused role-plays in group warm-ups like timelines, floor checks, and sculptures. Psychodrama's shape-shifting technique of role reversal seamlessly opened clients to and trained them in the capacity to step into another's experience and see a conflict in the round, from both sides. Role reversal solved a problem I hadn't yet known how to name. It moved clients beyond reactivity into relational empathy, coherence, and perspective, which is where real repair lives.

I also marveled at the joy and creativity these methods intentionally released in each group. Psychodrama was not just about resolving old pain; it was about restoring spontaneity, laughter, and connection. I was hooked. I immediately began to imagine how this approach could be further tailored to work with ACAs, complex trauma, and addiction recovery.

Breaking Down RTR Processes

There is no more direct route to accessing buried relational pain than embodying it through role-play and psychodrama. Speaking to the mother we once had, as the child we once were, can create a powerful, immediate connection to that relational dynamic, as it still lives within us. Simply talking about it often keeps us in our heads, merely describing what we're not fully feeling. Psychodrama, on the other hand, allows us to feel the emotions that are connected to the interaction. It lets us experience it in its fullness, to enter and exit each side and each role in the relationship and loosen the frozen relational memories or states we carry inside. As we do this, we begin to gain perspective. We see ourselves—and the other person—from the inside through doubling, and from the outside through role reversal. And as we move back and forth between these roles, an interesting thing happens: Rather than weakening the self, we strengthen it.

As a trained psychodramatist, I also became a sociometrist. *Sociometry* is the method Moreno developed to chart the unspoken dynamics of human connection: whom we're drawn to, whom we avoid, and where we feel positive, negative, and neutral connections with others. While psychodrama brings the past into the present moment so we can experience it in the here and now, sociometry deals with the connections and disconnections in the present moment, and it reveals the relational patterns that live beneath the surface. It's a system of both mapping and embodying relational dynamics so they can be explored and repaired in real time. On these foundations, I built *Relational Trauma Repair*, or RTR, to make this kind of healing more accessible, structured, and safe, allowing clients to move out of frozen states and into greater flexibility. RTR isn't just about understanding trauma and the grief, anxiety, depression, and distortions in thinking that surround it; it's about experiencing repair in the body, in relationships, and in the here and now. You don't just talk about your story; you *step into* it, and out of it, and that changes how it lives in you.

Let's break down some of the RTR processes we will read about or work with throughout our time together. Simple **embodied role-play** gives us a way to enter the hidden theater of the mind—the place where old roles and relational dynamics still play themselves out, often outside of awareness. Here, we can see how our internalized dysfunctional role relationships from the past might be driving repetition compulsions that keep us reenacting painful patterns in the present. The idea in trauma-informed role-play is to slow reality down enough so the thinking mind can wake up and come back on board, witness the self in action, and view an old interaction through new, more mature eyes.

Role reversal lets you step into the emotional, psychological, and even physiological shoes of someone else. In that shift, the spell of being stuck in your own head begins to break. As you stand in someone else's shoes, you can directly experience both sides of a relational dynamic, and with that comes awareness of the scripted patterns you may be reenacting in your life today. Taking perspective in this way isn't just a soft skill; it's neurologically and relationally transformative. Research shows that even brief role-based exercises, like the ones we'll explore throughout the book, can significantly increase empathy and shift perspective.[1] Stepping into another's role interrupts projection, turning empathy from an abstract idea into a more full-body experience. Over time, your nervous system can learn to tolerate difference, recognize boundaries, and stay present with someone else without you losing touch with yourself. You can develop a felt sense of where someone else ends and you begin, and where the neutral zone is.

Doubling gives voice to the parts of you that even you may struggle to hear; it helps to make the unconscious conscious and translate what is felt (or shut down) into words so that it can be thought about and shared through language. Done well, doubling connects your limbic world of images, sensations, and urges with your reflective, thinking mind. It bridges the inner disconnect that often leaves you stuck in your head and cut off from your body and emotions. Doubling helps shift the head, body, and heart back into coherence and relationship.

I created **floor checks** as a psychoeducational approach to healing relational trauma, and because of their immense effectiveness, they have become the core processes in RTR. Floor checks engage participants with one another in an interactive exploration that brings groups to life. They offer a structured way to practice the relational skills that trauma can disrupt and build the skills of self-awareness, emotional literacy, perspective taking, and nervous system or self-regulation. In group settings, participants become choice makers in their own healing process. Rather than being told what they feel, they move among cards placed on the floor, each labeled with a feeling, symptom, nervous system state, or core concept. When they reach one that resonates, they pause and give voice to what they're experiencing inside, then listen as others do the same. In this book, you will have the opportunity to identify and explore your emotional states as well, though in a slightly different way.

The recognition of emotional and psychological inner states is a simple but profound skill that opens the door to self-awareness, gives us the capacity to self-reflect, and allows us to build skills of emotional literacy, intelligence, and regulation.

Timelines are a powerful way to gently explore your story, especially if trauma has left parts of your past blurry or fragmented. You'll begin by drawing a simple **attachment wound timeline** in your journal, marking key moments or periods of time that shaped how you learned to connect, protect, or withdraw. This gentle process helps repair the split between your childhood and your present, bringing forward the parts of yourself that were left behind. It invites you to witness your younger self on the page and begin to integrate and embody those experiences in a new way. In these pages, you'll be guided through this practice and invited to speak directly to a younger version of yourself, offering the support, safety, or acknowledgment you may have needed then or still long for now.

A **resilience timeline** invites you to trace, consolidate, and celebrate the strength, courage, and adaptability that you developed in meeting life's challenges. These are the moments—large or small—when you endured, found support, or surprised yourself with inner resources you hardly knew you had. As you map these points, you begin to see that your story is one not only of pain but also of persistence, growth, courage, ingenuity, and possibility.

Letter writing is among the most remembered techniques in many therapy treatments, as it is the simplest form of role interaction. But unlike traditional journaling, RTR letters are made embodied and experiential, as we read them aloud, speak them to an empty chair, or role-play with them. Throughout the book, you will be invited to write letters to your parents, parts of yourself, inner states, substances, or imagined future selves. You can write a letter to your dog, a substance or behavior you want to say goodbye to, or even your home. You can ask for—or offer—forgiveness, express unmet needs or resentments, or say thank-you to someone who was there for you when you needed it (including yourself).

Your **social atom** is a map of your relational world. In chapter 4, you'll be given time and space to create a map of your familial dynamics, placing figures or symbols on the page to represent key people in your life and their proximity relative to you. As you do, you'll start to see patterns: who feels close, who feels distant, who is overlapped or isolated, and where ambivalence lingers. What emerges here is more than just a picture; it's a living representation of how connection and context have shaped you. When you do this in person, you can move it into **sculpting**, a living representation of any relational groupings you choose to explore in order to revisit and repair relational dynamics. As a final remapping you can resculpt role relations as you might have wished they had been or would like them to be going forward.

Don't worry if any of these approaches feels a bit ambiguous right now. As we journey through the book together, I'll offer guidance around how all of this works and what's expected as you try them out for yourself. For now, just become familiar with what these techniques are, why they're important for ACA, trauma, codependency, and addiction recovery, and how they can contribute to your lasting healing.

Your Path of Healing

Whether you're an ACA, codependent, a GCoA, or someone working with or through cPTSD, if you're holding this book, something in you is reaching out—maybe for understanding, maybe for words that match what you've long felt but never fully named. You may not call it "trauma." Many ACAs and GCoAs don't. We call it "normal," "not that bad," "colorful and eccentric," or "just the way it was." But beneath those phrases lives a story: your story. And it deserves to be met with care.

This book isn't here to fix you. It's not a treatment plan, nor is it a replacement for therapy. It won't pathologize you into change. Instead, it offers a path home to the parts of you that learned to survive before you had a choice. It's a map, not a destination. It's meant to help you recognize where you may be stuck and what supports can move you forward, not just with insight, but with action. It offers language for what has been hidden and direction toward healing that is intentional, supported, and entirely possible. It will show you how your story lives in your body, your relationships, and your beliefs, as well as how to work with it gently and honestly. I am not here to sell you false hope. Your potential for healing is everywhere if you're willing to walk the walk rather than just talk the talk. In our last chapter, I lay out the kind of support network that I have seen work in my own life and in the lives of thousands of people I have worked with over the decades of my career.

Healing rarely moves in a straight line; it isn't linear because trauma isn't logical. It lives in the body, in sensation, in the patterns we repeat without knowing why. But the body also holds your key to recovery. As you move through this book, you may begin to notice a shift: a softening, a new awareness, a growing capacity to stay present. These are signs that something is reorganizing inside you. That's how healing begins: not all at once, but in moments of safety, connection, and embodied knowing.

If you're reading this, you are already partway there. Your curiosity is your portal. My hope is that you read the pages that follow not as instructions, but as an invitation. An invitation to tend to the parts of you that have yet to be seen and felt, that have sat inside of you waiting for you to turn toward rather than away from them. This book is not a head trip; it's an offer to engage. You don't have to know where this is going. You don't have to do this alone. In fact, your support network and your changing relationship with life itself will help much of your healing happen spontaneously as you discover that you can survive feeling and sharing your painful emotions and remain open to receive the beauty that is always surrounding you. You just need to develop the skill set to be with your inner self—not to do a deep dive and get stuck there, but to dip into this profound pool and come up with more self, more aliveness, more of you. These macro and micro experiences in and of themselves are transformative. You just have to take the next right action.

It's Never Too Late to Have a Happy Childhood

I used to bristle at this phrase. It sounded sentimental, even naïve. But I've come to understand what it really means: The story isn't over—*your* story isn't over. The parts of you that went underground haven't disappeared. They've simply been waiting for the right conditions to return. And through your recovery—and the support you surround yourself with—you can begin to create those conditions.

Trauma steals both your present and your future. It robs you of the now, dulls your sense of wonder, and hijacks your ability to imagine something better. It closes the door not only on memory but on the felt experience of joy, spontaneity, and safety.

Healing makes space for those forgotten feelings. It makes space for *you*. Because recovery isn't just about remembering what hurt; it's about remembering what felt good. Recovery asks us to turn toward that pain, to process it gently, and to build habits that support healing. As you thaw the frozen places within, you reclaim what trauma forced into hiding: your lightheartedness and your ability to calmly think, hope, and dream. The simple delight of being a child on a sun-drenched afternoon. The comfort of a familiar voice. The ease of loving without hesitation.

Recovery can give you your life back. It gave mine back to me. Now I can remember being that happy child: grateful to be alive, to wake into a new day filled with sunlight and possibility. I remember the happy times in our family. That is my quiet victory. The very fact that you've made it this far is a testament to your strength, even if it hasn't always felt like it. That strength may have looked like withdrawal, people-pleasing, perfectionism, or shutting down. But it was you, managing the best way you knew how, trying to stay safe.

Healing and real, grounded, nourishing connection require a different kind of attunement. They ask us to stay present when it might be easier to disappear. To hold difference without collapse. To listen without needing to attack or defend. To sit in discomfort without rushing to fix. They require a nervous system that can tolerate proximity without fusing or fleeing. And they invite a different kind of strength, the kind that softens your defenses and opens you to relational maturity. They give you the space to choose curiosity over control. Not all at once, and not without fear. But slowly, a day at a time.

You're allowed to be messy and still make progress. You can be unsure and afraid and still heal. You're worth the time you spend with yourself. With this in mind, let's begin to examine this legacy together. My hope is to help you follow your yellow brick road to come home to yourself and to learn that you never really left to begin with.

1

Understanding Your Past, Reclaiming Your Present

The Cost of Addiction and Relational Trauma to the Family System

Growing up as the child of an addict is disorienting, like trying to take a full breath but never quite reaching the end of the inhale. Or like driving through thick fog, straining to see the road ahead. The atmosphere is changeable. Things can feel warm and alive to begin with, then become thick with tension, then suddenly feel so eerily still that you can hear a pin drop. You learn early that intimacy can be unpredictable, that safety is not something you can take for granted. In a home shaped by addiction, emotions are high but not often expressed... which is hard. And when they are finally expressed, they've been bottled up for so long that they are explosive... which can be worse. Unspoken needs feel urgent but are often ignored, so you learn to pretend they don't matter. Normal sibling dynamics—competition, jealousy, imbalance—can become intensified. Because the truth is in families dealing with addiction, no one is really getting their needs met all that well. The undeclared rules are clear: Adapt or be left behind. Figure it out for yourself.

You may not have had the words for it then, but your nervous system knew. It learned to read the room before you even stepped inside. It tracked the slightest changes in tone, the subtle shifts in expression, the difference between the good days and the bad ones. It taught you how to become small when the storm hit and how to come alive when things felt safe again. You likely savored the times of fun and easy intimacy, enjoying them almost with a kind of giddiness, but you also probably didn't allow yourself to let them feel *too* good, because you knew that they would disappear again as mysteriously as they came, and that you'd have no idea how to get them back. But that didn't keep you from trying.

There's a certain skill set that comes with being raised in emotional unpredictability. You learn how to anticipate mood swings before they arrive, how to read between the lines of a conversation for the hidden threats, and how to manage someone else's feelings while pretending you don't have any of your own. It's like growing up in a never-ending improv performance where the stakes are high and the implicit demand is "Don't get caught off guard."

You might think, having made it to adulthood, you'd be rewarded with a lifetime of ease, a nervous system that's made out of iron, a deep and unshakable sense of self-worth, and the ability to casually say, "I might have misunderstood you," without experiencing an existential crisis. But no. Instead, you get hypervigilance as a personality trait. You get an uncanny ability to detect other people's discomfort at a hundred yards while remaining baffled by your own emotions. You get to spend decades undoing the lessons you never wanted to learn in the first place.

Understanding Relational Trauma

While we often think of trauma as a single devastating event—a car accident, a natural disaster, or a sudden loss—many of us carry a quieter, more pervasive kind: relational trauma. This isn't the wounding of one catastrophic moment; it's the accumulation of countless moments, lived day after day, primarily in relationships where we reached for safety but found inconsistency, where we loved and needed but were met with something that made loving and needing hurt. Unlike a singular event, relational trauma leaves no clear before and after. Instead, it weaves itself into the fabric of our lives and nervous systems, shaping how we react and how we see ourselves and the world. It can leave us questioning our worth, mistrusting safety, and disconnecting from our feelings and needs. But it can also create a deep yearning for healing and connection, because something inside of us longs for wholeness.

Relational trauma begins in the most vulnerable of places: childhood. It arises when the people we depend on for love and protection become a source of confusion, criticism, or manipulation, when those we'd normally go to for help in unpacking and understanding painful moments are the ones causing them. Relational trauma isn't just what happens *to* you; it's what happens *within* you.[1] Healing from this kind of trauma requires more than words, because its residue doesn't live in your rational brain. It lives in your body—in the rhythms of your nervous system, in the felt sense of safety or the lack of it, in the ways your body learned to tighten, flee, freeze, or fawn long before you had words for what was happening. Healing takes time and, dare I say it, discipline. It requires an embodied process, one that invites you to gently reconnect with the parts of yourself that trauma taught you to ignore, dismiss, or bury; to feel what went unfelt and unprocessed; to say what went unsaid. And it also requires trading dysfunctional habits for functional ones, finding healthy ways to self-regulate and practice new ways of living within yourself and your relationships. As you move these pieces of your lived experience through a process of feeling, healing, and reflection, you can reintegrate them one by one into the whole of your being.

Sometimes I see adult children of addicts (ACAs) or even grandchildren of addicts (GCoAs) hope that saying the right words will be enough to create deep internal change or else give up in frustration when that isn't enough. It's hard to convince someone who has learned to take refuge in their thoughts that they cannot simply think themselves better. But if our behavior doesn't genuinely match what we say, we are simply postponing healing and using the same denial and manipulation on ourselves that our parents used when we were young. Trauma is a cunningly adaptive bedfellow, and if you imagine you can get the better of it by simply saying the right things, it will show up where you don't want it and act up when you least expect. Try if you like, but it will save you a lot of time if you can accept that *you can't outsmart your trauma.*

We have to feel to heal. This can prove to be difficult at first, because when we revisit those hurt parts of us, we may want to shut down all over again. Experiencing them overwhelmed us when we were kids, and reexperiencing them as adults isn't necessarily any easier. But healing happens when we reconnect with that wounded child sitting in the corner of our hearts and invite them to stand up and take a step toward us. When we befriend our wounded child parts rather than "exile" them, as Richard C. Schwartz, creator of internal family systems therapy, describes it. When we *feel* the emotions now that we had to *shut down* then, so that we can get to know how they made us who we became and invite them into who we are becoming.

We know we're healing when the situations that once left us frozen, frantic, or confused no longer hold the same power. Where there was reactivity, there is now a level of choice. Where there was fear, there is now a willingness to be present. This is the quiet revolution of healing—when what once felt inevitable becomes something we can meet with creativity and spontaneity. This is what J. L. and Zerka Moreno cited as a hallmark of change and growth.

Every child begins life with a kind of curiosity, freedom, and unshakable trust in the world. But ACAs experience many challenges to this innocence. Because of that, we can carry a sense of loss over something we can't quite name. This is why recovery is more than a second chance at life; it's a second chance at childhood. It's an invitation to uncover the incorruptibility beneath the pain and frozenness, and rediscover the parts of us that trauma taught us to hide. Beneath the survival strategies and protective walls, our aliveness—our essence—has been waiting for us to return.

Healing is about reclaiming the parts of you that went underground in order to stay safe. It's about rediscovering wonder, curiosity, and creativity—qualities that trauma buried but never destroyed. And it's about understanding how your nervous system adapted to try to stay regulated or became dysregulated when it got overwhelmed by growing up in a chaotic, unsettling world.

You Are Not Alone

You may feel terminally unique in your situation, as many ACAs do, but you're far from alone. Approximately one in eight children in the United States live with at least one parent who has a substance use disorder, which encompasses both alcohol and illicit drug use. Additionally, children of alcoholics are three times more likely to experience physical, emotional, or sexual abuse due to the lack of inhibition and the emotional dysregulation that surround addiction.[2] ACAs are four times more likely to develop alcoholism and other process addictions than those without alcoholic parents, and daughters of alcoholics are more than twice as likely to marry an alcoholic than daughters of nonalcoholics. And these are only the reported cases. How many more children grow up in homes where substance addiction and process addictions like compulsive eating, food restriction, spending, working, or sexual activity remain hidden?

As an ACA, you may find yourself repeating painful relational cycles, recreating dynamics that mirror the dysfunction of your past, or struggling with shame, mistrust, and emotional numbness. These patterns aren't who you are; they're the residue of what happened to you. But here's the good news: You can create a new way of seeing and living your life.

I know this because I have lived it myself. I've felt the weight of wounds I couldn't name as they shaped my relationships and distorted my sense of self. I've seen how unresolved pain shows up in the present in the ways we love, the ways we protect ourselves, and the ways we pull away when we most want to connect. Healing, I've learned, isn't a final destination. It's not about fixing yourself; it's about finding yourself. It's about becoming curious, compassionate, and deeply honest with what you're carrying and how it continues to impact your life and relationships, then doing the inner and outer work to change.

Embodied Healing for Relational Trauma

We all long for connection. It is written into our nervous systems, imprinted in the rhythm of our first breaths, the warmth of our first touch. Before we had words, before we had ideas about who we needed to be to belong, we simply *were*—reaching, sensing, attuning. But somewhere along the way, connection became conditional. We learned which parts of ourselves were welcomed and which were too much, too messy, too inconvenient. We adapted. We played roles. We twisted ourselves into shapes that fit the spaces available to us. And yet beneath all of that—the performing, the pleasing, the self-protecting—the longing remains to this day. Our bodies hold this imprint of intimacy, of what it felt like to be sensed, met, and held. Healing is not only about learning connection; it is about reclaiming our humanness and remembering that we were never meant to do this alone.

There are moments in experiential group work—sacred, electric moments—when a room comes alive in a way that words can barely hold. Through floor checks (discussed in the introduction), I have witnessed miracles happen. Rather than a leader figure telling a participant what they feel, floor checks allow participants to choose for themselves, and as a result, something shifts—not just in the individual, but in the collective nervous system of the room. I have watched a single floor check, a simple act of standing in one's truth, turn silence into tears and then laughter or isolation into ease and connection. The unspoken wounds we carry rise to the surface, and as they do, they become something new: seen, felt, held. A room of strangers becomes a room of friends, bonded by shared humanity, by connection, by presence. Coregulation takes over, nervous systems sync, and what once felt too hard to share begins to feel natural, bearable, felt, not in isolation, but witnessed by others. This is the alchemy of experiential, embodied healing—of working through relational trauma.

We all, even as adults, have a child within us who may still carry past attachment wounds that we need to work through. Processing the frozen and often unconscious pain of these childhood parts helps us grow up these immature selves so we can become more whole. And the beauty of being an *adult* child of an addict is that you get a second chance. A second chance to re-invite these inner parts to show themselves and claim space, to slowly experience who they are and what they have to show you about yourself and your childhood. You don't want these inner selves to show up unconsciously in your relationships and sabotage your interactions. Instead, the goal is to let them tell you—through role-play or journaling as a part of self—about the pain, hurt, and resentment they have carried for you. Then you can welcome them back to where they always belonged, alive and inside of you! You will have a freer and more integrated self to take into your relationships as an adult.

As I shared in the introduction, my model, Relational Trauma Repair (RTR), combined with psychodrama, uses tried and true processes that I have developed over the past thirty years to hone in on the kinds of issues that are specific to growing up or living with addiction and/or family dysfunction. Embodied healing transforms the invisible into the visible, turning our relational wounds into something tangible—something we can see, give voice to, and ultimately reshape. Throughout this book, you'll be introduced to some of the core teachings and exercises of RTR. Through floor checks, we teach the fundamentals of social/emotional learning, emotional regulation, and literacy. Timelines help us place our experiences into a developmental framework. They trace the path of our developmental wounds as well, pinpointing how we may have carried and recreated these early wounds in our adult relationships. They also help us to identify and own the resilient strengths we built through meeting the challenges we faced, strengths that we're still using today. And social atoms illuminate the gravitational pull of our relational world, showing us who occupies space in our psyche and where we may still be orienting ourselves around absent figures or outdated roles. We can also use social atoms to envision both role repair and the development of new roles and new ways of being. You can see film clips of how these processes look on relationaltraumarepair.com.

In these embodied processes, healing isn't an abstract idea; it's a lived experience. By engaging with these processes, we change not only our understanding of our relational history but also the way it actively shapes us today. The entrenched dynamics we once internalized—through which we unconsciously replay old roles and patterns with new people—begin to loosen their grip. We step out of inherited relational scripts, incorporating the body into the healing process. In the words of trauma healing pioneer Peter Levine, "We store the imprint of trauma in our bodies as 'snapshots' frozen in the nervous system that tell the story of how the body-mind experienced trauma. [This] approach to embodied therapy using psychodrama informed by Somatic Experiencing allows the body's unspoken voice to come forward and be heard."[3]

Through incorporating Levine's groundbreaking Somatic Experiencing (SE) work, I look to the body to understand what's going on emotionally within the client, or the person we call in psychodrama the *protagonist*. The use of this word is intentional: It comes from the Greek words meaning "first actor," the person whose story is being told. As you, the protagonist, begin to manifest emotion physically, for example, through collapse inward, tension in your throat or chest, or trembling limbs, I as the director simply ask, "If that part of you could talk, what would it say?" This seamless integration of SE and psychodrama allows the body to speak in its own authentic voice. In this way, you're able to engage with deep inner states and hear what they have to tell you.

Psychodrama Is Profoundly Relational

Unlike healing modalities that focus on the individual, psychodrama reaches into the relational fabric of your being to unravel the dynamics that can keep you stuck in unhealthy cycles. The stage provides a living rehearsal space where you can work through and break free from old patterns, try on different ways of being, and begin to embody the changes you long for in your relationships and within yourself. It involves the body as well as the psyche in the healing process, making healing more organic and integrated. For example, when you role-play a scenario where you talk to someone you imagine sitting in an empty chair (the person is not physically present), you are excavating the full relational dynamic that lives inside of you for further exploration.

Remember, we don't just internalize the other person's behaviors; we internalize the relational dynamic we experienced with them. We internalize not only an "I" but a "we." It is that dynamic—for better, worse, or both—that we continue to replay throughout our lives, unconsciously choosing people who are in some way stand-ins for them or for us. If we learned what repair felt like, we know how to find it again. If we remain stuck and silent, we fear sincere connection.

When it comes to releasing withheld hurt or, for that matter, withheld love, role-play allows you to say what you never got a chance to say and feel what you may have buried deep inside out of fear. How many conversations have you played out in your head, saying all the things to someone that in real life you held in silence, sometimes for decades? Psychodrama lets that genie out of the bottle. A profound sense of inner connection and aliveness happens when you intentionally step into a role rather than merely describe it, as you would in talk therapy. In that present moment of embodiment, your eleven-year-old self, for example, has the opportunity to talk *to* the parent you had then or the kids who bullied you at school and relieve yourself of the pain that has sat inside your mind, heart, and body.

From there, you can reverse roles and become the parent or kids talking back to your eleven-year-old self. This allows for a perspective shift that many clients report as freeing. With this healing method, not only do you see yourself from the outside, but through the magic of role reversal, you experience the parent or relationship you had then, from the inside, as someone separate from you with their own thoughts, beliefs, and problems. Suddenly, the dynamic that has locked you into place for decades pops open, and the trapdoor holding this frozen relational dynamic in place releases.

Again, true healing is not an intellectual exercise; it is something you feel and sense your way into, something you directly experience. Trauma isn't stored as a story you can simply rewrite with words; it is embedded in sensations, impulses, and states of being. The good news is that just as relational wounds were formed in connection, they can also be healed in connection—through these new experiences and through trying on new roles or old roles in new ways.

In the pages ahead, you will explore some of the unspoken rules that have governed your relationships. Slowly, you'll begin to rewrite those rules, learning to inhabit your body with more ease, openness, and trust. This is the journey from bracing for danger to opening to life—a shift from merely getting through your life to being more fully alive in the present.

How Relational Trauma Creates Codependency

The family is much more than a collection of individuals; it is a tapestry of interconnected lives, woven together by bonds of love, loyalty, and shared experiences. Our families serve as our first classroom on relationships. In a nurturing family atmosphere, you develop a sense of security and comfort in connection that enables you to engage with the world around you with effortlessness and confidence. But when addiction and relational trauma enter this delicate human fabric, it can impose strains and stressors that threaten to pull it apart at the seams.

As a child, you absorbed lessons about safety, communication, closeness, and emotional regulation from those who raised you, and you made them your own. The hand that stroked your head, the arms that rocked you, the eyes that met or did not meet yours—all those left an imprint that sank down into your emotional body, providing a direct experience of how it felt to be in intimate connection with another human being. These early interactions shaped your internal blueprint for intimacy, teaching you whether closeness was a source of safety, a signal to brace for danger, or both. When the natural daily ruptures that are part of any connection were followed by repair, you learned that relationships can lead to deeper understanding of both yourself and another person; when they were not, you learned that hurt festers and grows.

The unpredictable nature of the kind of parenting that often surrounds addiction—one moment warm and connected, the next rejecting or punishing—can create confusing and dysregulating emotional and psychological dynamics that can lead to codependency. This intermittent reinforcement is even more destabilizing than consistent neglect or hostility, because the brain craves predictability. When love and rejection intertwine, your nervous system remains on high alert, making it difficult to fully relax and be yourself in relationships. Some inconsistency is normal and even good training for living in the real world, but the kind that you find in troubled homes can be too much to metabolize; it can feel unbearable.

When connection is inconsistent, conditional, or unsafe, we adapt, becoming who we believe we need to be to belong or feel safe. As an adult, you may still carry the imprint of these early adaptations: anxiety, mistrust, or frozenness around authentic connection. Your nervous system, shaped by past experiences, may brace for rejection or conflict before it even arrives, or you may roll over your own boundaries and live below the radar in a misguided effort at self-protection.

The World Revolves Around Me: The Natural Egocentricity of Childhood

In the most innocent way, children are naturally egocentric. When they're very small, they think that the sun rises just above their bedroom window and sets over their sandbox. So it is only natural that if unspoken pain and resentment are suspended in the atmosphere of their home and no one is helping them understand what it is about, they use their egocentric thinking to make it about them, worrying deep down that something they did or, worse, something they *are* just isn't okay. You may have wondered as a child, *What am I doing wrong to make Mommy so distressed?* or *Why can't I seem to get anything right so my parents can be happy instead of frazzled and edgy?* And you may have taken your magical thinking one step further: *It is my job to fix this.* But in the face of addiction, you can't be good enough, smart enough, forgiving enough, or bossy enough to get your family to behave normally or to get your addict parent sober.

If the gradual crescendo of addiction remains unnamed and unaddressed, children are left to manage their increasing distress alone. If there was no caring adult helping you translate your fear and anxiety into words so you could feel seen and understood, you were left to make sense of them on your own. You had to use your childlike reasoning to understand an adult-sized problem.

In the absence of steady, reliable parental guidance, some children take on a role far beyond their years. In a desperate attempt to help the family and create order and stability, they become the caretakers—the ones who try to manage the unmanageable. You may have been one of those children. Perhaps it fell to you to gently guide your intoxicated parent to bed, to make breakfast or lunches for your siblings, to shoulder the weight of getting everyone out the door each morning, to worry. In the long hours of your childhood, you might have found yourself on high alert, your senses finely attuned to every subtle shift in mood or movement around you. Scanning your parents' faces, noticing the way they held their bodies, and listening for the tone of their voices likely became second nature. You learned that keeping the peace depended on anticipating trouble before it fully surfaced. The people around you became your compass, their moods dictating your next move. Codependency in the making.

Over time, this external focus may have solidified into a belief that your worth was tied to keeping others safe and happy. You silently colluded with your family in hiding what everyone feared: that your family was falling apart. You may not have succeeded in managing your family, but that didn't mean you quit trying. You may have created a false self: a competent and upbeat face you showed to the world that said, "Everything's just fine." Beneath that, though, was another you kept hidden—the sad, hurt, or angry face. The face you thought no one saw, because your family didn't see it or couldn't see it because they were in hiding too. So you might have wound up looking big on the outside but feeling small and empty on the inside.

Over time, you learned to prioritize the feelings, needs, actions, and moods of others, sidelining your own. This hypervigilance can lay the foundation for codependency. You remained on alert around others, scanning their faces and bodies for evidence of why you felt anxious. And because your questioning was often met with denial, you got stuck in prioritizing the moods of others over your own, believing that if you could just keep everyone else safe and stable, then perhaps you, too, might find some measure of peace. But the truth is, you often didn't learn how to care for the most intimate person of all: yourself.

Codependency has been known in pop culture since the 1980s, but it actually has its roots in the addictions field, describing those whose lives revolved around someone dependent on a substance. They were called codependents because they were often seen as mirroring dependent traits. As Dr. Janet G. Woititz and other leaders in the field such as Claudia Black, Sharon Wegscheider-Cruse, Robert Ackerman, and I talked about ACAs and adult relational trauma, countless others recognized themselves in those lists, whether or not addiction was present in their families. Almost overnight, the framework of codependency became a language for something larger: the experience of confusing your needs with what you perceive to be the needs of others. We think we're attending to others, but in truth, we're often acting out of and projecting our own unmet childhood needs, unconsciously hoping that by taking care of the the other person, our needs will somehow get met in the exchange.

At its core, it is a trauma response. It's how we learned to stay safe—through fawning, through hypervigilance, through tuning in acutely to others' needs while our own remain something of a mystery. If this sounds like you, you're absolutely not alone.

Take a look at the following list of common codependency traits and see if you identify with any:

- **Excessive people-pleasing**: You may feel responsible for other people's feelings, needs, and problems, even at the expense of your own. Saying no feels like rejection, so you say yes, even when it doesn't necessarily work for you.

- **Difficulty setting boundaries**: Boundaries can feel unsafe because they risk causing loss or disconnection. You may merge with others emotionally or tolerate mistreatment to preserve the relationship.

- **Caretaking and overfunctioning**: You may feel compelled to fix, rescue, or manage others' lives. Your worth becomes tied to being needed, even when it leaves you drained.

- **Low self-esteem and self-doubt**: Internally, you might carry harsh self-criticism, shame, or a sense of not being enough. External validation becomes a primary source of self-worth.

- **Fear of abandonment and rejection**: You might tolerate unhealthy relationships to avoid feeling alone. The prospect of someone leaving you can activate deep emotional distress, rooted in early attachment wounds.

- **Emotional suppression**: You learned to suppress or dismiss your own emotions to maintain family harmony. Over time, this may leave you feeling disconnected from what you need or want.

- **Control as a coping mechanism**: You might try to control people, situations, or outcomes to manage your anxiety and feel safe. Control becomes a substitute for secure attachment.

- **Hypervigilance to others' needs and moods**: You scan for signs of conflict, disapproval, or rejection. This attunement, once a survival skill, becomes exhausting.

- **Difficulty receiving help or support**: You're comfortable giving, but receiving seems foreign or makes you feel too vulnerable. You may struggle with asking for what you need, believing it's safer not to need anything at all. Or you may reject support from others, perhaps seeking to meet your needs surreptitiously through appearing to take care of others, convincing them that they're the ones who need you.

- **Emotional enmeshment**: Your sense of self can blur with those you're close to; you may have trouble seeing yourself or others as separate people.

Trauma, cPTSD, and ACAs

In 1980, the American Psychiatric Association made a groundbreaking move by officially recognizing post-traumatic stress disorder (PTSD) as a diagnosable condition in the third edition of the *Diagnostic and Statistical Manual of Mental Disorders* (DSM-III). This wasn't just about attaching a label to a collection of symptoms; it was a powerful act of acknowledgment. It validated what those of us who grew up with relational trauma had long known deep within: that trauma leaves lasting, sometimes invisible, wounds. This moment shifted the conversation in psychology spaces and in a broader, social discourse, expanding our understanding of trauma's reach. Trauma was no longer confined to soldiers on battlefields or survivors of catastrophic events. Instead, it was understood that trauma can seep into the lives and nervous systems of anyone who has faced prolonged threat, stress, or instability, no matter the cause.

Judith Herman, another pioneer in the trauma field, expanded this understanding in her 1992 book *Trauma and Recovery* by introducing the concept of complex PTSD (cPTSD). Unlike the classic form of PTSD, which often follows a single shocking event, cPTSD emerges from repeated exposure to relational trauma over time. For those of us who have experienced this, the effects can feel woven into the fabric of our being. It's not just that we've been hurt; it's that the hurt has been imprinted into our nervous systems, resurfacing again and again as a complex post-traumatic stress syndrome in which we recreate dysfunctional dynamics from childhood in our adult relationships. It shows up in the way our body tenses at a certain tone of voice, how we either shrink or explode in the presence of conflict, or how love itself can feel like a trap. In essence, our past dictates our present before we even have the chance to choose.

This revelation, along with Bessel van der Kolk's groundbreaking work on how trauma is stored in the body, began a lifelong mission for me to learn how to use psychodrama and eventually my own RTR model to heal cPTSD in ACAs, adult children of relational trauma, and codependents.

Building off of the work of ACA pioneer Tony Allen, Dr. Janet G. Woititz shared a "laundry list" for ACAs in her groundbreaking 1983 book *Adult Children of Alcoholics*, detailing the common characteristics observed in this group and broadening the understanding of how growing up in such environments impacts adult behavior and relationships. In the forty years since, scientists have done research on the brain, trauma, neurobiology, and the nervous system, and throughout that time, I have slowly developed my own up-to-date laundry list of symptoms that ACAs and those with cPTSD may experience.

Emotional and Psychological Symptoms of Adult Relational Trauma and cPTSD

Childhood trauma can overwhelm your nervous system, making it difficult for you to process or integrate what happened. As an adult, these unprocessed experiences can continue to affect your emotions, thoughts, and body in various ways.

- **Emotional dysregulation**: You may experience strong emotional waves on a continuum from intense reactions to emotional numbness, making it hard to sense a middle ground.[4]

- **Emotional flashbacks**: You might suddenly feel flooded with intense fear, shame, or helplessness, as if the past is happening all over again—yet without a clear causative memory to explain the reaction.[5]

- **Chronic shame and guilt**: A sense of guilt, shame, or self-doubt may linger, even if you try to push it away or mask it with achievements, analysis, or self-criticism.[6]

- **Anxiety and hypervigilance**: Your nervous system may feel like it gets stuck on high alert, constantly scanning for potential threats even in safe situations. This can lead to persistent anxiety or a sense that something bad is about to happen.[7]

- **Depression and hopelessness**: At times, joy or motivation may feel out of reach, leaving you emotionally drained or disconnected from things that once mattered to you.[8]

- **Dissociation**: You might feel distant from your emotions, surroundings, or even your own body, experiencing moments of fogginess or detachment as a way to cope.[9]

Relational Symptoms

Trauma affects the way you connect with others, making trust, closeness, and communication more complicated to develop and maintain.

- **Trust and attachment issues**: You may struggle to trust others or maintain emotional closeness, instinctively protecting yourself out of fear of abandonment or betrayal. Or you might alternate between anxious clinging and pushing away or disconnecting.[10]

- **Fear of intimacy**: Emotional or physical closeness may make you anxious. Vulnerability can bring fears of rejection or loss, or you may not know how to maintain your sense of self while allowing another person to do the same.[11]

- **Codependency**: You may feel responsible for managing others' emotions and behaviors, believing that their well-being—or approval—determines your own sense of safety. This can lead to self-sacrifice, people-pleasing, or even attempting to control others' choices to maintain your own sense of stability. To avoid conflict or abandonment, you may fawn, prioritizing agreement, self-erasure, or even identity fusion over autonomy.[12]

- **Relationship reenactments**: You may find yourself trapped in repeating relational dynamics that mirror childhood trauma, unconsciously recreating familiar patterns of hurt, control, or neglect.[13]

- **Fear of abandonment**: Even subtle signs of distance or withdrawal may trigger intense anxiety and emotional pain, making relationships feel fragile or unpredictable.[14]

Physical Symptoms

Trauma often leaves an imprint on the body as well as the mind, showing up in subtle and not-so-subtle ways.

- **Chronic pain or tension**: Unresolved trauma can manifest as headaches, digestive issues, muscle tension, or pain—symptoms that often flare up under stress.[15]

- **Sleep disturbances**: Falling or staying asleep may be challenging, with anxiety, racing thoughts, or trauma-related nightmares disrupting rest.[16]

- **Hyperarousal**: When the nervous system stays on high alert, you may feel jumpy, overly sensitive to noise or touch, or easily overwhelmed by your environment.[17]

Identity and Existential Symptoms

Early relational trauma can shape your sense of self, making it hard to feel solid in who you are or what gives your life meaning.

- **Uncertainty about who you are**: If you've spent years adapting to others' expectations, you may struggle to know what *you* want or believe.[18]

- **A persistent feeling of emptiness**: You might carry a sense that something is missing—an emotional void that feels hard to fill.[19]

- **Loss of meaning or purpose**: Trauma can make it hard to feel like your life has a steady thread running through it, leaving you feeling detached from your inner world or unmoored to your own history. Over time, you may lose touch with the inner compass that once guided you.[20]

Resilience: The Strengths You Built Through Meeting the Challenges in Your Life

I don't want to leave you thinking that all your emotions are pathological. Although my years in this field have shown me how deeply relational trauma can affect us, they have also revealed the resilient qualities that those who have experienced relational trauma developed by doing our best to cope with the challenges we grew up with. We can become deeply engaged with these qualities as well, because they too were our survival—in this case, survival of our spirits. A core outgrowth of trauma can be a sense of disconnection from the self, so to heal fully, you cannot stop at uncovering your pain. You need to also be open to the beautiful awakening that can emerge from it.

Trauma, while wounding, has the power to shape us in extraordinary ways, which is why ACAs can be so very funny, resilient, and talented. The very challenges that once threatened to break you have also built you. As an ACA, or someone who has experienced other forms of trauma, you have developed an extraordinary arsenal of strengths—among them intuition, resilience, and creativity. You learned how to adapt, manage chaos, find humor in the darkest moments, and sense what's unspoken before it's said.

Consolidating your gains and celebrating your strengths is as important as working through your woundedness! Which ones feel like you?

Resilience Traits Developed by ACAs

- **Awareness of others' needs**: Growing up in an unpredictable environment may have sharpened your ability to read people and sense unspoken emotions. This deep attunement can help you empathize and form meaningful, authentic connections.[21]

- **Adaptability and problem-solving**: Navigating chaos may have required you to think quickly and adjust to constant change. As a result, you may have developed an exceptional ability to handle challenges and find creative solutions under pressure.[22]

- **Emotional insight, empathy, and compassion**: Managing intense emotions from a young age may have fostered a deep curiosity about your inner world and those of others. This self-awareness now allows you to recognize and process your feelings with greater clarity and to understand what others might be feeling.[23]

- **Sense of responsibility**: Taking on significant responsibilities early in life may have made you dependable and conscientious. Others likely trust you, and you may take commitments seriously, sometimes even to a fault.[24]

- **Perseverance and determination**: Difficult experiences may have taught you endurance. You may have developed the resilience and inner grit needed to persist through life's challenges.[25] You don't expect life to be easy, and that helps you to work for what you want and tolerate setbacks well.

- **Self-reliance**: Inconsistent support may have required you to become resourceful and independent. Now, you may have a strong ability to manage life on your own, though learning to receive support may be part of your healing.[26]

- **Boundary-setting skills**: Breaking away from unhealthy family patterns may have taught you the necessity of boundaries. You may be learning to protect your energy and well-being by tending to your needs with greater confidence.[27]

- **Commitment to growth**: You may have actively sought out and relied on resources for healing and recovery—including reaching out and developing a support system, seeking therapy, embracing mindfulness practices, or engaging in recovery work—demonstrating a profound commitment to breaking generational cycles.[28]

- **Valuing stability**: Experiencing instability may have deepened your appreciation for consistency and security. You may prioritize creating a steady, safe environment for yourself and your loved ones.[29]

- **Advocacy for others**: Your lived experience may have fueled a passion for helping others heal. Whether through personal support, professional work, or activism, you may be an advocate for mental health, recovery, and emotional well-being.[30]

- **Self-reflection and insight**: Working through childhood adversity may have made you deeply introspective. You may have a gift for recognizing patterns, understanding their origins, and making intentional changes.[31]

- **Hope, optimism, and/or belief in something greater**: As a human, you may have used hopefulness as a survival tool.

You may believe in healing, growth, and the possibility of a fulfilling future for yourself and those around you.[32] This belief can offer resilience, helping you reframe your experiences, find meaning in adversity, and trust that healing is possible.[33]

Exercise

Feeling Floor Check

For ACAs, codependents, and those with cPTSD, emotions can sometimes feel distant, overwhelming, or hard to access, so it's important to develop emotional literacy. Floor checks allow you to connect with your feelings, name them, and translate them into words so you can think reflectively about what you feel. Here we're translating them for your journal so you can get to know what you carry on the inside.

Engaging with your feelings on this level is the first step in being able to understand and process them, which starts to give you choices. You can pause, reflect, and respond with more clarity and awareness. And this can help you temper your emotional responses, which in turn lets you communicate what you want to say to others with more balance.

The first time you try this floor check, you may have trouble naming what you're feeling. Feel free to refer to this list of core human emotions as you engage in your journal with the prompts that will follow:

Angry	Disconnected	Frustrated
Anxious	Disgusted	Grieving
Ashamed	Embarrassed	Guilty
Connected	Empowered	Helpless
Confused	Excited	Hopeful
Curious	Fearful	Isolated

Joyful	Resentful	Trusting
Numb	Sad	Vulnerable
Overwhelmed	Safe	Wounded
Playful	Stuck	
Proud	Surprised	

Now, setting aside some time when you can be quiet and undisturbed, reflect on the following prompts in your journal.

- Which feelings from the list do you identify with at this moment and why?
    - Where do you feel each of these emotions in your body?
    - If each emotion could talk, what would it say?

- Is there a feeling you tend to avoid experiencing?
    - What thoughts, memories, or body sensations arise when you feel this emotion?
    - How have you learned to push this feeling away, suppress it, act it out, feed it, or distract yourself from it?
    - What would it feel like if you were to gently sit with this feeling instead of avoiding it?

- Which feeling would you like to experience more of in your day-to-day life?
    - What do you imagine feeling more of this would bring to you?
    - What's in the way of feeling this emotion more often?
    - What small actions or shifts could help you cultivate more safety around feeling this emotion?

I will be the first to admit that devoting yourself to healing the pain from your past is no easy feat. As ACAs or those with relational trauma, we've experienced a variety of traumas that have left lasting wounds in our hearts and minds, wounds that have likely found their way into our current thoughts, beliefs, and behaviors. I want you to know, though, that healing is possible for you, and it starts with getting in touch with those parts of yourself that are tender to touch, the parts that require you to go beyond logical thought. This is what we'll begin to explore together in the next chapter.

2

What the Body Remembers

Why We Can't Think Ourselves Better

The face and body are intimate storytellers, living archives that quietly record our emotional history and reveal it moment by moment through expression, posture, and gesture. A confident stride, a relaxed jaw, or an open gaze may reflect a nervous system at ease, signaling trust in the world and readiness for connection. Conversely, a tightened jaw, slumped shoulders, or an avoidant glance may reflect imprints of unresolved pain or vigilance. The body isn't just a passive container for our experiences; it absorbs our lived experience and expresses it in subtle, often unconscious ways. With remarkable fidelity, it replays these emotional and psychological imprints through the way we hold ourselves and engage with others. This isn't metaphor—it's neuroscience.

If you were that child sitting frozen on the staircase, holding your breath as your parents' angry voices shattered the silence, your body tried to keep you safe by pumping blood into your muscles so you could run or fight and protect yourself. But let's face it: As a small child, you could do neither. You were too little to fight; you'd only lose or, worse, get hit, punished, or demeaned for your small efforts at self-protection. And where would you run to? This was your home, your shelter, your world, your family—the place that was supposed to be your safe haven. So because you couldn't use this adrenaline to *fight* or *flee*, you *froze*, and all those stress chemicals your body produced just stayed swirling around in your system, making it feel hard to live in your own skin. Your body went still, your breath became shallow or caught, your little shoulders hiked up, and your mind went blank. You attempted to make yourself invisible. And when freezing and hiding weren't enough to keep you safe, because someone demanded your presence, you might have *fawned*. You learned to stay small and invisible, to placate, to make nice—anything to maintain some semblance of a positive or workable connection with the caregivers you depended on for survival.

In an ideal world, a caring adult helps the small child unpack a moment like this so they can make sense of what happened, cry if they need to, and feel held and restored to relational safety and connection. But addiction and relational trauma are not an ideal world. If no one helps you understand what just happened, the experience can remain frozen inside you, unprocessed and unedited. The fear, confusion, or shutdown you felt in that childhood moment may settle into your nervous system like a blueprint that you default to when you're triggered even as an adult. Over time, that stuck activation can make it feel overwhelming just to be in your own skin. It's what we call in psychodrama "an open tension" that longs for completion. Then something in the present activates this imprint, and before you know it, you're back in that old emotional terrain, responding not just to *now* but to *then*. You react to what's happening in front of you as if it were your past. You say now what you couldn't say then. But you're saying it to the wrong person, at the wrong place and the wrong time. And this is how your past becomes reenacted in your present and you don't even know it's happening.

Let's take a deeper look at what goes on in our brain and body in these frightening moments. When trauma remains unresolved, it doesn't simply disappear. It lingers in the body and mind, often outside of conscious awareness. So instead of integrating the experience (because someone helped us understand it, work through it, bring it to closure, and feel better), it lives inside of us as a set of unconscious body memories. Some of the ways these body sensations and urges manifest are as follows:

- **Chronic anxiety or persistent hypervigilance**: A nervous system stuck in survival mode, scanning for danger even in safe environments.

- **Exaggerated startle responses that feel disproportionate**: The body reacts as if the threat is happening now, not then.

- **Physical symptoms like muscle tension, gut issues, or migraines**: The body carries what the mind cannot yet process.

- **A sense of restlessness or agitation with no clear cause**: A background hum of unresolved energy, seeking movement or discharge.

- **Emotional flooding, panic attacks, or dissociation**: The system becomes overwhelmed by internal stimuli that echo earlier trauma.

- **Relational reenactments**: We unconsciously cast people in our lives into old roles, replaying dynamics in an effort to find resolution, safety, or control.

- **Open tensions**: Unfinished relational or emotional moments that never had the chance to reach resolution. These incomplete experiences remain open inside of us, creating an ongoing sense of unease or inner push toward reenactment.

- **Act hungers**: Unmet needs or impulses for expression, connection, protection, or repair that were never fulfilled in the original experience. These hungers may resurface in our present lives, driving us to repeat old patterns in search of some form of completion through action. Someone who was hit becomes someone who hits.

A Post-Traumatic Reaction

These unresolved traumatic experiences are typically what present as part of cPTSD in ACAs or anyone who has experienced trauma.

The relational trauma you experienced as a child can go underground for months, years, or even decades and show up in adulthood as a post-traumatic stress reaction or disorder.

This is why soldiers are at highest risk for suicide—not when they are overseas, but when they return home. In battle, they went into survival mode and released adrenaline through fighting and fleeing. When they return home, though, their chronically keyed-up nervous system still gets activated—perhaps when they hear certain kinds of music or smell food that is reminiscent of where they were deployed or stationed. When the flashes of emotion and terrifying images of war come flooding back, they get lost in a post-traumatic moment, leading to overwhelm, disorientation, dysregulation, and anger. The past overwhelms and replays itself in the present as if no time at all has passed.

In ACAs, cPTSD is not so different. You may not remember every argument, every broken promise, or the exact moment you stopped feeling safe, but your body does. Maybe it remembers in the form of tension you can't explain; overreactions to feeling slighted, hurt, or humiliated; a sudden shutdown during conflict; or a panic that seems to come out of nowhere. But this "nowhere" may well reveal the truth of your deeper experience. And this remembering doesn't happen through logic; it happens through sensation. A tone of voice, a raised eyebrow, or an angry look can send you reeling back in time to recall moments, images, and flashes of emotion that you wish you could remember more clearly—or perhaps wish you couldn't remember at all.

One of the most disorienting features of trauma is how it collapses time. In ordinary memory, the past remains in the past, but this is not true for trauma memories. Instead, they become conflated. For many ACAs, the boundaries between then and now dissolve in ways that are invisible but deeply felt. You may find yourself reacting to something minor—a tone of voice, a canceled plan, your parent's opinion, a partner's silence, a sibling's comment—with a level of intensity that surprises even you. Your heart pounds. Your stomach drops. You feel shame, panic, rage, or dread but can't quite explain why. Maybe you withdraw or explode.

This is because trauma is not stored in the same way as typical memory. It's not filed away neatly with a date and time stamp. Instead, it lives in the body as scattered fragments of sensation, emotion, and impulse. When you were overwhelmed, rejected, or frightened—especially in childhood—your brain didn't prioritize making sense of what was happening. It prioritized just getting through. And in doing so, it rewired how those moments were encoded.

Here's some of the science behind what happened during moments that may have felt very hurtful, shocking, or traumatic to you, whether the trauma was emotional, physical, or sexual abuse; neglect; or disinterest.

- **When something feels traumatic, your amygdala—the brain's alarm center—takes over.** Its job is to scan for danger and signal survival responses. In those moments, your hippocampus (which organizes memory as to emotional significance, context, and sequence) and the prefrontal cortex (which makes meaning and helps you think clearly) down regulate; they are inefficient. Instead of becoming a clear story, the experience imprints as raw fragments—panic, shutdown, or flashes of image, sound, or sensation without a storyline.

- **Later, when you get activated or triggered, your past and present blur.** A raised voice, the smell of alcohol, footsteps in a hallway, or even a certain facial expression can activate the amygdala as if the old danger is happening right now. You may shut down, lash out, or collapse. And because of childhood trauma, you may sometimes misread neutral or safe signals as threatening, leaving you overreacting or pulling away when you long to connect.

- **Because your thinking brain wasn't online, the memory stayed fragmented.** Healing needs to move from the bottom up. When the body is involved, the frozen fragments can surface and integrate. As your nervous system finds safety, the hippocampus and prefrontal cortex come back online, allowing you to make new meaning.

So when something in your current life activates that early pain, your nervous system doesn't whisper, "This reminds me of back then." It screams, "This is happening right now!" The past bleeds into the present, and you react not just to what's in front of you but to what's still unresolved inside of you.

RTR, through the use of social atoms and sculpturing that create context and timelines that create sequence, helps the mind to reexperience, configure and reconfigure the memories, and process the emotions and the proxemics that are a part of them. Once clear thought can be rewoven into new meaning, the process becomes bottom-up and top-down giving you a clearer sense of how you developed throughout time and the context that surrounded you.

The Myth of the Trauma Narrative: Why You Can't Think Yourself Better

This is why healing isn't about convincing yourself you're safe. You can't just think your way out of complex PTSD, because trauma isn't a story in your mind; it's stored in your body, your nervous system, and the reflexes that activate before you even have time to think. Learning good ideas alone won't undo survival responses shaped by years of hypervigilance, unpredictability, or hurt. Trauma lives not just in memory, but in muscle, fascia, breath, and heartbeat. And when you get activated, your body reacts (or overreacts), and your thinking mind takes a back seat.

For those who've experienced relational trauma, we tend to feel safer and more in control living in our heads, alienated from the signals our body sends, whether it's to slow down, stop overeating or restricting food, or seek comfort or self-care. We analyze, overthink, and search for the perfect explanation, hoping that cognitive understanding by itself will bring relief. And when it isn't enough, we're frustrated. Why? Because the body still holds the fragmented imprints of past information, frozen and stashed away.

When activated, these imprints don't just remind us of old wounds; they pull us back *into* them, activating emotional spirals that feel inescapable and sending us tumbling down the rabbit hole of confusion and cognitive distortions (see chapter 5).

But paradoxically, as ACAs, we can also be endlessly preoccupied with our past, replaying who said what, how they said it, and why we have to hate them, amputate them, or just forget about everything. Trauma disrupts time: What should be long over continues to live in us as if it's still unfolding. Your nervous system is bracing for battles that belong to another time, expecting an assault on your self-esteem that never truly ends. The past collapses into the present, and suddenly, you're not just responding to this moment; you're reliving the original wound and the kite tail of reverberations and rewounding that came after. Because there was no resolution, no reflection on how those unprocessed, unspoken, and unfinished experiences build on each other, there has been no interruption of this chain of pain, so it keeps recreating itself in real time.

This is where experiential therapies like psychodrama and RTR become essential as part of an overall therapeutic strategy. They allow the body to become an active participant in the healing process, to release what was stuck, complete what was left unfinished, and reexperience in relative safety what felt too overwhelming to feel as a child, so it can be transformed into something coherent, witnessed, and whole. Something that makes sense and can be reintegrated into the self with new insight and understanding.

In psychodrama, we embody the role along with the sensations and memories that it carries. We show instead of tell, giving form to the invisible by incorporating posture, sound, and motion into therapy. We bring the unsaid into the space—or onto the "stage," as we say in psychodrama—and let it breathe. When you step into a role with the help of the director/therapist, you are remembering with your whole body. And in that sacred remembering, something profound happens: The limbic system no longer has to hold the experience in a frozen, unresolved state. The story moves from implicit memory—felt, but not fully known—into explicit memory, where it can be named, owned, processed, and integrated.

In a role-play, the gravity of the role interaction itself pulls the words and sensations from you, the protagonist, toward the person you are talking to through role interaction; you can say what went unspoken before and bring an interaction that feels incomplete to closure. You don't just talk *about* your fear—you *embody* it. You *speak* to it. Next, the director invites you to reverse roles and experience the interactions that live inside of you from the other side, helping you gain perspective. Then you go back and forth, always ending from your own role, and you allow the nervous system to experience a new kind of connection and a new kind of ending.

We don't simply store one side of a dynamic, we store both sides; role reversal frees us from both. We experience the full relational dynamic as it lives within us, gaining empathy and perspective on ourselves and the other person. Then we reintegrate this new experience and perspective back into our inner world in a more resolved way, with a felt sense of clarity that lands a bit differently in the body. What was once frozen begins to thaw; what was once fragmented begins to fit back together into a coherent whole. This is why it's so important that the director of the psychodrama not tell a protagonist what to say but instead help them come to the threshold of their own awareness and connect with the very deep and nuanced "reality" that lives inside of them.

As I've said earlier, and it bears repeating: Healing isn't about thinking our way out of pain—it's about reconnecting with our very personal inner world, replete with emotion, impressions, and imagery that long to surface to be felt and finally seen. As if searching through the darkness with only a torch to guide us, we're revealed to ourselves in pieces—an image, a scene, an important face. We see more as we cast our light about, first here to show fragments of experience and now there toward the rivers of emotions that are frozen over. We see our indistinct faces staring up at us through the ice of our unconscious. As we continue wandering our inner world, ghostly figures become visible. We can actually feel who we were and how we felt, and as we do, scattered pieces of our very self seem to acquire a magnetism all their own that draws them together into a coherent picture. Like a fractured bone sending out healing cells that miraculously know how to find each other, our inner world reknits itself back together, and we become "strong in the broken places," as Ernest Hemingway wrote.[1] And we see ourselves emerge out of this inner chaos now calmed, meeting parts of us, some for the first time—yet we feel we've somehow always known them.

What I have observed and now trust from my forty years of using psychodrama is that your body and inner being know how to heal. Moreno is remembered as having said, "The stage is enough." Emotions don't need to be forced; they need to be heard, they need to be expressed and shown. If we analyze events only on an intellectual level, we bypass the deeper work that engages the limbic system and body-based memory, allowing frozen survival states to thaw, find voice and action, and integrate. It's then that the nervous system can sense and reorganize itself, creating the possibility for new patterns of thought, feeling, and connection. To truly heal from cPTSD and our childhoods as ACAs, we need to create a new body to live in, one that no longer perceives life as if threats are always just around the corner.

The Lasting Impact of Childhood Trauma on Physical and Mental Health

The landmark Adverse Childhood Experiences (ACE) Study, led by Dr. Robert Anda of the Centers for Disease Control (CDC) and Dr. Vincent J. Felitti of Kaiser Permanente, is some of the most consequential public health research of our generation. This large and long-ranging study established the connection between trauma, or *adverse childhood experiences*, during a person's early years and physical and mental health issues later in life. Beginning in 1995, this study surveyed more than 17,000 adults to examine how childhood adversity—such as abuse, neglect, and household dysfunction—impacts health over a lifetime. The findings were striking: The greater a person's exposure to childhood adversity, the higher their risk of developing serious health conditions as adults. Specifically, individuals with an ACE score of four or more were found to be:

- Twice as likely to be diagnosed with cancer

- Four times more likely to develop emphysema or chronic bronchitis

- Seven times more likely to experience alcoholism

- Twelve times more likely to attempt suicide

- Five times more likely to struggle with substance use disorders in adulthood

- At significantly higher risk for depression, chronic disease, and early death[2]

These statistics underscore the profound impact that unresolved childhood trauma can have on long-term health, including creating a higher risk of chronic illnesses like heart disease, diabetes, and cancer, along with mental health challenges such as depression, anxiety, and addiction. For adults who experienced trauma during childhood, this research validated a deeply held truth: Our past, when left unprocessed, imprints itself on us, living in our bodies and shaping our well-being in ways we may not fully comprehend.

Allowing the Inner Child to Show Her Story

When Dierdre, a client of mine, was eight, her mom started calling her "my rock." It sounded like a compliment, and Dierdre wanted to live up to it. Her parents had split up after her dad's drinking took a turn for the worse, and her mom was overwhelmed—crying often, venting about money problems, and sharing details of her heartbreak. Dierdre would sit on the couch, holding her mom's hand, absorbing emotions too heavy for a child, wishing she could do something to steady the ship that felt like it might capsize at any moment.

Without realizing it, Dierdre's nervous system adapted. Her neuroception—her body's subconscious ability to detect safety and danger—began prioritizing her mom's needs over her own. Instead of tuning into her own cues for safety or distress, she learned to scan for her mother's moods, gauging how much space she could take up, whether she should stay quiet, whether she needed to step in and help. Her body learned that her own discomfort didn't matter as much as maintaining stability for someone else. This became her survival role.

By the time she was a teenager, Dierdre had actually become her mom's rock. Her mom relied on her for everything—keeping her younger sister in line, managing the house, even offering advice about dating. Guilt crept in anytime she thought about putting herself first. If she left her mom alone too long, she worried she'd get lonely. Her nervous system had learned that her worth, and even her security, depended on being needed and acting as a caretaker.

Fast-forward to adulthood, and Dierdre found herself in relationships where she was constantly overgiving. Conditioned through years of prioritizing others' needs, she struggled to say no, feeling an almost physical discomfort when she tried. Setting boundaries triggered guilt, as though she was abandoning someone. It took Dierdre years to recognize that her body and the emotions that coursed through it had been trained to bypass its own signals. She had learned to suppress exhaustion, ignore resentment, and push aside her own needs or feelings of being used in favor of keeping others close.

To help Dierdre gain a sense of context around her childhood experiences, I invited her to create a timeline of her relationship with her mother that included key moments and overarching relational dynamics, like times she felt needed, times she felt unseen, and the points during which she began and continued to feel responsible for her mother's well-being. As we've been discussing, trauma memories are often foggy and disjointed, so by including those hurtful or confusing moments or relational dynamics on a timeline, Dierdre was able to more easily identify periods in her childhood that felt highly charged. As she looked over her timeline, Dierdre chose age eight as the point where everything shifted—when her father left and she first became her mother's rock. This was the age when she learned to silence her own needs in favor of emotional caretaking.

I then invited Dierdre—armed with this focus and context—to do a role-play, to put the mom she had when she was eight in an empty chair and talk to her as her eight-year-old self. "What would you like to say to Mom?" I asked.

"Mom, I miss Dad. I miss being a family. I don't know what happened. I miss playing. I miss being eight. I think it's nice you call me your rock, but I wish I could be myself again," she said.

I then asked Dierdre to reverse roles with her mother and talk back to her eight-year-old self as if she were her mother at that time.

"Dierdre, you're my rock. You're such a special girl. I can count on you to do so much. I don't know what I'd do without you!"

"But I'm not a rock, Mom, I'm a little girl. I want a family, I want to play."

We went on like this, reversing roles back and forth, as Diedre continued to pour out her real feelings of how burdened she felt carrying the weight of being her mother's partner rather than her child. Through the deep, unconscious pull that Dierdre felt when talking to the past version of her mother, fragments of emotion, sensorial imprints, and bodily reactions surfaced seemingly out of nowhere.

"How could you do this to me? Didn't you see what it did to me? To my childhood? How different I felt from other kids?"

As Dierdre released her anger, bottomless tears followed, and her body shook with sobs. Then her childlike desire to connect and feel nurtured came forward like a full-speed train.

"What about me? See ME, damnit! Take care of me—I'm sick of taking care of you!" She felt empowered enough to risk the vulnerability of letting go of control and allowing her wounded inner child to have a voice.

With Dierdre, the role interaction itself did the heavy lifting, pulling from her unconscious both the anger and the longing she'd felt as a child. All of this is reparative in terms of getting blocked feelings out; however, another part of the repair came when Dierdre could be vulnerable enough to tolerate feeling her own needs—the ones she had buried beneath the hurt, resentment, and brave face. She asked for her mother's arms to open and just embrace her, to give her what she longed for. And through role reversal, she gave it to herself.

This is what healing looks like. It's not necessarily the brilliant insight of the therapist. Rather it's the protagonist's inner world made manifest on the sacred space of the stage, whether that stage is in person or on a video call. It can even come through role-based journaling that we'll explore together later in this chapter or a role-based letter-writing exercise, as in our next chapter. Once we can externalize our problem through some form of role-play, we can see how trapped we were as a child in an addicted family system. And sometimes we begin to sense how trapped our parents felt as well. In any case, we recognize that they had their own story; they brought in their own history. It wasn't us, after all, who made them act as they did. We weren't the problem, even though we felt like we were.

In order to get to the truth of these inner dynamics, it is important that we allow the protagonist to do the talking in both roles. I do not give the protagonist or other role players lines to say, nor do I let role players make things up. These common mistakes can override the protagonist's delicate connection with their own inner truth. We play out the relational dynamic as it lives inside of the protagonist, distorted or otherwise, and when we do a repaired role-play, it is the protagonist who says what they longed for, who vulnerably asks for what they need or want, and who opens themselves to receive it.

In Dierdre's case, once she had moved through her psychodrama, I simply asked her to rearrange the relationship with her mother to reflect how she wished it had been. She immediately moved their chairs apart to create space between them. Then she acted on her blocked urge—her "act hunger," as we say in psychodrama—and ran out the back door to meet her friends and play. She became the eight-year-old she didn't get a chance to be and opened the door to the life she wanted to have.

Again, the repair is up to the protagonist. Had Dierdre said, "I long to be held by you, Mom," that is what the repair would have looked like. The goal of psychodrama is to connect you to the delicate and nuanced dance you have carved into your neurobiology over decades, to allow you to revisit and reshape it. Who but you can access this inner pattern in all of its complexity, imagery, and emotion? You need to speak your own truth, not someone else's.

Neuroception: The Building Blocks of Safety, Attunement, and Attachment

Love really does make the world go round. It is the core of our human experience. Attachment is how it finds safe haven and expression. Attachment is as complete a mind/body experience as we can have. Our nervous systems and bodies know it first and foremost.

In early attachment relationships, neuroception plays a crucial role. A baby doesn't just respond to words—they respond to tone of voice, facial expression, body tension, and rhythm of interaction. If a caregiver is consistently attuned, warm, and emotionally available, the child's nervous system registers safety, laying the groundwork for secure attachment. But if the signals are inconsistent, frightening, or emotionally absent, the child's neuroception may remain in a state of vigilance, shaping anxious, avoidant, or disorganized attachment patterns. In this way, attachment isn't just psychological—it's deeply physiological. Our earliest relationships literally tune the settings of our nervous system, influencing how we relate to others and to ourselves throughout life. *Neuroception* is the nervous system's subconscious ability to detect safety, love, danger, or threat in our environment without involving our thinking brain. It's how we automatically sense whether we can let our guard down and connect or need to self-protect. If you grew up with "good enough" parents who responded to your cries, felt your pain, and held you till you felt better; who nourished you with a dependable combination of food and care; and who met your basic needs, chances are you will be able to be curious about your world and learn more each day about how to be a person navigating a life.

But if you grew up in an environment marked by stress, chaos, or emotional unpredictability—especially when no one acknowledged or soothed what was happening—you may have learned early on to override your own instincts just to stay connected. As a child, you couldn't afford to see a caregiver as unsafe, so you turned the volume down on your own fear, anger, or hurt. Over time, this taught your nervous system to doubt itself. Your neuroception—the body's built-in surveillance system for detecting safety and threat—can become miscalibrated when you have to ignore or deny what you're feeling in order to make sense of those you depend on. Now, as an adult, your system might still misread cues: neutral or even safe experiences can feel threatening, while genuine danger may not register clearly. Faulty neuroception can make it hard to recognize real danger. This is why so many ACAs describe struggling to know who is truly safe to let in and who they should protect themselves from. The result can be a disconnection from self, difficulty with boundaries, and a distorted sense of what's safe or unsafe, real or imagined.

When neuroception gets stuck in survival mode, it limits your life. It narrows your choices, keeps you stuck in reflexive reactions, and pulls you out of the present moment. This is why learning to regulate your nervous system is such an essential part of recovery—it allows you to shift from automatic survival responses to conscious, embodied choice.

The good news? Just as trauma reshapes our neuroception, healing can rewire it. With the right support, you can retrain your nervous system to recognize safety when it's there. You can gently reintroduce your body to cues of connection, grounded presence, and coregulation. Healing doesn't mean erasing your past—it means reclaiming your capacity to respond to the present with clarity, rather than from old survival scripts. Processes like floor checks and other RTR practices offer a structured, embodied way to gently recalibrate faulty neuroception. In a floor check, participants can choose to stand near a card that names their internal state, then they can share a sentence or two about why they choose it. This simple act of bringing vague, somatic feelings into conscious awareness within a relational and communal setting allows emotions that were once silenced to surface safely. As individuals witness others sharing similar experiences and feel the subtle resonance of group attunement, their nervous systems begin to register these social moments as safe. Over time, repeated exposure to attuned, nonjudgmental connection helps the body soften its survival-based patterns and relearn how to trust both self and others.

While we can't do a physical role-play within these pages, the next exercise offers an adaptation through role-based journaling. In this exercise, you're making friends with the child who lives within you, welcoming them back into your full, integrated self so they can relax and feel safe, so they can have a friend: you.

Exercise

A Dialogue with Your Body

Warm-Up: Recall a Recent Moment of Activation

Think of a recent moment when you felt emotionally or physically activated—perhaps anxious, overwhelmed, frozen, or reactive—and consider the following prompts. Answer them in your mind or, better yet, respond to them in your journal.

- Where in your body did you feel it? Describe the sensations (tightness in your chest, buzzing in your hands, heaviness in your limbs).

- What emotions came up in that state? Fear? Frustration? Sadness? A wish to connect?

- What did you want to say in that moment?

- What did you want to do? Run? Withdraw? Fight? Collapse? Freeze? Fawn?

Now that you're familiar with your internal state at that time, let's take it a step further and trace these emotions back to your past.

- Can you recall a time in your childhood when you felt this same way?

- Who was there? What was happening? As you bring up this memory, notice if your body reacts similarly to how it did in the recent moment.

- In this past space, ask yourself these questions:
  - Where do I feel the emotions?
  - What emotions did I feel back then?
  - What did the child in you want to say?
  - Whom did you want to say it to?

Action: Dialoguing with Your Younger Self

This part of the exercise is not about writing a script—it's about having a conversation. A meeting between who you were and who you've become. Let it be spacious. Let each voice take its time. You'll begin by writing from your adult self, then reverse roles and let your younger self respond. Move back and forth a few times—taking turns with each one listening, each one speaking—until the exchange feels complete. Let yourself write freely. There's no right way to do this. You just need a willingness to share and feel witnessed by your inner self.

- **Begin as your adult self.** Speak to the child within you. Say what you want to say to this part of yourself; open up and be honest. Maybe you remember their loneliness, their confusion, or their longing. Maybe you don't remember much at all—only that something went quiet inside for a long time. Begin wherever you are.

- **Now, reverse roles and become your younger self.** Let that younger voice emerge. Let them say what they've been holding. There may be questions. Silence. Anger. Or tenderness. Let whatever is true rise to the surface and be said.

- **Return to your adult self.** Write back. Not to fix or explain—but to remain in connection. Stay close. Offer your presence. Let your adult self respond honestly.

- **Reverse roles one more time and let your younger self speak again.** Give them another moment to say what's still there. You don't have to rush the closing. Just give them all the space they need.

- **End from your adult self.** Close the dialogue in any way that feels right to you. Whatever feels true, reassure this part of yourself that you see and welcome them, that you are here to listen, to connect, and to hold a loving space for them.

Sharing: Offer Repair to Yourself

From here, journal about the following prompts:

- How do you feel now?

- Has anything shifted in your body or your thoughts?

Take your time and journal about what took place for you and any takeaways you may have received from this process.

Creating Safety Within You

Now, find a quiet space, relax, close your eyes or soften your gaze if it's comfortable, and take slow, intentional breaths. Inhale deeply for four counts, hold your breath for two counts, then exhale slowly for another four counts. Take your time here. Your breath is a direct bridge between your sympathetic (activation) and parasympathetic (at rest) nervous systems, so taking a moment to slow your breathing will help your nervous system begin to settle. Repeat this breathing pattern for as long as you'd like, until you feel a sense of ease flow through your body from your head to your toes. Whenever you're ready, open your eyes! Welcome back to the present moment!

This is a practice you can return to again and again. Some days, your younger self may have more to say; you're building a bridge between the child in you and the adult. Sometimes we talk to the world as our wounded child and then feel disappointed when the world doesn't want to listen. We need to learn to turn toward the adult in us when we're stirred up. Our adult self can listen to our child self and help us to feel seen and to translate our feelings into coherent thoughts so when we communicate them, we do so with enough balance and clarity that we can be heard and then actually listen to what another person has to say as well.

As we've just seen, role-play and role reversal are key ways we can gently interact with the hidden parts of ourselves. Understanding our attachment patterns—which we will discuss next—will help us understand how the way we were raised impacts the way we partner, parent, work, and make friends.

3

Attachment Patterns

Our Blueprint for Connection

From the moment you were born and separated from your mother, every part of you—body, brain, breath—was instinctively reaching to reattach. With a kind of marsupial wisdom, you were driven to root, to be held, to feel the familiar rhythms of heartbeat and warmth. This deep inborn pull toward connection helped you begin to orient—to make sense of life beyond the womb, to find your place in the arms of another. To refind intimate connection in the world after birth. To attach. You were wired to seek the pouch—not just for nourishment, but for safety, for belonging, for the felt sense of being protected in the world. Staying close wasn't a preference; it was survival. So when that rhythm of closeness was disrupted, when the reaching was met with absence or unpredictability, it didn't just hurt, it disoriented. It confused something fundamental inside you. Because connection isn't just comforting. It's how you first learned who you were.

Just as ducklings imprint on their mother and orient their tiny bodies to follow her, to stay close, to survive, your nervous system, too, came into the world searching for a face and body to follow. From your earliest moments, you were wired to track the emotional energy of your caregivers, scanning their microexpressions, the cadence of their breath, and their vocal tones for signs of safety or threat. As Stephen Porges explains in his 2011 book *The Polyvagal Theory*, these early interactions shape your body's instinctive ability to sense safety or danger, not through logic, but through felt experience. When the signals are clear and consistent, your nervous system settles. Your body knows it can rest. But when those signals are absent, inconsistent, rejecting, or fear-inducing, your system does not feel safe; it prepares to self-protect. And long before you had words, your body already knew the difference.

Before you could speak, you were already engaged in one of life's most profound conversations—a wordless, rhythmic exchange between your body and another's. Ed Tronick, in his groundbreaking Still-Face Experiment, showed us how babies are exquisitely sensitive to emotional attunement and how quickly they go into deep distress and disorientation when that attunement disappears. What this tells us is that regulation is not something you were meant to do alone. You were meant to borrow calm from the nervous systems around you. When your caregiver smiled at your smile, felt your tears, soothed your cries, or simply made eye contact with their caring presence, your brain and body learned, *I'm okay. I matter. I exist in someone's heart.*

This back-and-forth—what Tronick calls "mutual regulation"—was how you began to know yourself. Through attuned touch, mirrored emotion, and consistent care, your earliest sense of self was shaped. This isn't just poetic—it's physiological. Your developing brain actually wired itself through these moments of coregulation. Emotional literacy began here: sensing what you felt, connecting it to a response, and eventually finding the words to name and talk about what you were feeling.

Babies are born with a fully developed amygdala—the part of the brain that triggers fear and stress responses—so they can signal distress and alert caregivers to their needs. But the neural circuits for self-regulation—particularly in the prefrontal cortex, especially the medial prefrontal cortex and its connections to the amygdala—are immature and build up over many years. Much of this capacity is acquired outside the womb. In those early months and years, babies depend entirely on the adults around them to help them navigate emotional extremes. It's through a caregiver's steady presence—soothing their cries, meeting their gaze, calming their tiny bodies—that a baby learns how to move from the emotional edges back to middle ground. These thousands of micromoments of attunement begin to wire the nervous system for self-regulation. As neuropsychologist Allan Schore puts it, "The attachment relationship mediates the experience-dependent maturation of brain structures that regulate affect and thereby determines the individual's characteristic patterns of affect regulation for life."[1]

But what happens when the caregiver is emotionally absent or overwhelmed by addiction or trauma themselves? The child's body still seeks connection—it's hardwired to—but the responses they receive may be inconsistent, misattuned, or even frightening. Without a reliable external regulator, the child's nervous system is left to manage what it cannot yet handle alone. Instead of learning how to move from distress back into calm through the presence of another, the child learns to shut down, brace, or overfunction emotionally.

Babies can't fight or flee, so they protect themselves through the only means available. Some shut down, or their bodies enter a freeze state or retreat into stillness or sleep when the environment feels too overwhelming or unresponsive. Many learn to silence their emotional expression altogether, to dissociate, sensing that their needs are too much or too often unmet. Some become hyperattuned, scanning their caregiver's face for cues, adapting themselves moment to moment in a kind of wordless vigilance, shaping their personalities around what the caregiver can tolerate. They fawn, becoming quiet, easy, or overly attuned long before they have language. Many do a combination of all of these. The baby's body is doing exactly what it was designed to do: Preserve connection at all costs. Because in infancy, disconnection doesn't just feel painful; it feels life-threatening. The tragedy is that these very strategies—once brilliant forms of protection—can become the barriers to genuine intimacy with yourself and others in adulthood.

These early experiences form your attachment style, the blueprint your body and mind carry forward into all your relationships. They influence how you reach for others, how safe you feel being vulnerable, how you protect yourself when connection feels uncertain. But here's the very hopeful and real truth: Attachment is adaptive, not fixed. It changes and heals through new experiences of safe, embodied connection. It repairs through repetition.

New experiences of coregulation—through therapy, support groups, safe relationships, and group work, particularly floor checks—can begin to rewire those early patterns. What the nervous system didn't receive early on, it can still learn later. The doorway to repair is always open, thanks to neuroplasticity, the brain's remarkable ability to form new neural connections and adapt throughout life.

Children growing up with addiction may learn to override their own instincts and felt boundaries in order to stay connected, which influences their future ways of attaching. Others can be forced to become independent far too soon, so later in life they may find it challenging to navigate intimate connection, with its vulnerability, need for emotional intelligence, and necessity of finding emotional middle ground and felt safety. Part of healing is learning to identify and celebrate these hard-won strengths, while also noticing where old attachment patterns from your past are still creating unhealthy ways of connecting in your present.

The exploration of attachment styles offers a path toward changing generational cycles of relational trauma. In this chapter, you'll learn how your attachment styles developed from your childhood dynamics and how they continue to influence your relationships today. We'll also look at how your particular patterns show up in partnering, parenting, friendships, and work dynamics. Attachment patterns are not fixed; they are shaped by experience and can be reshaped through new, reparative experiences. By doing the deep inner work and developing and practicing new attachment behaviors, you can use the brain's capacity for neuroplasticity to change and grow. Healing attachment is not just about personal change; it's about intentionally creating a better tomorrow for yourself and those you love. It pays itself forward. And if you are a parent, one of the greatest gifts you can give your children and grandchildren is to heal your own attachment wounds so they don't move through the generations that follow you. This is how you break the chain of pain.

Attachment Theory

To truly understand the depth of attachment and why it wields such a powerful influence over our lives, we can look to the work of John Bowlby and Mary Ainsworth, pioneers in the universe of attachment research. Bowlby, a British psychiatrist and psychoanalyst, developed his groundbreaking work on attachment by using a multidisciplinary approach, integrating insights from psychology, developmental biology, and ethology (the study of animal behavior). He saw attachment as a fundamental survival-based drive that shaped the long-term development and mental health of the adult.

Mary Ainsworth, Bowlby's collaborator and an American-Canadian developmental psychologist, took his ideas into real-world settings, examining how attachment unfolds in the delicate exchanges between infants and their caregivers. In her seminal Strange Situation experiments in the 1960s and 1970s, Ainsworth observed infants during brief separations from their mothers, studying their responses to both separation and reunion. From this research, she identified three primary attachment styles that develop on the basis of how consistently caregivers respond to their child's needs. A fourth style was introduced in the 1980s by Mary Main, a psychologist at University of California, Berkeley, and Judith Solomon of London's Tavistock Clinic and later Yale University.

- **Secure attachment**: Infants with reliably responsive caregivers most often displayed confidence, eagerly exploring their environment yet seeking comfort when necessary. These children developed a foundation of trust and self-assurance, feeling secure in the knowledge that their caregiver would respond to them and that they could explore the world safely and not lose their secure base. These children could refuel with their caregiver.

- **Anxious/ambivalent attachment**: Children with inconsistent caregivers—sometimes responsive, sometimes distant—tended to develop anxious attachment. They clung to their caregivers, distressed by any separation, and were preoccupied with maintaining closeness, fearing that connection could suddenly be withdrawn.

- **Avoidant attachment**: When caregivers were emotionally unavailable or dismissive, children learned to suppress their need for comfort, often avoiding their caregivers even when distressed. Avoidant children behaved as though they were self-sufficient, exploring without seeking comfort, but often their bodies reflected inner isolation as they faced a wall, dropped their heads, turned away, or shrugged off attempts to connect.

- **Disorganized attachment**: A fourth style emerged later when Main and Solomon observed that some children did not fit into the established attachment categories from Ainsworth's research. These children exhibited conflicting behaviors, such as approaching a caregiver but freezing or retreating in fear, simultaneously seeking and avoiding comfort.[2]

If you'd like to get a better idea of your own attachment style, you can take an online quiz by trauma expert and author Diane Poole Heller on her website: traumasolutions.com. It is important to note that we can exhibit different attachment styles, depending on who we are communicating with and what life stage we are in, so try to avoid forcing yourself or anyone else into a box. For starters, we can form different attachment styles with each parent. Take a moment to think about how your attachment style with your using parent may differ from the one with your nonusing parent. (In a seeming paradox, I was more securely attached to my alcoholic father, particularly when sober, than to my sober mother.) Additionally, keep in mind that parenting takes place over many years, and kids grow and change, as do parents, so our way of attaching may change over time. This is why I love psychodrama's capacity to let us embody and talk to the parent we had then as the child we were then, as I described in Dierdre's story in the previous chapter.

How Our Attachment Styles Affect Our Romantic Relationships

When you enter an intimate relationship, your body and mind are not simply responding to the person before you. They are, in many ways, replaying the emotional choreography you learned long ago—how you sought comfort, how you coped with rejection, how you adapted to the unpredictability of love. For ACAs, this choreography is often complex.

Attachment is not just an emotional process; it is deeply biological, drawing on your neuroception (discussed in chapter 2) to scan for signs of safety or danger in your interactions with others. For example, when your partner seems distant, your established attachment pattern may cause you to react with heightened anxiety or withdrawal, activating old survival responses that once protected you from emotional harm. Yet the very behaviors that once kept you feeling safer as a child may now sabotage your desire for connection in adulthood.

Luckily, as I mentioned, attachment patterns, though powerful, are not fixed. The concept of "earned secure attachment," according to Mary Main, describes a gradual process of relearning trust in both one's self and others.[3] Columbia University neuroscientist and psychiatrist Amir Levine emphasizes that it isn't about making a complete transformation, but rather about noticing subtle changes: the ability to pause before reacting, to practice expressing needs with less fear, and to feel moments of connection without immediate anxiety.[4] Over time, these small but significant interactions and shifts can help you build a more stable foundation for navigating relationships and the inner experiences they activate.

Let's take a look at a few case studies and explore the natural push and pull that takes place between people's attachment styles in relationships.

Anxious Attachment: The Fear of Losing Love

If you have an anxious attachment style, relationships may feel challenging when it comes to steady intimacy. You may crave closeness but fear abandonment, leading you to seek constant reassurance. Even small changes in your partner's behavior—delayed replies or a quiet mood—can activate feelings of rejection or even panic. You may overthink, mentally replaying past conversations and looking for clues that something is wrong. When you're caught in the grip of one of these moments, your body may register it before your mind does. Heightened arousal and a sense of inner restlessness may be trying to tell you something about how you attached as a child.

CASE STUDY: EMMA AND JASON

Emma grew up in a household where emotional security was either intermittent or just out of reach thanks to her addict parent's secret drinking and her nonaddict parent's preoccupation with keeping everything together. Now, in her relationship with Jason, Emma often wonders if he will show up for her and is hypersensitive if he doesn't respond to her nonverbal or verbal messages right away. Her mind races with fears of rejection, and she seeks reassurance by pressuring him for constant interaction or texting him repeatedly. Jason loves Emma, but he feels exhausted by the constant need to prove his commitment; and Emma's continuous demand for reassurance triggers his more avoidant tendencies. They both need to understand their attachment styles and how they play off of each other.

STEPS TOWARD EARNED SECURITY

Emma's healing journey can involve gently exploring the space between her past fears and present experiences, allowing herself to feel the pain of these past ruptures, and recognizing them as the source of much of her panic. This would enable her to ease up on projecting fears from her early relationships into the attachment she is creating as an adult. It's important that she begins the process of separating her past from her present. And as she grows more self-aware, she can own her feelings and question them. She can risk being vulnerable with Jason and check in with him to see if her worries have a real basis, rather than insisting that she's right in feeling anxious or being critical of him. This in turn gives Jason a chance to be understanding of her and of his own urge to distance (having an avoidant attachment style) in order to feel safe.

Avoidant Attachment: The Fear of Dependence

With an avoidant attachment style, intimacy may feel like a threat to your autonomy. You've likely learned to equate vulnerability with risk, perhaps because in your early life, emotional needs were met with neglect, criticism, or dismissal. As a result, you became fiercely self-reliant, suppressing your own needs and keeping others at a distance.

In relationships, this can manifest as emotional detachment. You may focus on practical aspects of the relationship—offering support or solutions—while avoiding deeper emotional engagement. You may feel more comfortable with transactional or somewhat distanced relationships, where you feel more in charge or in control. You're not indifferent; your nervous system has simply learned to protect you by downregulating emotional intensity. However, this emotional distance can leave your partner feeling unseen or disconnected, even as you quietly long for closeness.

CASE STUDY: CALIN AND AVA

Calin was raised in a home where expressing vulnerability was met with cold indifference. Now, he struggles to engage emotionally with Ava, who often feels frustrated by his emotional distance. When Ava tries to share her feelings, Calin retreats into himself, overwhelmed by the unspoken fear of being engulfed or judged. Calin's avoidant attachment style becomes more ingrained rather than more flexible because their styles play off of each other.

STEPS TOWARD EARNED SECURITY

Calin can begin to heal this response by practicing small moments of openness. When Ava shares something emotional, he can focus on staying present rather than succumbing to the urge to retreat or get busy with something else. He might start with simple acts, like acknowledging her feelings with, "That sounds really hard." He might share his own vulnerable fears of being engulfed in her needs.

Together they might practice being more present in ways that feel unthreatening, like taking a walk or cooking a meal together. As they gradually build greater trust in the safety of these simple connections, they can both gain a felt sense of sharing an activity and letting it feel safe. As they allow themselves to grow in emotional intimacy, Calin can discover that being vulnerable often strengthens his sense of connection rather than threatening his independence, and he can see that letting someone in can feel good. And Ava can learn to check out her anxieties with Calin rather than projecting them; she can come to understand that distance doesn't always mean rejection. They can each give each other space to be who they are, and they can work with their own styles toward greater understanding and connection.

Disorganized Attachment: The Push and Pull of Connection

For those with disorganized attachment, relationships can feel like an emotional minefield. You may crave closeness but also fear it, caught in a painful cycle of approach and withdrawal. This dynamic often stems from early experiences where caregivers were sources of both comfort and disengagement. Your nervous system learned to exist in a state of chronic ambivalence, oscillating between hyperarousal (fear of abandonment) and dissociation or numbing (fear of intimacy).

In romantic relationships, this can create profound confusion for both partners. One moment, you might feel deeply connected, and the next, you might be overwhelmed by a sudden need to push your partner away. This inconsistency leaves both of you unsure of how to build lasting trust.

CASE STUDY: RACHEL AND ALEX
Rachel's childhood was marked by chaos—her mother and primary caregiver would be loving one day and frightening the next. As an adult, Rachel struggles to maintain emotional stability in her relationship with Alex. When things feel too intimate, she pulls away, retreating into solitary activity. But then the distance

feels intolerable, so she reaches out for reconnection. She cycles between anxious clinging and disconnection. This push-pull pattern creates instability in their relationship, slowly eroding Alex's trust and comfort in their connection.

STEPS TOWARD EARNED SECURITY
Rachel's healing can involve learning to soothe the parts of herself that still carry fear and confusion from the past. Grounding techniques—such as focusing on the sensation of her breath or the feel of her hands resting on her lap—can help her stay present during moments of emotional overwhelm or when she feels the urge to withdraw. By communicating openly with Alex about her fears, Rachel can slowly build trust in both herself and their relationship. Over time, the push-pull cycle can lessen as she experiences the safety of a more reliable connection.

My big tip for couples: Try not to project your discomfort and make it about your partner. For example, if Alex seems distracted, Rachel might assume, *He's angry with me, he's playing with my emotions.* In doing that, Rachel is personalizing his behavior and making it about something she is doing, when in reality he's just preoccupied with work. Instead, she can pause, stay with her body, tune into her overreaction, and gently ask herself, *Did I feel this as a child?*

And remember, it takes two to tango: It's important that each partner understands their own attachment style and how they are playing it out in their partnership. We can learn to *reflect* before we *react*, to *check it out* before we *check out*. We can create peace or recreate chaos. We can live in and model a nourishing and supportive relationship for our children, or we can pass down pain unconsciously.

How Our Attachment Styles Affect the Way We Parent

If you grew up in a home shaped by addiction and/or relational trauma, it's no wonder you carry a deep, unspoken hunger to feel wanted, cherished, and admired. That longing comes from the silenced voice of your inner child's unmet needs—to be loved without conditions, to matter simply because you exist. When you become a parent, the wide-eyed adoration of your child can feel like a balm on that old wound. It's so sweet, so powerful, that it can be easy to lose sight of where your needs end and theirs begin. Without realizing it, you may start relying on their love to soothe the parts of you that still ache. Your child's dependency and need of you can feel like proof that you're finally enough—while some of this is natural, it can make it hard to see them as their own person. And in this confusion, you may unintentionally create the very dynamic you swore you'd never repeat: a subtle (or not so subtle) holding on that keeps your child from developing their own sense of self.

One of the greatest gifts we can give our children and grandchildren is to heal our attachment wounds so we don't misread our children's normal life circumstances as out of the ordinary, confuse our childhood pain with theirs, or conflate *our* past with *their* present. Our love for our children can be a profound motivator for personal growth. We don't have to visit the pain from our childhoods onto theirs; we can turn the tide.

Take a look at how specific attachment styles can show up while parenting and notice how you do or do not identify with these descriptions and examples.

Anxious Attachment: The Emotional First Responder

As an ACA with an anxious attachment style, you may find yourself highly attuned to your child's emotions—an acute sensitivity shaped by the need to navigate unpredictability in your own childhood. This deep attunement, though rooted in love, can sometimes lead to you becoming too protective or enmeshed, overreacting to shield your child from distress. You might rush to rescue them when they are perfectly capable of working something out themselves or with their friend, causing you to get in the way of them building their own resilience and autonomous skills for managing connection. Next time you feel the tendency to fix too fast, pause and ask whether it's your child or *the child within you* who needs saving.

For another example, imagine your child comes home from school upset and doesn't want to talk. Instead of giving them space, you feel a rising sense of anxiety—maybe even panic. You press them with questions, try to coax them into sharing before they feel ready, or begin offering solutions before they've said a word. When they pull away, you feel rejected or even hurt, thinking, *Why won't they let me in? Don't they know I'm trying to help?*

Maybe what's happening underneath is that your child's emotional withdrawal activates your own attachment wound, say, from a time when your needs for comfort were dismissed or ignored. Their silence taps into an old fear of disconnection or rejection, and suddenly, it's not just about *their* feelings, it's about *yours* too. From this place, it can become difficult to distinguish where your child ends and you begin. Your well-meaning efforts to connect may start to feel intrusive to them. They may shut down further—not because they don't love you, but because they need emotional breathing room. And your fear of that distance may feel intolerable to you.

As a parent, finding the balance between closeness and independence is so freeing. If you lean toward anxious attachment, this might mean giving your child space to explore and make mistakes without constantly stepping in. This balanced approach nurtures both confidence and resilience (in both of you, actually), encouraging your child to build a healthy sense of independence and giving you opportunities to heal and do things differently.

CASE STUDY: MARIAH AND HER DAUGHTER, MIA
Mariah grew up with a parent who was unpredictable and emotionally unavailable, making her feel anxious and fearful. As a result, in motherhood, she is quick to respond to her daughter, Mia, whenever she's upset, stepping in to fix things even before Mia asks for help. Mariah has a very hard time letting Mia have her own big feelings because they activate the big hurt feelings of Mariah's inner child that were rarely heard and often ignored. So she hovers, offering Mia solutions even when what Mia wants is the space to simply share her feelings openly so she can learn more about her current state, feel heard by her mother, and come to her own conclusions.

STEPS TOWARD EARNED SECURITY

Mariah needs to gently remind herself: *My child isn't me.* While Mariah grew up feeling alone or emotionally unsupported, her daughter, Mia, might not feel the same way. The idea isn't for Mariah to pull away or to overcompensate—it's to stay present. To listen. To be there for Mia without trying to fix or control her emotions and to learn to tolerate the feelings that get triggered inside of her without projecting them onto her daughter.

When Mariah allows Mia to feel her feelings—without rushing in or shutting her down—she teaches Mia something powerful: that it's safe to feel and safe to share. Over time, Mia can build confidence. She can learn that she is able to explore her more difficult emotions and come out the other side. And, eventually, she can discover that she's capable of handling things even when Mariah isn't right by her side.

The deeper healing for Mariah can come when she begins to own and work through her own attachment wounds, so she can clearly see the difference between the child who lives inside of her and the child she is parenting.

Avoidant Attachment: Emotional Distance and a Focus on Independence

If you identify with an avoidant attachment style, you may approach parenting with a strong emphasis on independence and self-sufficiency. For many ACAs, this attachment style reflects early experiences of emotional neglect or dismissal, so closeness and vulnerability came to feel risky, like a bad idea; managing on your own felt safer. In parenting, this may manifest as a tendency to keep a comfortable emotional distance, meeting your child's physical needs but sometimes struggling with the softer emotional skills of nurturing and calmly listening.

CASE STUDY: JUAN AND HIS SON, LEO

Juan grew up in a household where emotions were considered a liability: Tears were brushed aside, and vulnerability was quietly shamed. As a boy, he learned that strength meant silence and composure meant survival. Now a father himself, Juan wants the best for his son, Leo. He encourages resilience, independence, and self-reliance, offering phrases like "You're strong, you can handle it" whenever Leo shows signs of distress.

But what Juan sees as empowering, Leo sometimes hears as dismissal. When he cries after a rough day at school or withdraws after a conflict with a friend, he senses that his emotional world makes his father uncomfortable. Juan often redirects or downplays his son's feelings—changing the subject, trying to fix the problem, or offering pep talks instead of presence.

Over time, Leo begins to internalize the message that his more tender emotions are not welcome. He stops bringing them to his father—not because he doesn't crave closeness, but because he fears he will be met with distance. Inside, he still longs for something simple and profound: to be seen, soothed, and supported by the person he looks up to most.

STEPS TOWARD EARNED SECURITY
Juan's journey toward earned secure attachment starts with a shift in perspective: understanding that emotional openness is not a threat to strength—it's the foundation of it. Each time Juan pauses to validate Leo's feelings rather than bypassing them, he sends a powerful new message: *You don't have to be alone with your emotions.*

Small moments matter. Sitting beside Leo during a tough moment, saying, "That sounds really hard," instead of "Forget about it," or simply offering quiet presence, warm, hearing ears, and a reassuring touch without fixing—these are the building blocks of relational safety. Over time, these consistent, attuned responses create a new emotional blueprint. Leo learns that his father can hold space for both his courage *and* his sadness. He discovers that vulnerability doesn't push love away—it draws it closer. And this listening is what actually lets Leo walk away feeling stronger for having shared his feelings and receiving his father's caring presence throughout.

Disorganized Attachment: When Love and Fear Get Fused Together

For many ACAs with a disorganized attachment style, parenting can stir up a deep mix of emotion: on the one hand, a tender yearning for deep closeness, while on the other, a deep fear of being rejected or hurt, with underlying feelings of ambivalence, confusion, and overwhelm. This attachment pattern often develops in childhoods where the very people you depended on for comfort were also a source of fear. Love was intertwined with unpredictability—sometimes you were held; other times, hurt or abandoned. The result is a nervous system caught between the longing for closeness and the instinct to protect itself from it.

This can become a push-pull dynamic. You may feel deeply bonded to your child one moment, then suddenly feel emotionally flooded, responding by shutting down, withdrawing, or reacting harshly. These inconsistencies aren't intentional—they're unconscious reflexes rooted in early survival strategies. But for your child, they can feel confusing and destabilizing. When a parent's responses fluctuate between warmth and withdrawal, it becomes hard for your child to trust their emotional footing. Over time, this can interfere with their ability to develop a strong internal sense of safety—the secure base they need to explore the world and form healthy relationships of their own.

CASE STUDY: MARISSA

Marissa is a single mother of two young children. She loves her kids deeply, but parenting often feels overwhelming and confusing. Some days, she showers them with affection and is fiercely protective. Other days, she becomes easily triggered by their emotional needs, withdrawing suddenly or snapping with a sharpness that surprises even herself. When her four-year-old cries or clings, Marissa sometimes freezes, unable to comfort or even approach them. At other times, she overcompensates with smothering care, fearing that she's already failed them.

Marissa grew up in a home where her own mother struggled with untreated trauma and addiction. She remembers needing comfort and being met with rage—or, worse, silence. As a child, she never knew whether her mother would be soothing, terrifying, smothering, dismissive, or drunk—which could mean she cycled through all of the above. That unpredictable mix created a deep inner conflict: *I want to feel close, but closeness feels scary, even dangerous.*

Now, as a parent herself, that same push-pull dynamic replays with her children. She is sometimes their safe harbor and other times emotionally unavailable or reactive—especially when her kids express intense feelings she doesn't know how to handle. Inside, Marissa carries both a desperate longing to protect her children and a haunting fear that she might harm them the way she was harmed.

STEPS TOWARD EARNED SECURITY
When Marissa begins therapy, she slowly starts to see this pattern not as evidence that she's a bad mom, but as a survival strategy rooted in her own trauma. Through using the timelines in RTR and doing embodied role-plays with both her developing inner child and her alcoholic mother, she learns to tolerate the historical pain of her own inner child, which allows her to respond to her children's emotions without dissociating or lashing out, and build more consistency in her responses to her children. Most importantly, she learns that rupture can be followed by repair.

Parenting often activates the parent's unhealed wounds, which then get projected onto the child, so seeking support through therapeutic resources, ACA or other support groups, or parenting groups can help support Marissa in her dual journey of self-healing and child-rearing.

How Our Attachment Styles Affect Our Ability to Make and Keep Friends

For adult children of addicts, and codependents, friendships often carry a unique emotional weight. They can feel profoundly important, sometimes even like chosen family, yet also bring up subtle challenges that are hard to name.

Anxious Attachment: Are We Still Okay?

If you tend toward anxious attachment, you might notice that you feel things strongly in friendship—you care deeply, and you're often exquisitely attuned to shifts in tone or energy. This sensitivity comes from growing up in an emotionally unpredictable environment, where staying alert helped you navigate the moods of caregivers. It was adaptive then, and it still makes you a thoughtful, attentive friend.

But this hyperattunement can sometimes leave you feeling unsure of your place. If a friend takes longer than usual to respond to a text, for example, or seems distracted, it may stir up old fears: *Did I do something wrong? Are they pulling away?* In response, you might find yourself overapologizing, reaching out repeatedly, or minimizing your own needs to preserve closeness.

The invitation here is not to stop caring, but to include *yourself* in the circle of care. You can honor your longing for connection *and* learn to anchor in your own self-worth, even when things feel uncertain.

CASE STUDY: MARIA

Maria treasures her friendships and puts a lot of thought into making others feel valued. But when a close friend doesn't reciprocate in kind, Maria's thoughts spiral. She replays conversations, searching for missteps. Her instinct is to reach out again, just to make sure everything is okay. Or she feels critical, as if her friend isn't as nice and caring as she is.

STEPS TOWARD SECURE RELATING

For people like Maria, the path toward secure connection begins with pausing in the moment of worry and gently asking, *Is there room for another possibility here? Can I trust this friendship without needing immediate reassurance? Or can I let my friend take a different tack than me and still be close?*

Avoidant Attachment: The Thoughtfully Boundaried Friend

If you resonate with avoidant attachment, friendship might feel most comfortable when there's a little space built in. You may enjoy companionship but find it difficult to open up emotionally. This isn't because you don't care; rather, it's often the result of learning early on that being too vulnerable wasn't safe or helpful. So you adapted. You became self-reliant, strong, and good at managing on your own.

In adult friendships, this can sometimes look like being the easygoing or uncomplicated friend, fun to be around, dependable in a crisis, but a little hard to read emotionally. When others try to get closer or express a need, you might feel an impulse to pull back, not out of disinterest, but from a reflexive need to protect your inner world, your "space."

The invitation here isn't to change who you are, but to explore what it feels like to let someone in, just a little. To risk small acts of closeness and gradually discover that it's possible to share more of yourself without being overwhelmed.

CASE STUDY: ELLIOT
Elliot grew up in a home where people didn't talk much about feelings. Today, he's known for being steady and upbeat, but friends sometimes sense a wall. He's quick to offer help but slow to reveal what's going on inside. He doesn't mean to keep people at arm's length—it just feels more natural to manage things on his own.

STEPS TOWARD SECURE RELATING
For people like Elliot, building secure friendship starts with allowing a bit more transparency. It could be as simple as saying to a friend, "I've been going through something," or accepting support when it's offered. Letting others see small glimpses of his inner life can deepen connection and help him feel more at ease being known.

Disorganized Attachment: I Want You Near . . . Until I Don't

Disorganized attachment often reflects a past where love and fear were deeply intertwined. If you resonate with this style, friendship can bring both joy and nervous system activation. You may find yourself craving closeness one moment and needing distance the next, not because you're indecisive, but because connection can feel both nourishing and overwhelming.

You might bond quickly and deeply with someone, then feel flooded or uncertain and retreat. Or you might fear being abandoned and yet struggle to trust when someone stays. These dynamics aren't failures. They're reverberations of earlier relationships where you had to protect yourself emotionally, even from those you loved.

The invitation here is to bring awareness to this dance. To stay present through the waves of closeness and retreat. To tell yourself that the most likely scenario is that nothing is wrong and that your obsessing about it might even create the distance you're fearing. Instead, offer yourself the slowness and space to build calm at your own pace. The world is full of potential friends. It's not like parents—you're not trapped. Call someone else, go to a twelve-step meeting, find community. Twelve-step groups can feel like a safe place to slowly build a sense of safe connections.

CASE STUDY: JAMIE
Jamie forms close friendships quickly: intense late-night talks, shared secrets, fast connection. But when a friend cancels plans or says something offhand that stings, she starts to worry the bond isn't real. She might pull back, withdraw emotionally, or even ghost the friend, not because she doesn't care, but because it feels safer than risking hurt.

STEPS TOWARD SECURE RELATING
For people like Jamie, the work is to stay present in relationship through moments of discomfort. Practicing small repair conversations, staying with a difficult feeling without acting on it, or simply texting back even when she's unsure: These are the building blocks of trust. Over time, she can teach her nervous system that connection can stretch without breaking.

How Our Attachment Styles Affect Us at Work
In the workplace, your attachment style shapes how you relate to colleagues, handle authority, manage stress, and approach collaboration.

It may influence whether you thrive as a team player or need to be in an authority role to feel safe. It may show up in how you receive critiques, how you feel and operate at meetings, or how you maintain boundaries like being on time, asking for help, or cultivating work friends. Let's take a look at how attachment styles commonly manifest for ACAs and codependents in the workplace.

Anxious Attachment: The People Pleaser

If you have an anxious attachment style, you may find yourself frequently seeking approval and validation from supervisors and colleagues, working hard to maintain harmony and avoid conflict. Growing up, you may have learned that acceptance was conditional or unpredictable, leading to a nagging need for reassurance and a bit of fear of rejection. In the workplace, this can translate into overextending yourself, taking on too many responsibilities, and struggling to set boundaries—all in an effort to avoid disappointing others. You may be sensitive to feedback, sometimes interpreting even neutral comments as criticism or overweighting criticism and discounting positive comments. This hypervigilance can create a cycle of anxiety or burnout, where external approval drives your actions, sometimes at the expense of your own well-being.

CASE STUDY: PRIYA

Priya, a marketing manager with an anxious attachment style, constantly seeks praise from her supervisor and takes on extra projects to prove her worth. She often sacrifices her personal time, fearing that declining any task might make her seem unreliable. Over time, Priya realizes that her efforts are more about seeking validation than achieving her own career goals, leading to stress and diminishing her job satisfaction.

STEPS TOWARD EARNED SECURITY

By recognizing her attachment pattern, Priya can begin to practice self-validation. She can set realistic boundaries and gently challenge her internal need for constant approval. Over time, she can learn that saying no and prioritizing her well-being don't necessarily compromise her value at work; in fact, they may just enhance her creativity, value, and balance.

Avoidant Attachment: The Lone Wolf

If you have an avoidant attachment style, you may find that work feels like a sanctuary of independence and self-reliance. Perhaps you grew up in an environment where depending on others felt risky, and you learned to prioritize autonomy, keeping vulnerability at bay. In the workplace, this often shows up as a reluctance to collaborate closely, delegate, or ask for help, preferring instead to handle projects on your own terms.

You might be seen as distant or overly self-sufficient, consistently meeting deadlines but avoiding deeper engagement with the team. Feedback can feel intrusive, and conversations that require emotional openness may be uncomfortable. While this approach supports strong individual performance, it can also limit opportunities for connection, mentorship, collaboration, or being a team player.

CASE STUDY: AHMED

Ahmed, a software developer with an avoidant attachment style, prefers to work independently and finds team meetings uncomfortable. He rarely asks for help, fearing it may make him appear less capable. Though he consistently delivers high-quality work, his team perceives him as withdrawn, which limits his opportunities for promotions that require visibility and engagement.

STEPS TOWARD EARNED SECURITY

To modify his avoidant tendencies, Ahmed can begin taking small steps toward collaboration, like seeking feedback from a trusted colleague or joining a team project. Over time, he'll likely discover that sharing his work strengthens his team's respect and lightens his load as he learns to rely on others for support and input.

Disorganized Attachment: The Ambivalent Performer

With a disorganized attachment style, you may experience conflicting feelings about connection and authority, resulting in inconsistency or ambivalence at work. Perhaps in childhood, caregivers were a source of both comfort and fear, leaving you uncertain about relationships. At work, this can create a push-pull dynamic characterized by periods of high engagement followed by withdrawal, intense productivity followed by burnout, or a mix of craving validation yet fearing authority figures.

This dynamic with supervisors and colleagues can result in intense bonds or attachments to your work followed by doubt, anxiety, or distrust when conflicts arise or feedback is given. You may struggle with loyalty, sometimes feeling devoted to your role and then questioning your value or struggling with insecurity, creating challenges for you and your team.

CASE STUDY: ALICIA
Alicia, a project coordinator with disorganized attachment, forms close bonds with her team and shows dedication. However, when she receives critical feedback, she becomes overwhelmed and pulls back from work relationships. Her productivity fluctuates, and her supervisor notices that she struggles with stability in her professional connections.

STEPS TOWARD EARNED SECURITY
With self-awareness and support, Alicia can begin to address her attachment-driven responses, developing grounding techniques to stay balanced during stress. By seeking therapy or mentorship, she can learn to process feedback constructively and navigate work relationships with greater stability, reducing the emotional highs and lows that once disrupted her performance.

Projection: Where Attachment Wounds, Cognitive Biases, and Distortions Collide

One of the most powerful—and humbling—steps in healing is learning to recognize when you're projecting your attachment wounds, which are rooted in your past, into your current relationships. Projection happens when, instead of recognizing your painful feelings as yours, you make them about someone else. You experience the distress as something *they're* doing to you rather than something *you're* feeling and responding to from your own history.

When old attachment wounds get activated, they can feel overwhelming, frozen in time, or too painful or confusing to fully sit with. So instead of staying with that raw vulnerability, the mind scrambles to make sense of it, often landing on the person who activated the wound. *They're abandoning me. They're rejecting me. They're unsafe*, your brain may tell you. It feels real. It feels immediate. But often, what you're feeling is not only about them. Projection can be yet another attempt to self-protect, but it comes at the expense of the other person and the relationship.

Our unresolved attachment ruptures, and wounds can leave us with a lack of closure. You become the child waiting for the apology that never comes, the partner who clings too tightly or distances too quickly, or the parent who inadvertently passes down the very wounding behaviors you swore you would never repeat. These are all instinctive ways that you try to make the unconscious conscious so you can find some sort of closure.

Without intervention, this trauma cycle continues, recreating reenactments and shifting unprocessed pain from one generation to the next. These dynamics can be intense, charged, and confusing. But they're also invitations. If you can learn to pause and get curious when you're activated, you can start to untangle the past from the present. You can begin to ask yourself, *What does this really remind me of?* or *Where have I felt this before?* In doing so, you reclaim your ability to respond rather than react, to own rather than disown and project.

Recognizing your projections doesn't mean denying your feelings. It means becoming curious enough to ask where their intensity *really* comes from. And the more you can identify when you're projecting, the more freedom you build to stop recreating painful relational patterns. You may not be able to change other people, but you *can* change how you see, interpret, and respond to what they say or do. And that changes everything.

Remember, our knee-jerk trauma responses are largely *unconscious*. We don't know we're recreating dynamics from our past and projecting them onto our present until we take a pause. We need to learn to *reflect*, not *react*. To own and get curious about what we might be importing from our past into our present.

And bear in mind, trauma isn't just about what happened, but about what didn't happen: the connection and warmth you didn't feel, the invisibility, the lack of the love you longed for. Your body, mind, and heart yearn to complete the interactions that were interrupted by rupture or neglect, to unfreeze and come alive, to say what you didn't get a chance to say then and feel what you didn't feel safe enough to feel. This is the beginning of healing.

Exercise

Role-Based Letter Writing: Putting Memories Back into Context on a Developmental Timeline

As I worked with clients with cPTSD, I noticed they had trouble remembering key parts of their lives; they would get foggy, go blank, and lose sense of time. When I asked them to put their experiences on timelines, they found it so helpful, and so did I. They were able to notice how they continued to carry and reenact pain from childhood throughout their lives. And as they wrote their timelines, they remembered more. Try it for yourself!

Draw Your Timeline

On a blank piece of paper, draw a horizontal line across the page. Mark your ages at five-year intervals. At the corresponding ages, gently jot down moments or arcs of time when you froze, carried hidden pain, experienced dysfunctional relational dynamics, or lived out negative self-conceptions and cognitive distortions. Take your time—there's no need to rush. You may notice more memories arising as you go; welcome them and add them to your timeline as they come to you.

Write a Letter to Your Younger Self

Choose an age on your timeline that calls to you. Write a letter to yourself at that age. Imagine speaking directly to this younger you. What would they need to hear most from you right now?

Reverse Roles and Let Your Younger Self Write a Letter in Response

Now, step into the perspective of your younger self. From their place in time, write a letter back to your adult self. What might they want to say if they finally had a voice? What feelings or needs would they share? What might they ask the adult you for?

Return to Your Adult Role for a Letter of Closure

Finally, write one more letter from your adult self to your younger self. This is your chance to offer words of protection and care, letting them know you are here now to keep them safe. This final step helps you anchor in your role as the loving, steady adult self.

As you do this exercise, pause often to notice what arises in your body—the quality of your breath, the sensations in your chest or belly, the emotions that arise in you. You can repeat this letter-writing process for any age along your developmental continuum. Another way to do the exercise is to imagine your younger self sitting in an empty chair across from you; read the first letter to the younger self in that chair, then reverse roles, change chairs, and read the letter from your younger self to your adult self, and finally return to the adult-self chair and read the letter of closure to your younger self.

In embodying and externalizing these hidden parts of yourself, listening to what they have to say, these once-silent roles can finally speak and be heard. The child who felt overlooked, the teenager who lost their footing, the young adult who dragged so much old pain into their young lives—as you bear witness to them with some perspective and distance, you begin to gain a sense of agency and connection you may not have felt before. You develop a more secure attachment to the child who lives inside of you. And this can serve you in attaching to others in deeper and more intimate ways.

When you begin to recognize the patterns that shaped you, you open the door to choice and change. You can bring more awareness to what you are passing down through the generations.

We all need to attach to our families. But sometimes, to stay attached to the people we loved, we had to modify and shape ourselves around what was needed or what was acceptable to them, even if it meant leaving parts of ourselves behind. I refer to these adaptations as *survival roles*. At first, they helped us feel protected or valued. But over time, they became masks we forgot we were wearing. In the next chapter, we'll take a closer look at these roles, not to judge them, but to understand how they formed and see how we can begin to outgrow them.

4

Survival Roles

The Masks We Wear to Feel Safe and Connected

As a child, your deepest need was to be loved and seen for who you truly were. In an addicted family system, however, you often had to become who you were *not* in order to get by. Seen through the lens of attachment theory, survival roles allow us to adapt to dysfunction and stay connected in a family that feels like it is constantly falling apart. When families feel fragile and overstressed, children instinctively learn how to adjust themselves to keep harmony, albeit it a compromised version of it. They learn, often unconsciously, how to be needed, useful, or at least invisible in order to preserve their feeling of attachment to those they rely on for their sense of safety and belonging. As a result, their identity forms around others—what they need, expect, or demand. This becomes a form of false-self functioning. We become what the family approves of, needs, and values, even if it interferes with our ability to grow into our own sense of self. "The looking-good family" is frequently used vernacular to describe family systems that are colluding to look good and hide their problems. It is very common for alcoholic families to hide their ever-increasing secrets and worries. Children are sent out like little representatives to prove to the world that all is well. They are expected to behave in such a way to keep the world from knowing what they fear is happening—namely, that they are falling apart at the seams—isn't happening. But the more deeply a family moves into dysfunction, the greater the gap between how they feel about themselves and what they present to the outside world.

Maybe you became the hero, always achieving and trying to hold everything together. Or perhaps you were the scapegoat, drawing attention away from everyone's real pain. Or did you learn to disappear like the lost child or bring relief through laughter like the mascot? These roles, discussed further throughout this chapter, helped you feel needed, and they enabled your family to continue to function. The cost, though, was that your real emotional needs and feelings may have become buried beneath the roles you learned to play. While the roles gave you a purpose that your family approved of, they also interrupted what every child needs to grow and mature: a safe space to experiment with being you. Over time, these roles may have hardened into identities, shaping how you see yourself, interact with others, and find purpose and belonging well into adulthood.

The more we use our survival roles to stay safe, the more dependent we become on them. Then if someone challenges our role, we might hang on because change would require that we feel the lack of safety that these roles were designed to hide in the first place. We feel like we might unravel on the spot. To understand how these survival roles may have set in for a family living with a parent's addiction, let's look at a dinner scenario. Dinner might start normally enough. Let's say it begins with everyone seated nicely at the table, catching up about their day . . . but then, about two-thirds of the way in, Mom quietly pours her third glass of wine, or Dad pours it for her. No one speaks about it, but everyone feels it. They have all learned that looking for confirmation can get them into trouble, so they stay under the radar. They move into behaviors. The atmosphere thickens, the energy in the room alters, and without a word, each family member brings out their mask and silently slides it into place.

The nonaddict spouse senses what's coming and steps into the enabler role, smoothing things over. "She's just tired," he says lightly, suggesting she go lie down. Maya, the eldest, instinctively goes into action to fill the void, directing her younger siblings to clear the table, do their homework, and get ready for bed while she loads the dishes into the dishwasher with Dad. Maddie, the middle child, doesn't have words for the creeping dysregulation she's sensing in her body, so she acts it out, bursting into tears about something, anything but what's really happening—becoming the scapegoat. Her outburst gives the family a safe place to unload their frustration; they redirect their discomfort from their mother onto her instead. And then there's Langston, the youngest, whose body tells him that the safest thing to do is disappear. He slips away to his room, sinking into video games and learning—without ever thinking about it—that retreat is his best option.

These automatic shifts help the family get through the evening without going on tilt, but they come at a cost. Because no one is talking about the elephant in the living room, they can't fully integrate what is happening. They just respond to their inner discomfort by filling in and finishing the jobs that need to get done to keep the family moving forward into the evening. Their actions are now designed simply to pick up the dropped balls and get through, then to try to settle themselves down inside, to lessen the feeling of their stomach dropping down two inches, carving out spaces in their body to hold pain. The day finally ends, someone puts someone to bed, someone kisses someone goodnight, and someone closes the door on the bedrooms.

The next morning, when their mother comes downstairs smiling, acting as if nothing happened the night before, everyone follows suit. The children are expected to remove their masks, temporarily give up their roles, and return to being just kids. Their father blows a kiss as he heads out the door, saying nothing. And then the cycle starts all over again.

In families shaped by addiction, children are often forced to grow up too soon. The *parentified* child takes on adult responsibilities, becoming the caregiver, protector, and emotional anchor in a household that feels adrift. The *spousified* child, on the other hand, is pulled into the role of an emotional surrogate spouse, offering companionship, affirmation, or even intimacy that is absent between the parents. In both roles, the child learns to prioritize the needs of others, leaving their own tender longings and developmental needs unmet.

Do any of these patterns sound familiar? When you see these as survival roles, automatic adaptations to a confusing and disequilibrating environment, you can begin to shift from blame to understanding. If you took on those sorts of roles, know that they were your best attempt to create stability and connection in a family that felt precarious and unpredictable. But what once was adaptive, what once protected you, can become a liability in adulthood, keeping you hyperattuned to others while disconnected from yourself. Family systems therapist Sharon Wegscheider-Cruse created and introduced the roles hero, scapegoat, lost child, and mascot into the addictions field. They represent each member's best attempt to grow up with parental addiction and the chaos it creates.[1]

How Our Nervous System Shapes the Roles We Play to Stay Safe

Neuroception relies on the seamless integration of sensory input, emotional responses, and external validation to create a coherent sense of reality and of self. But when, as a child, you were repeatedly told that what you saw wasn't real, what you felt was wrong, or what happened didn't happen, your mind and nervous system were forced into a state of confusion and dysregulation. Instead of learning to trust your body's signals, you learned to override them. And without a reliable signaling system, you were left vulnerable and disconnected from your real feelings, at the mercy of external definitions of reality. You may have become scared of the pulsating anxiety that your family was constantly feeling but trying to hide, and you may have started to look toward others to tell you who and how to be. You may have taken on a role. This wasn't just a set of behaviors; it was an emotional strategy meant to protect the family system from going into free fall.

But we don't want to throw the baby out with the bathwater, so I have added the superpowers you may have developed along the way. Most people play more than one role or play overlapping roles. The idea here is to give you a sense of how family members adapt in various ways to maintain peace and balance and to help you understand that you may have developed a form of false-self functioning as you operated from a persona or mask rather than from your more genuine self. Take a look at the following roles and reflect on where you and your family members fit.

The Addict: The Center of the Family Storm

The addict is trying to survive by using substances or compulsive behaviors as a way to self-regulate and manage their inner turmoil. They are trying to numb pain, but this is a synthetic form of soothing and self-regulation, so they don't develop their own capacity to manage distress. Over time, they become increasingly dependent not just on the substance but on the relief it provides. Instead of learning how to settle from within, they rely on something external to feel okay, and they model that for their children. Their addiction often becomes the focal point of the family system, their substance use dictating the rhythm of daily life. Their behavior sets off waves of chaos and emotional turbulence, leaving the family orbiting around in the bedlam it creates.

- **How it shows up**: The addict's actions, whether overtly destructive or subtly manipulative, create an atmosphere of instability. They may deny their problem, shift blame, or promise to change without follow-through. Their presence often requires the family to adapt in ways that prioritize managing the individual's addiction over addressing other needs.

- **The cost**: The cost to the addict is life as they previously knew it and their normal role in the family. Their identity suffers, their emotional development comes to a screeching halt, and they create countless complications for themselves and others. The cost to the family is their sense of safety, reliability, and dependability. Family members also suffer as they absorb shock after shock and hurt after hurt because of the addict's erratic behavior and the chaos it throws the family into.

- **The superpower**: When the addict begins the journey of recovery, their healing can transform the entire family system. They hold the potential to rebuild trust, model accountability in a way that creates lasting change, and demonstrate for the children that healing can happen and that lives on a path of destruction can be turned around.

The Enabler: Maintaining the Status Quo

The enabler shields the addict from consequences in an attempt to feel safe, soothe their own growing sense of internal dysregulation, and keep the family looking and feeling "normal." They believe they are preserving harmony, but their efforts to manage the situation often end up prolonging the addiction and enabling the addict's behavior.

- **How it shows up**: The enabler covers for the addict by making excuses, cleaning up after their mistakes, or assuming responsibilities the addict neglects. They may deny the family member's addiction and minimize and/or rewrite the many mortifying changes both in the addict and in the family. Their rewrites can slowly morph into all-out gaslighting and lies.

- **The cost**: Enablers often lose themselves as they overuse defenses like denial, intellectualization, and minimization. In their efforts to normalize what's happening, family members begin to lose their own grip on "normal." Exhaustion, resentment, and a growing sense of unworthiness can take root as they lose touch with who they are. The enabler's denial of the truth leaves children constantly questioning themselves.

- **The superpower**: When the enabler begins to get honest with themselves, the family can begin to get honest too. The enabler's honesty becomes a new permission structure for the family, who can start telling the truth, relax, and be their authentic selves. They can trust their neuroception again and connect with themselves and each other in healthier ways.

The Scapegoat: The Family's "Identified Patient"

The scapegoat, or the family's designated flash point of acting-out behaviors, sometimes referred to as the "designated patient," gives the family someone to blame and a way to postpone looking at their own problems. Scapegoats absorb the family's unspoken tension. Scapegoats act out denied family pain, often in self-destructive ways, sometimes blurting the truth out to those who might be trying to shut it down.

- **How it shows up**: Scapegoats often rebel, act out, or develop behavioral issues, becoming the family's black sheep. Their rebellion says, "Blame me, not the addiction or my parent's problems." Their actions create just enough chaos to distract from the real source of the family's pain.

- **The cost**: Over time, scapegoats may internalize the belief that they are flawed or bad. They don't learn to relax and self-regulate, because their behaviors tend to increase their internal sense of dysregulation. Beneath their defiance can lie a deep well of shame and the sense that they are somehow to blame for other people's struggles.

- **The superpower**: The scapegoat possesses a remarkable ability to confront uncomfortable truths. Scapegoats are used to being called the problem, so when it comes to recovery and the self-examination it requires, they can tolerate the idea that they have problems they need to own and work on. In fact, it can be a relief to discover that they aren't the entire problem and that their behaviors were an attempt to stay safe in a dysregulated system.

The Symptom Bearer: The Family's Emotional Mirror

The symptom bearer expresses the family's pain more vulnerably than the scapegoat, embodying the unspoken distress through anxiety, depression, or physical symptoms. Unlike the scapegoat, their behavior doesn't distract, but instead reveals the emotional cracks in the system. The scapegoat and symptom bearer roles, however, sometimes overlap.

- **How it shows up**: The symptom bearer may develop anxiety, depression, eating disorders, or chronic illnesses or express distress through behaviors like excessive crying or school refusal. Their symptoms make the family's pain visible.

- **The cost**: Being labeled "the problem" isolates the symptom bearer, leaving them feeling broken or defective when their struggles are actually reflections of the family's dysregulation and unacknowledged pain.

- **The superpower**: The symptom bearer's sensitivity and astute emotional insight make them a powerful force for change. In therapy, their struggles often become the key that unlocks the portal to hidden family dynamics, and it can catalyze healing.

The Lost Child: Invisible but Not Unscathed

In the chaos of addiction, the lost child fades into the background, adopting invisibility as a safety strategy; they need nothing, ask for nothing, and take care of themselves. They often learn to self-regulate on their own, sometimes in isolated worlds and activities.

- **How it shows up**: Lost children avoid conflict by retreating into hobbies, books, screens, or fantasy worlds. They become quiet, self-sufficient, and disconnected, disappearing to avoid adding to the family's stress.

- **The cost**: As adults, lost children often struggle to feel entitled to attention or self-care. They can also be uncomfortable with being seen and can have trouble asking for help. Their independence can mask a profound sense of loneliness, hurt, and/or resentment due to emotional neglect.

- **The superpower**: When the lost child begins to reconnect with themselves and others, their quiet strength and deep introspection can become powerful tools for building meaningful relationships, and their ability to sustain their own often creative interests gives them a deep inner life and frequently a satisfying and purposeful career path.

The Hero: The Family's Savior or Pride and Joy

The hero strives to bring dignity to the family and maintain a sense of normalcy and the appearance of functionality to the outside world. They may take over functions that parents drop, like gathering the family or maintaining rituals. They feel safe in accomplishment, whether in academics, in sports, or in social or powerful positions within the family.

- **How it shows up**: Heroes excel in school, work, or other visible arenas, projecting competence and perfection. They take on responsibilities far beyond their years, trying to hold the family together and sometimes even shielding others from the dysfunction.

- **The cost**: The weight of perfectionism can leave the hero feeling isolated and exhausted. The hero may struggle with imposter syndrome, perfectionism, or fear of failure.

- **The superpower**: When they release the need to be the hero to feel good about themself and save everyone, their determination and discipline can help them build a life of purpose and meaning. They can be a good actualizer of their own dreams.

The Mascot: The Family's Comic Relief

In the tension-filled environment of addiction, the mascot lightens the mood with humor and charm. They serve as the family's entertainer, deflecting attention from the chaos while bringing brief moments of relief, laughter, and connection. They feel safe when deflecting, often through humor or antics. When they sense family dysregulation, they enter with a joke, a distraction, or an attention grabber to break the growing tension and feel less anxious.

- **How it shows up**: The mascot becomes the class clown, the eccentric, or the family jokester, masking their pain with wit. They excel at reading the room, diffusing tension, making others laugh, or entertaining them. Sometimes they are also hiding their own pain and anxiety from themselves.

- **The cost**: Beneath the cheerful exterior, mascots often feel unseen or misunderstood. They may struggle with expressing vulnerability, fearing that without their humor or talent, they have little to offer.

- **The superpower**: When the mascot allows themself to be fully seen and gives up the role of being the tension breaker and comic relief, they can start to know who they really are. Then their wonderful talent for humor, creative expression, and even changing the energy in a room can be a superpower that they're in charge of instead of it being in charge of them.

The Whistleblower: The Emperor Has No Clothes

Naming the dysfunction in one's family system is often met not with gratitude, but with exile. Truth tellers are frequently cast as the problem—scapegoated for breaking the unspoken contract of silence. Yet in doing so, they realign with their own inner authority. They begin to trust what they see, sense, and know, reclaiming their own neuroception from the grip of collective denial. This act, however isolating, ends the psychic split of living one way and knowing another. I have added this role to the list so that if you have been a whistleblower, you will know you're not alone.

- **How it shows up**: Whistleblowers talk directly and openly about the elephant in the living room, the addict's using, and the family's dysfunction and denial. Often they are simply saying what they see, not to obstruct, but to feel sane.

- **The cost**: There is grief for the whistleblower in letting go of the hope that others will see what they see. But part of maturity is accepting that not everyone shares the same risk tolerance for truth. The whistleblower's task is not to convert them, but to remain faithful to their own perception. That, too, is belonging.

- **The superpower**: The whistleblower took a risk to tell the truth because denial became too obvious to them and the pain of lying too costly to their sense of integrity. Most whistleblowers' sense of personal ethics and desire to be authentic wouldn't allow them to keep silent anyway, so their best bet is to continue building their identity and living their truth. This is their superpower: giving themself permission to be them. The sticky part is wanting others to see it their way. For the whistleblower, part of finding inner comfort will be to allow themselves to be them and the family to be the family, to give everyone some space.

All of these roles play a part in disrupting the child's natural development, often leading to issues with boundaries, self-worth, and relational enmeshment in adulthood. These adaptations are signs not of dysfunction in the child, but of emotional survival in a family system where the adults are unavailable or impaired. It's important that they are understood so they don't turn into long-term dysfunction. If you recognize yourself in any of the roles above, healing involves facing and working through the pain and losses you experienced while playing these roles, recognizing the power playing the roles gave you in your family system, being willing to soften or relinquish the roles where they are in your way and in the way of others, and taking responsibility for building your own identity.

Exercise

What Are Your Roles?

Take a moment to reflect on the following prompts to help you explore your family roles and how your nervous system adapted to your early experiences. Respond to these prompts in your journal to deepen your self-understanding.

Mapping Your Survival Role

Think back to your childhood. What role did you play when things felt tense or unpredictable? Were you the mascot, the hero, the scapegoat, or the one who disappeared? How did this role help you survive at the time? Now consider: How might this survival role still show up in your adult relationships? What patterns do you notice?

Listening to Your Nervous System

Close your eyes if it feels comfortable and take a few slow breaths. Bring to mind a moment from childhood when you felt like you had to adjust yourself to maintain connection or avoid conflict. As you recall this memory, notice what happens in your body. Does your breath change? Do you feel tension, restlessness, or numbness? Now, write about how your nervous system learned to read the room and anticipate others' moods. How has this shaped your ability to trust your own instincts? How does it influence how and where you get activated in relationships today?

Reclaiming Your Inner Compass

If you no longer had to manage or scan for the emotions of others, what would shift for you? What gains would you make? What would you be losing or afraid of losing? Describe this new awareness. What attitude shifts and new behaviors can you take on to make it more real in your day-to-day life? Remember to keep the focus on yourself here and not on others.

Unconscious Family Dynamics: Emotional Undercurrents that Shape Family Patterns

Now that we've explored the masks you may have worn and the roles you took on to feel safe, connected, and needed, let's turn to something more hidden but just as powerful: the emotional undercurrents that shaped your family system. These are the forces you may have felt your whole life but never had words for, the silent pulls that keep you stuck when part of you is ready to move forward. Like survival roles, these invisible dynamics are rooted in a search for safety. They show up in how families align or divide, compete or disconnect, all in an unconscious effort to manage anxiety and create a sense of stability, however fragile.

Parentification and Spousification

In families shaped by addiction, children are often forced to grow up too soon. The *parentified* child takes on adult responsibilities, becoming the caregiver, protector, and emotional anchor in a household that feels adrift. The *spousified* child, on the other hand, is pulled into the role of an emotional surrogate spouse, offering companionship, affirmation, or even sexual intimacy that is compromised between the parents. In both roles, the child learns to prioritize the needs of others, contorting their own developmental needs.

Enmeshment/Overcloseness: When Boundaries Blur

Enmeshment can be a training ground for codependency and blended identities. In families without clear boundaries, emotions, decisions, and even identities begin to overlap, leaving little space to explore and develop your own individuality.

Disengagement: Undercloseness, or Building Emotional Walls

Maybe you learned to retreat behind emotional walls or hide in plain sight using a false face of ease and positivity to cover up your stress and worry. Or maybe you used these walls to avoid being brought into hard truths, like why Dad disappeared for days. These strategies were useful when they helped you buffer the pain at home, but you may be using those same walls now to keep you at a distance from the people who matter most; they may be making vulnerability and letting in hard truths about yourself or those close to you feel like risks you can't afford to take.

- **Avoidance/disengagement**: Silence may have been your safe haven; you might have been adept at dodging difficult questions to keep the fragile peace. But the truths you avoided didn't just vanish; they lingered beneath the surface, creating emotional barriers that can still make genuine connection—both with yourself and with those closest to you—feel daunting.

- **Compartmentalization**: Pouring yourself into work, studies, or hobbies may have been a safe anchor—a way to create structure and predictability in a world that felt chaotic. This kind of focus can be a powerful adaptation, allowing you to move forward and build a life of your own. But there can be a hidden cost. When compartmentalization hardens, it can leave parts of your emotional life sealed off, even from yourself. You may become so identified with achievement, success, or other roles like sexual attractiveness that gave you relief and a sense of identity, that without them, you feel unmoored. And/or vulnerability and closeness might feel dangerous, leading you to live behind invisible walls—not fully knowing the parts of you that long for connection.

Invisible Divides and Factions

Addiction doesn't just disrupt families; it fractures them, creating invisible factions that pit family members against one another. You might have found yourself choosing sides: defending one parent while a sibling defended the other or feeling torn between loyalty and resentment. These rifts often leave scars that outlast childhood, shaping your adult relationships in subtle but enduring ways.

- **Family factions**: Once-close bonds may now feel strained by mistrust or resentment. Taking sides or navigating shifting alliances within the family can leave lingering emotional wounds. Some members band together for safety, leaving others out.

- **Parent/sibling overcloseness**: When a parent leaned too heavily on one child, perhaps treating them as a confidant, other siblings may have felt neglected or resentful, creating lasting fractures. This can turn what would otherwise be normal sibling rivalry into deep envy and rifts.

Covert and Overt Alliances: Invisible Ties That Bind

In chaotic families, often some members form alliances to maintain balance, minimize conflict, gain power, or feel safe. Sometimes these alliances are explicit; for example, you might have become your parent's confidant or emotional caretaker. Other times, the alliances are unspoken, like when you silently agree with a sibling to avoid certain topics or form pacts to gain power or to keep the peace. These patterns helped you survive, but they can linger into adulthood, leaving you unable to talk directly about the childhood you shared and all that went on.

- **Overt alliances**: Visible and clearly defined, overt alliances place one family member in a stabilizing role, often at great personal cost. You may have sacrificed your emotional well-being to soothe a parent's anxiety or shield siblings from conflict—again, another manifestation of parentification.

- **Covert alliances**: Silent, unacknowledged agreements that bind family members together in subtle ways. These unspoken pacts to engage in certain behaviors, like avoiding certain topics or bonding together for safety or power over others, can last into the future.

Triangulation: Indirect Communication Patterns

Triangulation is a common family pattern where two people avoid dealing with conflict between them by pulling in a third person. Instead of facing each other, they go through someone else—turning that person into a go-between, an ally, or even a gossip partner or dumping ground for their emotions. It might feel like a way to keep the peace, but it actually spreads tension, creates confusion, and it blocks real healing. Families often use triangulation to avoid uncomfortable emotions or quietly shift power. Pulling in a sibling for comfort or power: One sibling complains to another about a third sibling or parent they want to avoid talking with directly. This can put the sibling who is being "triangulated" in a painful, loyalty bind, and it can cost them their comfortable relationship with the other family member.

- **The child as go-between**: One parent complains to the child about the other parent, expecting the child to take sides or deliver messages.

- **Emotional surrogate**: A child is placed in a spousal or confidant role, meeting the parent's emotional needs instead of the parent's partner doing so.

- **Sexualized triangulation**: This occurs when a parent, caregiver, sibling (generally older) places a child in a sexualized role, either explicitly, through sexual abuse, or implicitly, by burdening them with adultlike relational needs or desires. Triangulation can happen when:

- A parent treats a child as a substitute spouse
- A parent engages in inappropriate flirtation or boundary violations
- The child is placed in a role to compete for the attention or affection of the other parent
- Incest or covert incest occurs, where a child is expected to meet emotional or sexual needs that should exist between adults, namely the parents

Emotional Contagion: Identity Blending/Fusion

A parent's, caregiver's, or sibling's anger, worry, or sadness may have felt like it seeped directly into you, as if their emotions were yours to carry. This lack of separation can leave you second-guessing your own emotional reality, unsure where their feelings end and yours begin. Over time, you may have come to believe that by absorbing their pain, you were somehow protecting or caring for them.

But this enmeshment comes at a cost: It can leave you disconnected from your own needs, emotions, and desires. It's codependency in the making. Untangling from this emotional web isn't about abandoning those you love—it's about reclaiming your inner space and learning to discern what belongs to you and what never did or should.

Exercise

Mapping Your Unseen Family Dynamics

This exercise will help you *see* the invisible family dynamics that have shaped you. Though this may dredge up some uncomfortable feelings, I encourage you to also let yourself be creative. You can draw and write out the family map, or if you prefer using your own photos, drawings, or other images, you can make a scrapbook or collage.

Map Your Unseen Family Dynamics

Beyond individual roles, family systems are shaped by alliances, splits, and fractures. To bring these patterns into focus, create a simple family map or social atom. Using circles to represent females, triangles males, and rhombuses for gender neutral, first place yourself anywhere on the page that feels right to you, then locate and label all others in the family including caregivers, pets, and relatives who were an incorporated or otherwise important part of your family system. Make symbols reflect size differentials, distance, closeness, enmeshment/overlap, disengagement, factions and so on. Draw connecting lines or add words to describe the dynamics:

- "Thick as thieves" (fusion/enmeshment)

- "Cut off" or "isolated" (disengagement)

- "Two against one" (factions or triangulation)

- "Schism" (a split or fracture)

- Close and connected

- Confidants

- Covert alliances

- Overt alliances

Next, in your journal respond to the following questions.

- What stands out to you?

- What surprises you?

- What feelings come up as you look at this map?

- Where are you in this system, and how do you feel about it?

- How does it feel to look at these dynamics and groupings?

- Do you still play out these dynamics today in your life?

Now, redo your map to reflect how you wish it had been or how you'd like it to change now or in the future. You can answer the same questions from your previous map with answers related to this second one. Leave out the last question and replace it with this:

- How does it feel to look at your new, repaired map?

How Addiction Suspends Family Development

One of the most profound impacts of addiction is how it arrests a family's natural evolution midstream. It's as if they become frozen in time, a family locked together somewhere in the past, unable to move forward. And if the stress of living with addiction is compounded by other family traumas like divorce, poverty, or mental illness, your family can be even more vulnerable to fissures and to the damage that comes with leaving wounds unresolved. As time moves on, family members are more likely to cling to the patterns they developed to cope with crisis because that feels safer than going back, peeling back the protective armor of their dynamics and roles, and feeling the pain that lies underneath the surface. Instead of growing together and adapting to the relational shifts that come when children become adults with families of their own, they hang onto old roles and patterns they learned when young. But this keeps the family from growing, adjusting, and thriving together. Embedded in these old roles is the pain they were designed to cover; the silent threat of crisis still lives beneath the surface. Arguments rehash the same wounds that never quite mend while deeper, unspoken emotions remain unaddressed. Family members can't just relax and be themselves.

Exercise

Reflection: Frozen in Time

In your journal, take a few quiet moments to reflect on these questions:

- If my family froze somewhere in time, when might that have been?

- What are some of the features of our frozenness? How do I see it play out in roles, rules, or repeated patterns?

- What does this frozenness keep us from seeing, feeling, or talking about?

- What has it cost us—as a family, and for me as an individual?

- What parts of myself might still feel frozen, stuck in the family's old story?

- If this frozenness could thaw, what might become possible for me on my own or for us as a family?

There are countless ways we learned to contort, mute, or mask our true selves to keep the peace—both within our families and within our own bodies. As children, these adaptations helped us belong and get through. But in adulthood, they often keep us locked in roles and patterns that no longer serve us, leaving us disconnected from our own emotional truth.

Real healing begins when we stop managing other people's emotions and start attuning to our own. Instead of scanning the world for cues about how to stay safe, we learn to listen inward—to our nervous system, our feelings, and the quiet signals of our body.

This is the doorway to change and to breaking cycles that may have traveled through generations.

To take this work deeper, we now turn to another layer: the cognitive and somatic distortions and biases we developed in childhood in a desperate attempt to take on responsibility for the deep, unspoken terror floating around the family system. These conclusions we came to became the seeds of subtle, often unconscious patterns that shaped how we see ourselves and others. In the next chapter, we'll begin to untangle these distortions and biases, so we can see more clearly.

5

Guessing at Normal

Cognitive and Somatic Distortions and Biases

If there is one chapter in this book that I hope you'll read and reread, it is this one. Cognitive distortions and biases are a key to unlocking ACAs' deepest problems around creating emotionally healthy and balanced relationships as adults. Picture a parent who is high on pills or alcohol and what that state of mind looks like to the developing, magical mind of a child, which is fundamentally detached from reality and inhibitions. In many households with an addicted parent, guardrails are rarely, if ever, enforced; reasoning is questionable; and the parent is disturbingly unpredictable. Now, add to that a well-meaning coparent who is trying to manage the child's anxiety with excuses like "Dad's just happy" or "Mom has the flu again," essentially rewriting reality to keep the peace. Then there's the reality that the traumatized brain and body don't function normally in high-stress environments, and you have a recipe for survival-based, distorted reasoning that embeds itself into the child's mind and body, then shows up with a vengeance as they grow up and try to create their own "normal," "balanced" life as an adult.

Young children don't have the psychological maturity to see their parents' struggles as separate from them or to put them in perspective. They live in a world of magical, egocentric thinking. With a wave of their little arm, they believe they can summon fairies, subdue dragons, alter the course of the moon, and bend truth. In their minds, they are powerful enough to shape reality, grant their parents' wishes, and bring their family peace. But if children can imagine they have the power to change their families, they can also believe they are responsible for the pain they see but don't understand. When parents deny or minimize what's clearly wrong, children assume the truth must be too terrible to face. So they make up their own story to preserve some sense of control and connection: *This must be my fault* or *If I pretend everything is fine, maybe it will be, and I can still feel safe.*

Accepting a distorted version of reality is often less terrifying than facing the unbearable possibility that the people they depend on are in fact not so dependable. And these beliefs don't go away by themselves. We carry them straight into our adult identities and relationships.

Cognitive Distortions and Relational Trauma

Cognitive distortions are mental shortcuts that enable us to make quick decisions and interpretations without overthinking every detail. Helping the stressed brain simplify complex information, they allowed us to function in a world of information overload by speeding up decision-making, reducing cognitive load, and allowing quick mind/body responses in uncertain situations. However, because these distortions in your thinking and assessments are conclusions you came to in the middle of emotionally charged moments when you weren't thinking clearly, when you were scared and anxious, they can lead to serious errors in judgment. They cause you to come to conclusions that are designed to explain away fear.

An addicted family system puts *everyone* on cognitive overload, so these distortions offer a fragile sense of safety and control for anxious children. They provide a quick explanation, however flawed, for denied or out-of-control family dysfunction. They helped you as a child feel a small measure of control in an environment where chaos surrounded you and threatened to upend your sense of basic security.

When the nervous system senses threat, the *survival mind* takes over. This is not the calm, reflective mind that weighs options and considers context; it is the fast, reactive mind wired to keep you alive. As we discussed in chapter 2, in states of high activation, the amygdala sounds the alarm, flooding the body with stress hormones and pulling resources away from the prefrontal cortex—the part of the brain responsible for reasoning, perspective taking, and impulse control. The thinking mind takes a back seat while survival circuits drive behavior.

In this state, logic becomes narrowed, and thought patterns often shift into extremes—black-and-white thinking, catastrophizing, overgeneralizing, mind reading, and assuming the worst. These distortions or mental shortcuts were your brain's attempt to make rapid sense of chaos and keep you safe, even if the danger was long past. But this shift has profound effects on cognition. Threat states limit access to perspective taking and flexibility, instead favoring rapid, reflexive judgments. Subtlety collapses into absolutes; situations are perceived as safe or unsafe, people as friends or foes, outcomes as successes or failures. Cognitive distortions emerge as the brain scrambles to impose order on chaos. In developmental trauma, these patterns often become ingrained, embedding survival logic into the architecture of identity and shaping adult relationships long after the original threat is gone.

To help you get a sense of the cognitive and somatic distortions you may default to when your fears and nervous system get activated, let's take a look at the most common ones, along with descriptions of how they might show up (both in your thoughts and in your body) and how they affect your behavior.

All-or-Nothing/Black-and-White Thinking: "It's either all good or all bad"

- **As a child**: Black-and-white (or all-or-nothing) thinking grows out of a dysregulated nervous system that shoots from zero to ten or ten to zero with no speed bumps in between. This dysregulation causes us to seesaw between hyperactivation on the one hand and emotional numbing or shutting down on the other. It is the body's survival system engaging to allow you to function without thought so you can gear up fast to fight, flee, freeze, or fawn. When you're in the throes of such reactions, you likely have trouble finding middle-ground solutions, swinging from one pole to the other. This state is a kind of ground zero for cognitive and somatic distortions and drives dysregulated thinking, feeling, and behavior.

- **As an adult**: This all-or-nothing pattern might show up as a need to be right in conflicts, because if you're not completely right, then you must be completely wrong. You can see only one solution and one side: yours. Middle ground feels unfamiliar and requires that you sit with the deep, anxious internal states that set the pattern up to begin with. Remember, in survival mind, it's almost impossible to take in new information.

- **In the body**: You may experience tight shoulders, a tense jaw; rigid posture; a loud, insistent voice; waving arms; redness in the face; or breathing that barely moves past your chest. In this state, your nervous system is in performance mode, braced to win or collapse.

Emotional or Intense Reasoning: "I feel this so strongly, it must be true"

- **As a child**: With emotional reasoning you base your conclusions not on logic, but on how intensely you are feeling something. You may have thought, *I am feeling this so strongly. My feelings are my evidence that I must be right and what I am feeling must be the truth.*

- **As an adult**: You might believe that if you feel something very intensely, you must be right; you get stuck defending what feels like your absolute truth. But feelings aren't facts. Trust how you feel, but also be open to questioning it, knowing that your emotions don't always tell the full story.

- **In the body**: You may feel overwhelm, foggy brain, shaky hands, or a sensation of being consumed by emotion. Without early support, these feelings became overwhelming. Your body and nervous system didn't have enough experience with having your intense emotions soothed and coming back to a calm, regulated state, so the neural pathways that could move you toward balance are underdeveloped.

Catastrophizing: "If something goes wrong, it will ruin everything"

- **As a child**: You may have thought, *If my parents argue, the whole family will fall apart.* In your anxiety, you swung to extreme conclusions, or you may have resorted to fawning in order to feel safe.

- **As an adult**: Today, you may find yourself constantly expecting the worst, which leads you to unintentionally get stuck in a negative feedback loop. Instead of going down this rabbit hole, pause and ask yourself, *What is true right now?* The present is often more manageable than your fears.

- **In the body**: You may experience anxiety leading to racing thoughts, a pounding heart, cold hands, or a tight belly. This is your nervous system sounding the alarm early. It learned to get ready for the worst so you wouldn't be caught off guard.

Shifting Blame: "It's all my fault, it's all their fault"

- **As a child**: You may have thought, *If I just try harder or take the blame, I can get this pain to stop.* Taking on blame gave you the illusion of control.

- **As an adult**: You might still carry self-blame or shift the blame entirely to others because nothing in between feels safe. Both serve as shields that protect you from sitting with the uncomfortable middle ground. Recognize that no one, including you, can *always* be to blame.

- **In the body**: This thought pattern can manifest as irritability, jaw clenching, shallow breath, or a wired, defensive energy just under your skin. Your nervous system may always feel cocked and ready to fire.

Personalization: "It's all about me, what I did or didn't do"

- **As a child**: You may have internalized the belief *If I were good enough, they wouldn't fight so much, or my parent wouldn't drink*. It was easier to carry the burden of responsibility for other people's pain than to face the fear that your parents weren't functioning well.

- **As an adult**: This pattern might show up today as you feeling responsible for others' emotions and well-being. You may have trouble staying in your lane, because other people's problems feel like yours to solve. But you don't need to fix or rescue others to prove your worth.

- **In the body**: This can show up as tension around your eyes or jaw, a tight chest or racing heart, or an almost compulsive urge to step in and smooth things over—even when no one has asked for your help. Your nervous system still registers others' discomfort as danger and tries to restore safety the only way it knows how: by overfunctioning.

Minimization: "I'm making too big a deal over this; it really isn't that bad"

- **As a child**: You may often have thought, *I must be exaggerating* as a way to ward off feeling unimportant or invisible when your pain was dismissed. Or your parents downplayed your worries or needs because it was easier than considering them.

- **As an adult**: You might still silence your struggles, thinking, *I'm making too much of this* or *I shouldn't feel this way*. But remember, you don't need to act on every feeling; just allow yourself the opportunity to witness how you feel. Practice becoming curious about your responses rather than automatically minimizing them.

- **In the body**: You might say, "It's no big deal," even as your chest tightens or your stomach knots. Minimizing can show up as a flat tone, disconnection, or a freeze response. This is your body's way of staying invisible.

"Should" Statements: "I should be better by now"

- **As a child**: You may have thought, *I should always agree or give in to keep the peace. I should always do the right thing so I won't get in bad trouble. I shouldn't be mad; it's not nice,* et cetera. Rigid rules gave you a sense of control.

- **As an adult**: Impossible expectations, like *I should be able to keep everyone from harm*, might still weigh you down. Letting go of the "shoulds" is freeing. Learn to accept that you can't fix everything. You can help, but fixing is another thing, and it's often based on *your* need for control rather than the other person's actual desires.

- **In the body**: This thought pattern might show up as a collapsed posture, bent shoulders, tightness in the chest, or pain in your muscles.

Overgeneralization: "This always happens to me"

- **As a child**: Early on, you may have formed this belief as a way to make sense of hurt. For example, if a caregiver frequently let you down or a friend betrayed you once, your young mind might have decided, *It will always be like this*. It was a defense you used to predict and prepare for further hurt.

- **As an adult**: Overgeneralization becomes a lens that distorts emotional reality. You might catch yourself using words like "always" or "never" after a setback, perhaps saying things like, "See? I always mess up" or "People never treat me fairly." This thought pattern is common when the brain uses past failures as templates for future expectations or when a single painful event becomes symbolic of a larger narrative of failure or danger. This "always/never" reflex shrinks your sense of agency. You may avoid new opportunities or relationships because your nervous system has come to expect repetition of past pain.

- **In the body**: You may notice a tight chest, slumped shoulders, or a sinking feeling in your gut. Your heart may race, or you might freeze in moments that resemble earlier experiences.

Labeling: "I'm a failure/He's the problem"

- **As a child**: When caregivers were emotionally unavailable, unpredictable, or blaming, your mind searched for a reason. Often, it landed on *you* or someone close to you. *I must be the problem* or *He's the messed-up one* became a way to make sense of the chaos. Labeling gave your brain a quick explanation and a fragile sense of control over what felt unfixable.

- **As an adult**: You may still use harsh labels, like *I'm broken* or *They're toxic*, to manage uncertainty or avoid deeper emotional discomfort. These labels are often fear in disguise. Healing begins when you pause, notice what you're actually feeling underneath the labels, and ask: *What am I protecting myself from right now?*

- **In the body**: Shame shows up physically. You might feel a collapse in your chest, a heaviness in your limbs, or an urge to look down and disappear. The body curls in on itself, as if trying to hide. This posture of shame is the residue of early experiences, when shrinking felt safer than being fully seen.

Mind Reading: "I know what they're thinking—and it's not good"

- **As a child**: You may have thought, *They're mad at me; I can tell*. Or you may have thought you knew what someone else was feeling; you could read their mind in a way. Imagining you knew what others felt became a way to manage your anxiety as a kid.

- **As an adult**: You might still assume others are upset with you or imagine you know their feelings and hence what they need—that is, your advice! Instead of guessing, try asking. Don't assume you're right just because you think or feel something.

- **In the body**: You may experience jittery energy, flickering eye contact, or tight muscles, especially in your neck or face. You learned to scan people for danger. Now your nervous system reads threat in every pause.

Discounting the Positive: "They're just praising me because they have to"

- **As a child**: You may have thought, *When they say they love me, they don't mean it* or *You're just saying I'm good because you're my mom.* Dismissing love and positive affirmation felt safer than risking disappointment.

- **As an adult**: You might brush off praise, affection, or kindness, feeling unworthy or afraid that someone's caring words aren't real. Or you might minimize the positive feelings others have about you so you won't learn to count on them or trust that they will continue. Dare to let in the good bit by bit; it can be profoundly healing.

- **In the body**: You may experience a shrinking; curved, slouched shoulders; a lack of eye contact; or a reflexive urge to disappear, even in moments of success. Excitement, trust, and ease didn't feel safe, so now your body flinches from these feelings like they're too good to last.

Control Fallacy / Overresponsibility: "If I don't do it, it won't happen"

- **As a child**: You may have thought, *If I don't take care of everything, this family will fall apart* (and perhaps this was true). Becoming the caretaker was your way of creating stability.

- **As an adult**: You might feel it's your job to fix everything, leaving no room for self-care or for others to care for you. You either overfunction, trying to manage everyone and everything, or you collapse in exhaustion. You didn't learn what shared responsibility looks like. You may have a hard time reaching out for or accepting help.

- **In the body**: You may feel chronic tightness (fight mode) or disconnection/dissociation (freeze mode). So your body only knows extremes: Either you feel wired, or you feel nothing at all. This is what chaos taught you. If you didn't control it, your world could collapse around you.

Fallacy of Fairness: "I never get the breaks; they have everything"

- **As a child**: You may have thought, *It's not fair that other kids have normal families*. Perceiving unfairness helped you see what was wrong, even if you couldn't change it.

- **As an adult**: Because this distortion emphasizes perceived unfairness, it can keep you stuck in anger and resentment when life doesn't go as you want it to go. Life isn't always fair, but gratitude can help shift your focus.

- **In the body**: You can experience a sinking feeling, slumped posture, or internal energetic collapse. Because your nervous system didn't learn what healthy balance and responsive caretaking felt like, you tend to give up and collapse.

Confirmation Bias: When Certainty Feels Safer Than Truth

Cognitive bias makes distorted thinking feel like fact. Your brain clings to familiar beliefs. It filters in only the evidence that supports them while ignoring, discounting, or dismissing anything that contradicts them. Evolution wired us for survival, not truth, and survival often depends on making quick, confident decisions rather than accurate ones. Because this was your way of staying safe, your brain became deeply invested in proving itself right; certainty felt like self-regulation.

Over time, a cognitive distortion, like *I'm not good enough* or *People can't be trusted*, can become *confirmation bias*. Confirmation bias is the tendency to search for, interpret, and remember information in a way that confirms what we already believe—while ignoring or discounting anything that challenges us. For example, if you believe someone doesn't like you, you're more likely to notice their frown than their friendly wave.

Your brain isn't trying to deceive you—it's trying to protect you. But in defending the distortion and rejecting anything that challenges it, you stay stuck; you can even feel threatened by intimate negotiation, changes in plans, or team playing at work. Here's why the brain clings to being right:

- **Predictability feels safe**: Uncertainty activates the same parts of the brain as physical pain. A predictable belief—even if it's distorted—feels more secure than vulnerability or the anxiety of not knowing. So the brain doubles down on what it already believes, even when new evidence suggests otherwise.

- **Energy efficiency (cognitive ease)**: It takes effort to consider new information, question our assumptions, or revise a belief. The brain prefers cognitive shortcuts—like biases and heuristics—because they save energy. Once a belief is wired in, the brain uses confirmation bias to defend it, scanning the environment for evidence that supports it and discarding what doesn't.

- **Identity protection**: Beliefs are often tied to our sense of self. If I've built part of my identity around beliefs like *I can't trust anyone* or *I'm the one who holds everything together*, then contradicting that belief can feel like a threat—not just to my thoughts, but to who I am. The brain resists that kind of subtle rupture.

Certainty may quiet your inner conflict, but it does so at a cost. Bias reassures the brain that its old beliefs are still true, so you don't have to feel fear, grief, or vulnerability. Yet this kind of certainty is rigid, not balanced—it closes your ears to others, making real dialogue and mutual understanding impossible. In short, proving yourself right—even when you're wrong—becomes the brain's way of feeling safe, but it keeps you stuck in isolation rather than connection.

As an adult, you may still default to the reasoning that once got you through the asymmetry of addiction at home. When triggered, your nervous system flips into survival mode, and without realizing it, you use childhood logic to navigate adult relationships. Because you feel all of this so intensely, you become sure you're right—yet in that certainty, you can't really listen. Healing begins when you can tolerate uncertainty, question old beliefs, and gently update your internal map of reality. With time, support, and practice, you can learn to slow down, take in another's perspective, express your emotions more clearly—and discover that true connection is possible only when you loosen the grip of distortion.

Name It, Reframe It, Rewire It: Changing a Cognitive Distortion or Bias

To change a cognitive distortion or bias, you have to interrupt the automatic neural pathway and begin to build a new one—a capacity known in neuroscience as *neuroplasticity*. First, when you catch yourself going black-and-white, catastrophizing, or feeling like you have to be right, name it: *I'm blowing this up—I'm catastrophizing* or *Feelings aren't facts; just because I'm feeling it so intensely doesn't mean I am right.* The act of naming activates the prefrontal cortex, helping shift the brain out of its automatic reactive mode and into conscious reflection.

Next comes developing *cognitive flexibility*, or intentionally considering alternative explanations or more balanced thoughts. For example, you might think, *Maybe I'm making more of this than I need to. Am I worried they're rejecting me?* Reverse roles in your head and try to take the other person's point of view for a moment. It's about training your brain to see more of the picture rather than just the part that matches the old belief.

Finally, repetition and emotional engagement are key. Each time you catch the distortion and reframe it, you weaken the old neural circuit and lay down new tracks. You're able to consider more possibilities and reflect rather than react. The more emotionally resonant and embodied the correction is, whether it's in your mind or through taking a different action than usual, the stronger the new pathway becomes. Over time, the brain learns to default to the new belief instead of the old one.

In short: Awareness disrupts the bias, conscious reframing creates choice, and repetition rewires the brain.

Case Study: How Ben Carries Childhood Fear-Based Reasoning into His Adult Relationships

Ben grew up in a household ruled by his father's alcoholism. If his father was in a good mood, Ben felt some hope for a good encounter. But if his father came home angry and with liquor on his breath, Ben, the little boy who loved his dad and looked forward to seeing him when he returned from work, felt a bolt of electricity shoot through his body, and he'd sprint up to his room to lose himself in games or something else that felt soothing and distracting. He learned to make himself scarce to stay out of harm's way. He learned to self-soothe, to find activities that helped him feel less sad and lonely. While this worked in the moment, it didn't help him process or feel his emotions, and he was left, over and over, with a mix of confusion, hurt, and anxiety in his young body and mind. Over time, Ben's nervous system got used to bracing for danger, making snap assessments, and acting quickly.

As an adult, Ben carries his particular cognitive distortions—catastrophizing and impulsively reacting—into both his intimate relationships and his interactions with authority figures at work. He has a hair-trigger sensitivity to perceived slights or criticism, with his emotions escalating quickly. To cope, he reverts to the strategies he developed as a child, often personalizing events and assuming that if something goes south, it's his fault, or if there is criticism, he must have done something wrong. This is, of course, his child mind taking over, and his big reactions cause him to somehow make everything about him. His emotional reasoning convinces him that because his feelings are so intense, he must be right, making him unable to consider other people's perspectives. This frustrates others and makes them irritated with Ben, which then confirms Ben's bias that the problem somehow centers around him, leaving him feeling hurt, blamed, and angry. His cognitive distortion of catatrophizing creates a perpetual vicious circle.

To heal this cognitive habit, Ben needs to take a step back, pause, and feel what might be lurking beneath his defenses. He needs to stop assuming he's right just because he has strong feelings and become curious about what might be driving his rigid reactions.

These patterns can get triggered in the blink of an eye, often beginning in the way the body reacts to someone or something before the mind even realizes it's reacting. Somatic markers are somatic distortions and biases that occur in the body, such as tensing up, pulling back, or revving up. When somatic markers get activated and in turn activate the cognitive distortions, the past and present blur. Then your body essentially does the same thing as your mind: You interpret or misinterpret internal signals as if what you are encountering in the present is exactly the same as what you encountered in the past. Of course, it isn't; it's a different time, a different place, and a different circumstance altogether. But try to tell your activated body and mind that! They just won't listen! They are loaded, locked, and ready to fire on command. And the command comes in the form of a trigger from the outside that activates what's on the inside.

Exercise

Listening to the Story in Your Body

This journaling exercise is designed to help you gently uncover how cognitive distortions are living in your body, where they came from, and what they're trying to protect.

Name the Pattern

Choose one distortion that shows up often for you—for example, all-or-nothing thinking. Write its name at the top of your journal page.

Let It Speak

Write in the voice of the distortion. Let it speak freely. No edits, no shame—just honesty. Use these prompts to get you going:

- "I show up when..."

- "My job is to protect you by..."

- "I learned this from..."

- "If I wasn't here, what might happen is..."

Tune into Your Body

Pause. Close your eyes if it feels comfortable. Ask yourself:

- Where do I feel this in my body?

- How does this make me feel? Tight, heavy, buzzing, cold, collapsed?

- If I breathe into it, what happens is...

Write down what you notice. Be gentle. You're gathering information, not fixing anything.

Write from the Compassionate Self

Now, respond to the distortion with your grounded, wise voice—the part of you that sees the bigger picture. From that compassionate self, write into these prompts:

- "I see how hard you've worked to keep us safe by..."

- "Here's what's actually true now..."

- "Here's what I want you to know..."

Let this be a conversation: one part still scared, one part finally listening.

How Cognitive Distortions and Biases Show up in Daily Life

Now that we've pulled back the curtain to reveal where our cognitive and somatic distortions may come from, let's take a look at how they become the fuel for dysfunctional generational patterns and how they can make our relationships much more chaotic than they need to be.

First things first: What is hurt in relationships needs relationships to heal. You are no longer a helpless child at the mercy of others. Your family members will heal—or not—in their own time. That is not yours to control. But you, here and now, have the power to reshape your cognitive distortions. As adults, we can use our relationships as arenas to reenact dysfunction or as mirrors to show us what we carry inside—or, realistically, both. Our most important relationships can motivate us to change, grow, and gain perspective on our family of origin through meeting the challenges of the partnership family we create.

Take a compassionate look at the following patterns, understanding that they were your lifelines as a child, things you told yourself so you could maintain your sense of belonging. The distortions you fall into as you try to develop an intimate and trusting relationship with your partner can become a portal through which you view the unconscious patterns you carry from childhood. If you unpack them, they can guide you toward transformation. Even in the ache of connection gone wrong, there is the seed of healing. Take it as your invitation to move toward personal growth and wholeness.

Cognitive Distortions and Biases in Romantic Relationships

Partnering is one of the most intimate experiences you will ever have in life, and often, it mirrors those early, deeply formative relationships you had with your parents. As a child, you learned whether or not you could trust love, whether you could expect the closest people to you to be there for you and with you. As an adult, when you fall in love, something in that primal space inside you awakens. Those early experiences of needing, depending, and connecting are stirred up, and often, without even realizing it, you begin to reenact what you once knew.

Let's look at how the cognitive distortions discussed earlier in this chapter might play out in your relationships today. Say that, as a child, you had experiences with your parents of dysregulation and alienation alternating with cloying and intense closeness. This might leave you with a tendency to think in **all-or-nothing** (or **black-and-white**) terms—for example, you might idealize your partner and then devalue them the moment they disappoint you. One day, everything feels perfect; they're your soulmate, the person who can do no wrong. But when they do something to hurt or disappoint you, the pedestal you've placed them on collapses, and you swing from one extreme to the other, struggling to hold onto the nuanced, complex reality of who your partner actually is: a human being with flaws and gifts, just like you.

The past keeps looping, disguised as the present. You might also **catastrophize** to the point where a small disagreement feels like it signals a deep fissure looming or even the end of the relationship. Maybe you have an argument and immediately think, *This is it, we're going to break up* or *I'll never be able to make this work*. These kinds of intense thoughts can lead you to act in ways that create conflict or distance, when in reality, the issue you're dealing with may be something quite manageable. Both catastrophizing and black-and-white thinking can make it hard for you to maintain perspective, and they can prevent you from seeing that relationships are full of ups and downs—none of which define the whole.

Then there's **emotional reasoning**, where your feelings—often anxiety or fear—become the lens through which you interpret and respond to relationship interactions. If you're feeling anxious, for example, you might assume something is wrong between you and your partner, even if there's no real evidence to support that conclusion. If you grew up in an environment where positivity felt fleeting or unreliable, you may even lean into a **negativity bias**, assuming the worst in your partner's intentions and even warding off their attempts to get along. These distortions, left unchecked, can create self-fulfilling prophecies, shaping the way you interpret your partner's words and actions and ultimately affecting the way you see and respond to them.

Another distortion that might creep in is **personalization**, where you find yourself feeling overly responsible for your partner's happiness. You believe it's your job to fix things for them and smooth over their struggles, so their problems don't become too big and derail everything.

But you're likely operating from your own, activated, sympathetic state and making your meaning from there.

Personalization can also show up as deciding your partner's moods begin with you, assuming their withdrawal, irritation, or silence must be somehow about you rather than just the mood they are in for their own reasons. Try seeing them as separate from you, a fellow human having their own thoughts and feelings, then check your feelings out with them. Don't assume you're right just because you feel this strongly (**emotional reasoning**). You may be **misreading** the situation because of your experience growing up in a family with a lot of pain and little open sharing. This can lead to a dynamic where your partner becomes afraid to say anything to you that may sound critical, because you use up all the oxygen in the room making what they say bigger than they meant it to be. And you make it all about you, so they feel misread and unseen. You **catastrophize** it, which makes it hard for them to take care of themselves in your presence.

For some ACAs, in moments of stress or conflict, it's easy to focus only on what's wrong, **mentally filtering** out all the good things that are happening in your relationship and disqualifying the positive. You might find yourself zeroing in on your partner's mistakes or shortcomings while overlooking the ways they show up for you, whether it's through support, love, or simply a steady, reliable presence. When you disqualify the positive, you rob yourself of the ability to see and savor the full picture, and it becomes much harder to trust in the good that's there.

You might also **jump to conclusions** or **mind read**, assuming you know what your partner is thinking or feeling without asking. If they're quiet or distant, you might immediately think, *They're mad at me* or *They don't care about me; they're selfish and preoccupied*. And because you've already decided what's true, and you feel it so strongly that your emotional reasoning says, "I am right," you might not check in with them, missing the chance to understand what's really going on, as well as depriving them of safety in telling you and yourself of hearing their truth.

ACAs often don't like feeling vulnerable. It feels risky. As kids, checking things out may have meant we got blamed for something, we were laughed at, or our feelings got minimized. Checking things out with your partner and letting them do the same with you can literally change a relationship, not only because you are developing the courage to ask rather than assume but also because, as you listen to what your partner is really telling you, your perspective changes; you make room for someone else's point of view, and your identity becomes more distinct, less blended with others. You have the opportunity to individuate today in a way you may not have been able to as a child. Your partnership in this way allows you to move through developmental stages that you didn't complete while growing up, giving both you and your partner richer, fuller identities.

And even if your partner isn't as good at this as you are becoming through your own recovery, you can become good at it and get healthier. It opens the door to feeling closer and more trusting and, it creates a positive, mutual goal of mining your repeating, dysfunctional patterns and conflicts to excavate hard-to-feel emotions as fodder for growth, to see more of yourself and each other.

Cognitive Distortions and Biases in Parenting

There is no role we play in life that has greater impact and influence on the people we love than being a parent. If ever there were a motivator to recover from ACA issues, it is to spare our children from ingesting our unresolved pain and distorted reasoning for breakfast, lunch, and dinner. Our children are our sacred trust, and we owe it to them and the children they will raise to do everything we can to clean up our side of the street.

Here are some of the ways cognitive distortions manifest in our parenting. Understanding them is the beginning step in our changing for the better. We can use our relationships with our children as mirrors to more clearly see and heal ourselves and thereby become more loving, healthy parents.

Personalizing Their Pain

When your child faces difficulties, you may feel a stab of guilt, as if somehow you're responsible for their challenges. Remember, to your inner child's mind filled with cognitive distortions, everything is personal; everything is about you. So if your actual child is upset, you can lose your sense of footing and separateness, the way a child would. Time collapses, autonomy collapses, and you become as young as they are. This is why doing your own healing is the greatest gift you can give your children. It makes it possible for the child in you to grow into the parent your real child needs to feel secure.

Overprotecting Versus Underprotecting

You might find yourself struggling with all-or-nothing thinking, swinging between overprotecting and underprotecting your child. Because you didn't get what you needed growing up, you may feel pulled in two directions. One part of you wants to shield your child from absolutely everything, and the other part is telling you to give them space, maybe too much space, in hopes they'll figure it all out on their own. You may find that it's tough to land in the middle, where you can offer both the structure and the freedom they need.

Middle ground just wasn't modeled for you when you grew up, so you lack a felt sense of where it is, especially when you're feeling anxious. Remember before you operate from an activated/sympathetic state, step back and breathe. Once you calm your nervous system, you may see things a bit differently.

Perfectionism

If you grew up in a home where "good enough" was never modeled, you may feel an unspoken pressure to be a perfect parent—to get it all right this time. This kind of thinking is both all-or-nothing and a form of personalization: You feel as if your child's mistakes reflect your own failings, as though their struggles are a mirror of your inadequacy.

The weight of that belief can be suffocating. And without meaning to, it can trickle down to your child. When you're too hard on yourself, they may start to believe that mistakes aren't just part of learning—they're proof that they're not enough.

But the truth is, your child doesn't need a perfect parent. They need a *present* one. When you model self-compassion—when you can tolerate your own setbacks, repair when needed, and keep going—you teach them something far more valuable: that being human means trying, failing, learning, and growing. You give them permission to be imperfect and still deeply loved.

Fixing Instead of Feeling

When you see your child in pain, your first instinct may be to fix the problem and take away their hurt—the way you may have felt it was your job to fix your parent's or sibling's pain. While it's natural to want to protect your child, sometimes jumping to solutions too quickly robs them of the chance to experience their emotions fully and find their own way through. When you catastrophize a problem that is a normal part of growing up, your child learns to catastrophize it too.

Kids are intuitive. They pick up on your energy before you say a word. So when you go into overdrive, when a forgotten assignment or moody silence triggers visions of a doomed future, they feel it.

What started as their struggle quietly becomes yours, amplified by worry and imagined bad outcomes. But most of the time, what they need isn't a rescue or a forecast—it's your calmness. Instead of rushing to fix things for them because their problems trigger your old pain, simply being present with them in their angst can teach them that feelings, no matter how difficult, are okay to experience. You're showing them that they don't have to be afraid of their emotions, a crucial step in developing emotional resilience. Remember, they have the adult you to parent them; you didn't have the adult you.

Comparing Your Child to Others or Yourself

You may find yourself comparing your child's progress to that of others—their classmates, friends, or even your own childhood experiences. If they're not achieving what you think they should, it can bring up feelings of disappointment or worry in you, a form of **mental filtering** and **discounting the positive**. You're focusing on perceived deficiencies in your child compared to others and dismissing their strengths and individuality. But every child is unique, with their own timeline for learning and growth. When you compare them to others, even unintentionally, it can make your child feel like they're not enough, fostering insecurity. Letting up on these comparisons allows you to see your child with more perspective and lets them feel accepted, valued, and loved for who they are to you.

They're already enough. And in treating them as such, you remind yourself: *So am I.*

Living Through Your Child's Successes or Struggles

If you didn't have certain opportunities growing up or didn't get the support you needed, it's easy to want your child to succeed in areas where you felt you fell short. You might push them toward achievements you wish you had pursued, hoping they will fulfill dreams you had to set aside. This is a form of **personalization**, where you tie your own worth or success to your child's accomplishments, making everything about you rather than them. This can create pressure for your child, leaving them feeling unseen or as if their worth is tied to their success or their ability to meet your unmet needs. But your children have their own dreams. In projecting your unmet dreams onto them, you rob them of their sense of choice and autonomy. By honestly checking in with your motivations, you can create space for your child to explore their own interests and passions, fostering a more authentic path for them to follow.

Overexplaining and Rationalizing

Sometimes, when your child is upset or confused, you might try to explain everything in detail, hoping to make them understand why they're feeling a certain way or why something happened. This can be a control fallacy, where you feel an overresponsibility for how your child interprets or experiences events, as if you can reach into their mind and control their thoughts. While it's important to provide guidance, overexplaining can overwhelm your child and make them feel disconnected from their own feelings. They don't need a huge explanation for everything; they need to feel heard, seen, and supported. When you focus more on listening and less on explaining, you're teaching them that it's okay not to have all the answers right away.

Ignoring Your Own Needs

Parenting can sometimes become so all-consuming that you forget to take care of yourself. You might put your emotional or physical needs on hold, thinking that sacrificing for your child is what makes you a good parent. While sacrifice is a normal part of parenting, erasing your needs can lead to burnout, resentment, or even unconscious expectations that your child should somehow make up for what you've given up. With this all-or-nothing thinking, you lose track of a healthy middle ground. Making sacrifices without taking care of yourself will ultimately teach your child that self-care is unimportant. By tending to your own well-being as well as theirs, you're modeling balance, teaching your child that it's not only okay but necessary to take care of themselves, too. This balance is foundational for a healthy relationship between the two of you and your child's healthy relationship with themself.

In all these moments, remember that one of the best things you can do for your child is to find healing for yourself, so you can separate *your* past from *their* present. It's important that you consider what you model. You are telling your child who you want them to be by what you show them through who *you* are. Children absorb us at such a deep level—our confidence or lack of it, our character, our movements, our emotions and behaviors. Be the person you want them to become. Who you are sends your strongest message.

Case Study: Sarah and Her Son

When my client Sarah's son throws a tantrum, she freezes, reliving the rage she grew up with that made her feel overly responsible. In that moment her past and present collide, and she feels as though she's done something wrong to make her child so angry, the same way she felt as a child in the face of her father's rages. In this state of activation, rather than seeing her child as a perhaps tired, hungry, or momentarily distressed child, she gets overwhelmed with his anger. She loses her sense of separateness, calm, and maturity because she's operating from her child mind; she just wants to shut him down or placate him, anything to get it to stop. Her mature thinking mind is less available to her, so she's not able to settle him down and identify what he might be feeling or might need. Momentarily, they're both little, dysregulated, and scared.

Sarah has learned to identify these moments and bring them to therapy, where we unpack them together. For now, her victory is that she doesn't act out through placating her son or trying to shut him down. As we examine her own childhood experience, she gains more compassion for herself. Through role-play she lets the child inside of her cry, get mad, tell her father how much he terrified her, and change the power dynamic that made her freeze and feel small. The little girl in her is able to move out of emotional and physiological frozenness, so that she can mother from a more adult version of herself. When she makes this shift, she can see her son as the little boy he is—one who needs his mommy to stay calm so he can feel safe inside himself, so he can feel boundaried and held.

Cognitive Distortions and Biases at Work

Work is one of the places where our inner narratives can run wild, shaping how we see ourselves in relation to authority figures and colleagues. It's where we grow skills, face challenges, and navigate high-pressure dynamics. It's also where teamwork and collaboration invite us to trade the solitary "I" for a more balanced, effective "we."

Here's how cognitive distortions can quietly show up in the workplace—and how noticing them can be the first step toward healing.

If you lean toward **all-or-nothing thinking**, feedback can feel crushing. Instead of hearing constructive criticism as a chance to grow, it might land as a personal attack: *Why don't they see how hard I'm trying?* or *Why are they being so mean?* What could be an opportunity for refinement instead becomes a source of dread, threatening to unravel your sense of competence.

In moments like these, pause. Imagine stepping into the shoes of the person offering feedback. What might they be seeing or needing? When you return to your own perspective, notice if anything has shifted. Can you sense that their words may not be about your worth as a person, but about keeping the work moving forward?

Then there's **filtering out the positives**. Even when you succeed, a quiet voice nags at you: *How did I get here? When will they figure out I don't belong?* You might land a promotion or lead a successful project, only to dismiss it with: *I just got lucky* or *It wasn't that big of a deal.* You discount the positive and rob yourself of the satisfaction and confidence you've earned and the good leadership that created your success. These distortions can make it feel like you're doing something wrong if you enjoy your accomplishments or give yourself credit, which can undermine the good feelings that should be yours. Instead of maintaining a constructive focus, you freeze, your ability to think clearly goes down, and you have trouble tossing around new ideas. Getting support to examine these distortions as they arise can let you use them as grist for the mill of exploration and growth rather than for self-sabotage.

Cognitive Distortions and Biases in Friendships

Friendships, with all their potential for warmth, fun, and companionship, can also stir up your insecurities, especially when cognitive distortions sneak into your thinking. You might find yourself wondering if your friends are as invested in the relationship as you are. These doubts can cast a shadow over even the strongest connections. Take a look at some of the ways cognitive distortions show up in your friendships.

If you tend to lean toward a **negativity bias**, you may find yourself zeroing in on the moments when your friend doesn't meet your expectations. Your **mental filtering** hones in on the times when they didn't return your call as quickly as you'd hoped, or perhaps they seemed distracted during a conversation, and you **personalize** and **catastrophize** these moments, making them all about you in some way: *What did I do? What did I say?* Meanwhile, the many times they did show up for you or the many good times you've had fade into your mental background as you **minimize** them. This imbalance can erode your easy trust in the relationship. As you amplify the negative, you make it harder to appreciate the natural ebb and flow that all friendships experience.

Mind reading is another common trap. When a friend seems quiet or distant, your mind might immediately jump to conclusions like, *They're mad at me* or *They don't care about me in the same way I care about them.* These assumptions often go unspoken, but they can quietly create distance. You may fall into **emotional reasoning**, believing you've already figured out the problem (*I feel this strongly, so I must be right*), and then you might withdraw emotionally, leaving your friend in the dark about how you're feeling. You behave in ways that confuse or distance them, and pretty soon you create the very issue you feared they had.

Or you may fall into the **control fallacy**, where you feel responsible for everyone else's happiness. Perhaps you're the friend who always checks in, offers support, and goes out of your way to make sure everyone's okay, but rarely asks for attention or help in return. Over time, this one-sided dynamic can leave you feeling drained, resentful, or unappreciated. You might hesitate to express your vulnerabilities, fearing that doing so would make you seem too needy or burdensome. Or you don't risk just saying, "I miss you. Let's get together."

Friendships, like any meaningful relationship, thrive on openness and vulnerability. It's okay to let down your guard and lean on your friends when you need support. In fact, it can make them feel more comfortable being vulnerable when they need to be. Remember, you don't need to be overly close or agree on everything to be friends. Just do you and let your friend do them.

Exercise

Unpacking Your Childhood Story

This exercise invites you to meet two parts of yourself: the *child* who created a story to survive and the *adult* who unknowingly hardened that story into a lens for seeing the world.

Connect with the Younger You

Choose a story you've lived with since childhood that you want to examine. Now, close your eyes and picture the younger you who first formed this belief. Maybe they're five years old or ten. Maybe they're sitting in a bedroom or hiding in a corner of your memory. Gently ask them:

- What was happening around you when you first believed this?

- What did you feel in your body? Fear? Sadness? Anger?

- What story did you tell yourself to make sense of it all? ("I'm not good enough," "I have to stay small," "People can't be trusted.")

- If you could speak freely, what would your child self say to the adults in your world?

- What were you longing for, deep down, that you didn't get?

Let this child speak. Let them pour it out without interruption.

Give the Adult You a Turn

Now turn to the adult part of you who carried that story forward. Ask yourself:

- What has it felt like to carry this story into adulthood?

- How have I reinforced it, maybe without realizing that I was?

- Where do I gather evidence of this belief in my current relationships or choices?

- What have I ignored or pushed away because it didn't fit the story?

- What feels scary about seeing the world differently?

Write as this adult part with honesty and compassion. See if you can notice the ways the adult you has used the story to try to protect you.

Listen to the Child

Now imagine the child sitting across from you. Don't rush in to fix them. Just listen. Ask them gently:

- What do you want me, the adult, to finally understand?

- What have you been carrying for us all these years?

- What do you wish someone had said to you back then?

Respond as the Adult

When they've spoken, respond as the adult—not with advice or judgment, but with grounded compassion. Consider:

- What do I, as the adult, see now that the child could not?

- What do I want to say to this child part about what I know today?

- What gentle reassurance can I offer about the safety and choices I have now?

Closing Reflection

Pause. Notice what's shifted. Reflect on these questions:

- What did I learn about these parts of me?

- How can I gently question the old story?

- What's one small way I can remind myself that I am not that child anymore?

In the next chapter, we'll discuss how unconscious triggers can reactivate old attachment wounds, pulling us into cognitive distortions that blur the line between past and present until it's hard to tell them apart. But triggers don't just sabotage us—they can also become windows into our unconscious, offering some of the best insights into our hidden, inner world we'll ever have, if we're willing to listen.

6

Triggers as Teachable Moments

A Window into Your Unconscious

A trigger is not just a fleeting moment of discomfort; it is a reverberation from a deep pool of unresolved pain, a piece of the past that erupts suddenly into the present, carrying the emotional charge of an old wound that has never fully healed. It can feel like it's coming out of nowhere, but it's not. It's your unconscious sending up a flare from an unhealed, shut-down place inside of you, pointing you to a place within you that's screaming for your attention.

When you get triggered, you're not simply reacting to the moment in front of you; you're being pulled into a physiological and emotional flashback, where the past hijacks your present. A car backfiring in a Target parking lot can send a former soldier to the ground in an instant, triggered by the unconscious memory of battlefield sounds, the body reacting before the mind can catch up. For ACAs, relationship cues are that car backfiring. Angry voices, cold silence, a raised arm, a smarmy touch, or a sudden shift in mood can activate the same kind of automatic survival-based response in us—not because the present moment is necessarily dangerous, but because it carries the scent of the past. It is your body's implicit memory reawakening, overriding conscious thought, and flooding your nervous system with open tensions and act hungers that belong to another time and place. Time collapses, and you experience, or reexperience, your intense reactions as if they are in response to what is happening right now. The present becomes saturated with the raw, unreleased energy of the past.

When your nervous system feels activated or triggered, you can feel unsafe inside your own skin, and when you feel unsafe, you can become catapulted into a state where your adult self is no longer fully in control, where the past is now dictating your reactions without you understanding that's what's happening. Because you're in an activated state, you misread what is coming toward you. A neutral expression may feel rejecting. A critical sentence is an indictment of who you are. A difference of opinion may ignite the panic of impending conflict. Your heart races; your breath grows shallow or catches in your throat; your mind scrambles to make sense of the intensity coursing through you; and you reach for the closest piece of information and turn it into fact. Your nervous system doesn't fact-check; it reacts. It doesn't ask whether the threat is real; it assumes it is. So your cognitive distortions kick in: *I am feeling so intensely angry, I am certain I'm right about holding you to blame for how I feel.* You personalize and catastrophize: *They're about to lose it. I knew this would happen when . . .* Your hidden emotions and body states from the past are replaying themselves in the present in an unconscious, repetitive loop. What your mind has not yet integrated is still searching for closure.

But reenactment is never closure.

Here is your choice point. You can act out unconsciously (again), making the conflict in the present impossible to solve because in this triggered moment your thinking mind is shut down, your fear system is hyperactivated, and your body is in a self-perpetuating trauma loop. Or you can take a deep breath, consciously feel your feet on the ground, reorient yourself, and attempt to name what is happening. You can say something like, "I am being triggered. This is probably old stuff. I need to hit the pause button, hard, now."

What you do from here will determine whether you begin a process of healing your past wounds by seeing, owning, and feeling them. Or you can continue to recreate them in your present by disowning your own unconscious wounds and making your intense reaction about whatever or whomever triggered it. This is the moment that counts. The path to healing begins with recognizing what is happening *and interrupting the cycle.* Instead of reacting from the urgency of your emotions, slow everything down. Understand that during these moments of unconscious triggering, your cognitive distortions will kick in with a ferocity that may make you aggressive or frozen. You might become rageful or withdrawn, accusative or collapsed. You might personalize, catastrophize, or think that because you feel so strongly that someone else is in the wrong, they actually are—and you will be blind to what you're importing from the past that is fueling your overreaction in the present.

But please know that within this very activation is your open invitation to heal. This triggered moment is actually opening a secret passageway into your unconscious that can let light in.

How "State Creates Story"

Your brain doesn't passively observe reality—it actively constructs it, moment by moment, on the basis of signals from your body and nervous system. As Deb Dana, a clinician and international lecturer on polyvagal theory, says, "State creates story."[1] When you're in a survival state—fight, flight, freeze, or fawn—your mind scrambles to make sense of the inner alarm, and the story it spins will reflect danger, distrust, or urgency. But when your nervous system is balanced and settled, the story can be entirely different: calm, open, and even filled with gratitude. In a regulated state, you're able to see possibilities, feel connected to others, and make meaning from a place of safety rather than fear.

This is why when you're triggered, your emotions and thinking feel so real—because in a sense they are. Your nervous system in a heightened state is braced for danger, and your mind weaves a narrative to justify the intense feelings.

It's also why trauma survivors often struggle with trust and safety, even in environments that are objectively secure. A nervous system still primed for threat turns that inner state into stories that reinforce fear and hypervigilance. But as your body learns to soften and settle, the stories begin to shift too—making space for connection, curiosity, and calm.

Recognizing that state creates story allows you to step back and ask: *Is what I'm making up in my head true, or is my nervous system reacting as if it is?* Shifting your physiological state—through awareness, breath work, movement (such as a brief walk), coregulation, or self-soothing—can change the way you experience your environment and your relationships, helping you see the present for what it is rather than through the lens of your activated nervous system.

If your nervous system is in a regulated, safe state, you're more likely to interpret interactions positively. A delayed response from a friend might evoke a thought like, *They're probably busy. I'll hear from them soon.* But if your system is dysregulated and you're stuck in a fight-or-flight state or a shut-down state, the same situation might trigger a completely different story: *They're ignoring me. They don't care. I always get ghosted like this.*

The Past Meets the Present

The past doesn't dissolve simply because we age. If issues are left unaddressed, they linger, tucked into the crevices and cracks of our present, showing up in ways we often don't recognize: in the fights we keep having, the relationships we struggle to maintain, or the fear that pulls at the corners of our mind, heart, and body. Triggers bring these fissures and fragments into view, acting as messengers from the past trying to tell us, "I still hurt and have a lot to say. I need you to hear my voice, and I need you to give me the stage for a moment so I can see myself more clearly."

Much in the way that psychoanalyst Carl Jung used dreams as a doorway into the unconscious, which he called "shadow work," I suggest we use what activates or triggers us as a window into our unconscious past and as a mirror that reflects back to us what still needs to be processed. Activations are rich with information; they point directly to the places where our pain is still buried alive. By looking into what activates us with open and curious eyes, we give ourselves permission to see what we're holding onto, we bring our disowned parts back to life, and we let them reveal truths to us that we didn't feel safe enough to know back then.

What Happens Inside When You're Triggered

Trauma, at its core, is any experience that's too big for your psyche to metabolize or too overwhelming for your body to process. So you don't. Instead, it sits inside of you, a buried landmine waiting to be stepped on. Even if you don't remember specific moments or incidents, those relational undercurrents are still with you. They live in your body, tucked away in your limbic system, in the patterns of your nervous system that remain vibrating and primed to react because those experiences were never completed and brought to closure.

Healing is a courageous process of sitting with the feelings that overwhelmed you at the time, finally giving them the space to come into your conscious awareness—as they've been asking to all along, albeit in a very dysfunctional way. As you do, you may feel young and vulnerable and scared all over again, but remember this: Packed away with your pain are your innocence, creativity, and capacity for connection and joy. If you can sit through the hard part, what you will get back will be so much more than worth it.

When you're triggered:

- **Your perception narrows.** You see the world through the lens of your past trauma. Your partner's silence, for instance, might not feel like quiet; instead, it may feel like rejection or abandonment. Your brain makes assumptions on the basis of past experiences, not present realities. Your cognitive distortions get activated. You see the person activating you as the entire problem, and you can be completely blind to the history you're bringing into your heated reaction. Checking out whether your perceptions are correct seems needless, because you already think you know what's going on.

- **You react automatically.** You move straight from trigger to action, shooting from zero to ten with no speed bumps in between. Without even realizing it, you might lash out, withdraw, accuse, or cling in an attempt to protect yourself from what you assume now to be true. These reactions are not logical; they're fear based, shaped by your nervous system's activated state.

Leaning In: Looking as the Window into Your Unconscious World Opens

The moment you stop fighting, fleeing, shutting down, or fawning, your nervous system begins to settle. With that shift, your thinking brain, which goes offline during a trauma response, can come back online and function more normally. Instead of being swept away by old fears, you develop the capacity to notice, pause, and regulate. You can see, hear, and interpret the present for what it is, rather than as a replay of the past. This is how you stop time traveling.

By allowing yourself to feel your way into those triggered states without acting out or shutting them down, you can see their root more clearly. The mist hanging over them lifts, and you're able to befriend your inner child and understand bit by bit the circumstances that created the intense pain you felt you had to numb or deny. Then you integrate those fragmented parts of your experience, tucking them back into the overall context of what makes you you. This is how you heal. So the goal isn't to eliminate activation, but to transform your relationship with it.

Exercise

Using Triggers as Windows into Your Unconscious

In your journal, place a photo of yourself that draws you—one where you sense there are unspoken words or unprocessed feelings beneath the surface. Choose an image that stirs something inside. Add thought bubbles or mentally give words to what you imagine was going on in your inner world at that moment but was not being spoken out loud.

Reflect on these questions:

- What emotions arise as you look at this younger version of yourself?

- What do you, as the adult you are today, want to say to this child?

- What does this child want to say back to you?

- What do they most long to hear from you? Say it now—on the page, aloud, or in your mind.

Your triggers are not enemies; they are messengers from the past, pointing to places where your nervous system learned to protect you. By listening with compassion, you begin to thaw what's frozen, soften old defenses, and reclaim the aliveness that fear once silenced. This is the essence of reparenting: becoming the steady, safe presence your younger self always needed.

The Difference Between Trigger and Activation

Originally, the word *trigger* was used to describe a powerful psychological reaction rooted in trauma or PTSD. One was triggered when an external cue activated the nervous system and caused intense distress. Over time, however, popular usage has blurred its meaning, often reducing it to signify that one is feeling mildly upset or annoyed. This shift in its interpretation can dilute the gravity of genuine trauma responses. That's why many psychologists now emphasize the importance of distinguishing between feeling *activated*, which is a state where you have awareness of what's happening inside you, and true trauma-related unconscious triggering, where the nervous system becomes involuntarily hijacked by your more unconscious and unprocessed implicit memory and history.

As you learn to tune in to early signs of emotional activation, you can take steps to calm your nervous system in the moment, interrupt your unconscious reactions, and avoid getting fully triggered. This helps you to catch your automatic unconscious reactions before they blow everything out of proportion and before you make up a story that will get you stuck in your head. Over time, with support and practice, you become more readily able to recognize and be with your implicit memories, allowing them to rise into consciousness, where you can witness them with awareness rather than reenact them without it.

Relational Reliving

Relational reliving is a term I coined to describe the specific way adult children of addicts reexperience early trauma through the dynamics of their adult relationships. While PTSD often involves flashbacks, nightmares, or intrusive memories tied to a specific event, relational reliving has a subtler—but no less powerful—presentation. It plays out through roles, reactions, and emotional states that reawaken ghosts from childhood.

In addicted family systems, the emotional atmosphere is often saturated with what we used to call "dry drunk" behaviors—rage without reason, blame, withdrawal, control, defensiveness, or icy silence. These patterns linger even in the absence of substances. And when conflict arises in your adult life—say, with a spouse or partner—it can trigger those old survival states. Suddenly, you're not just arguing about dishes or schedules—you're emotionally flooded, reliving the emotional climate of your childhood.

You may find yourself reacting from a younger place, thinking and feeling like the child you once were in the presence of a drunk, neglectful, or volatile parent. And if your partner has a similar history, you might both be standing there—two adults on the outside, two wounded kids on the inside—reverting to the same defenses you once used to survive. This is the essence of relational reliving: the past taking the wheel in the present, unless and until it's brought into conscious awareness.

Or you might even find yourself waiting for your partner to step in and fix your pain, just like you wished a parent would have done. When that doesn't happen, the hurt grows, and old wounds reopen and become recreated in the present. This is the essence of relational reliving: the past hijacking the present, driving your emotional responses until you bring your past into conscious awareness.

Role-Play Case Study: Emily and Jeff

I had been seeing Emily and Jeff for some time to help them resolve their chronic arguments. Their children were showing signs of anxiety and had begun to complain about their parents' fighting. I spent a few sessions listening to them talk about their families of origin. Emily grew up with an addicted parent, and Jeff grew up with a father who was a veteran and carried untreated PTSD; he was distant and at work a lot of the time. Jeff's mother had a compulsive relationship with food that really impacted the family, and his sister struggled with weight issues and learned from her mother how to self-medicate with sweets and ultraprocessed foods. Emily's father used alcohol. Neither had models of healthy conflict resolution, and they both bore those scars.

Jeff wanted to do a role-play so he could talk to instead of about his mother; he used the empty chair in my office to represent her. As Jeff sat across from his "mother," his shoulders immediately hunched, and his voice trembled. "You were so angry all the time," he said, blinking back the tears welling in his eyes. "I tried to be good, to not upset you, but it was never enough. You said Dad didn't care about us, and that hurt me so much to hear, but I felt like you didn't care about me either."

He paused, his voice breaking. "I wanted you not to hate me because I loved Dad. I needed you to tell me none of it was my fault. To really feel that. But I felt like I got stuck between your anger and his loss, his absence, I guess. I lost both of you."

I invited Jeff to reverse roles, stepping into his mother's perspective. As he sat in her chair, his posture shifted, and he spoke in her voice. He showed us the mother he had as a boy.

"Go to your room and do your homework. Your father's at the office late again, and I have to clean the kitchen. Take your dessert upstairs," his "mother" said.

"I don't like dessert," Jeff responded. "I don't like sweets."

The dialogue continued. When I asked him if he'd said all that he wanted to say, he nodded his head yes. Then I invited him to stand behind the chair representing his mother and double for her, meaning that he would talk from the position of what he imagined to be her inner self.

Jeff, as his mother's double, spoke what she could never have said then and perhaps still can't say—or, for that matter, even let herself feel: "I am drowning, Jeff. I'm so hurt and angry at your father, but I don't know how to handle it. I eat because I don't want to feel how alone I am. I don't mean to hurt you, but I can't see past my own pain."

I called for him to reverse roles, and Jeff returned to his own chair and talked to his "mother." He put his head in his hands.

"I always thought it was my job to make you happy," he said through tears. "But I see now that it wasn't. You were so lost, and it was way too big for me to fix for you. It wasn't my job; it was yours and Dad's job." Simply reversing roles opened the door for Jeff to be able to take her perspective. Once he could do that, he stopped feeling so blended with her feelings, and he started to feel his own.

In the discussion we had after the role-play, Emily had more empathy for Jeff than before, and Jeff had more empathy for himself. Jeff realized that one of his triggers was that when Emily had a complaint about him, he thought it was his job to fix it and keep her happy, which set him sailing into a transference with his mother, suddenly layering his mother's qualities onto Emily. He felt trapped in what he saw as her demands; he felt angry and activated; and he couldn't hear Emily, because all he felt was intense activation. Unconsciously, he was experiencing Emily as the mother he had as a child, and he was experiencing himself as the powerless child.

Next, Emily set up a chair to represent her father. As Emily faced the empty chair, her body tensed, and her hands clenched into fists.

"You're so hard on me," she said, her voice rising with anger. "Nothing I do is ever good enough. You always find something to criticize. And when I stand up to you, you make me feel small, like I am the one who is wrong." Her voice cracked as she continued, "Why can't you tell me you love me? Why can't you ever say that?"

I invited Emily to reverse roles, stepping into her "father's" chair. At first she resisted, as if by taking on his role, she'd permanently get stuck there or relinquish her own. But as she began to show us the father she had by standing in his shoes, speaking as him, and experiencing his role, the charge started to leave her, and she became more who he truly was rather than the frozen caricature of him she carried in her mind. The dynamic softened.

Paradoxically, through standing in the shoes of her father, Emily began to experience a greater sense of herself. Suddenly he looked small and vulnerable to her. Suddenly she had access to a side of him she'd walled off for so many years; her face and demeanor softened. As she saw him in this way, she could feel more of herself come into view as well. By the time Emily reversed roles again and wanted to double for her father, she was already, in truth, most of the way there.

"Hi, Dad," she said.

"Hi, Emily."

"May I double for him?" she asked.

As Emily reversed roles then dropped down into what she imagined to be her dad's inner self, speaking as him words began to pour out of her. "I don't know how to show love. My own father was so hard on me. I guess I think I am teaching you to be strong. I am hurting you instead, just the way I was hurt. No one saw me or my hurt, and when you want me to see yours, I just get mad like he did."

Emily was in essence repairing the frozen dynamic she had experienced as a child with her father, allowing compassion to enter in spontaneously as she became the father she wished she'd had. She was feeling something different, making a new memory.

Emily's tears flowed freely as she returned to her own seat. "I've been fighting you my whole life," she said to the empty chair. "But I don't want to fight anymore. I just want to let go. I love you so much."

One of the tragedies of being stuck in pain is that it also gets us stuck in love. The child in us yearns to feel the love we felt for our parent, but the unresolved, frozen pain and resentment block our ability to do that. Through embodied role-play, we experience both perspectives. We can reignite the connection, step out of our black-and-white cognitive distortions and triggers, and find middle ground.

As Jeff watched Emily confront her father, he felt a wave of compassion. "I see now why you fight so hard," he said afterward. "You're not just fighting me; you're fighting for the love you didn't get. And I'm sorry I've made you feel like I'm not here for you."

Emily turned to Jeff, her expression softening. "And I see why you pull away. It's not because you don't care; it's because you're scared. And me fighting you makes you more scared. I see you as my dad, and you see me as your mom. But I'm not your mom, Jeff. I don't want you to fix me, and I don't think it's your job to keep me happy. I get that it's my job. I just want you to stay. I don't want to lose you."

Own It, Own It, Own It

Two people can decide if they want to be each other's safe haven and build a happy, sane, and thriving life together or if they want to recreate and live out their unresolved wounds with each other, projecting unhealed pain from the past into their intimacy in the present and then pass pain down to their children.

When you begin to see your triggers not as doors slamming shut, but as doors being opened, you transform them into some of the most powerful entry points you can find for healing your unconscious wounds. Each trigger becomes a key, opening to the parts of you that were silenced—emotions, needs, and truths that went unspoken but never disappeared. They reveal the pain that's been reenacted in your relationships as your unconscious tries to find resolution for what it couldn't bring to closure back then.

We spend so much time rationalizing what's going on when we're stuck in relational reliving—making it about our partner and ignoring the piece of our history we're dragging in and playing out—that we create a whole new trap to get stuck in. Own your side of the conflict. Get curious about what is triggering you, why your reaction is so big, and why the current trigger might be providing you with a relational reason today to act out your relational pain of yesterday. Who are you shouting at anyway? What cognitive distortion are you operating from that is pumping up pain inside you? When you can stop making every fight about winning and losing—when you can pause, back up, breathe, wonder, and use what is triggering you as the beginning of exploration and healing instead of the foundation upon which you build a new generation of confusion, hurt, and resentment—you will have in your hands the keys to the castle. You will have a shot at freeing yourself from the grip of the dysfunction you grew up with and freeing the next generation as well.

Next time you're triggered, stop and let your mind float back to the painful moments from the past when you froze and where you may still remain frozen. Whatever these moments were, you can see more of them if you want to.

The mind, just like the body, wants to heal, and these turgid wounds within us will hurt and blast out pain until we attend to them. Be your own best friend and own your side of the street—not to blame yourself, but simply to hold yourself accountable, with compassion, for what's going on inside of you that's contributing to the unmanageable tension of the moment. This is how you will set yourself free.

You don't have control over what another person is or isn't willing or capable of seeing, but you do have control over yourself. Exercise that control. Explore the contents of your triggers for the unconscious pain, reasoning, cognitive distortion, or rage that could never safely come out before, then welcome and witness it today as it passes before your mind's eye. Treat yourself now with the attention and concern you longed for then. Be the parent you wish you had had and reparent yourself.

When it comes to your primary relationship, you and your partner have a choice. You can reparent each other and help each other grow into adulthood and build a relationship that is free (or at least freer) of reenactments from the past or reinforce dysfunction and pass it to another generation. You can learn to live as two loving adult partners in the present.

Exercise

Walking the V: Writing Your Soliloquy for Self-Regulation

When you're triggered, it can feel like parts of you are fighting for control—swinging between activation and collapse. This exercise helps you explore your activation using what I call the **V of Self-Regulation** through writing a short soliloquy, or inner monologue, from each perspective—activated, shut down, and balanced.

Draw a large **V** on your paper:

- Place an **X at the bottom point** to mark the *triggered moment*.

- The **left line** is your *activated self*—flooded with energy, anger, or panic.

- The **right line** is your *shut-down self*—collapsed, numb, or withdrawn.

- The **center space** between them is your *balanced, integrated self*—calm, steady, and connected.

The Trigger Point (X)

Think of a recent situation where you felt highly activated—an argument, a misunderstanding, or a moment of deep overwhelm. Close your eyes and picture what happened. Feel it in your body.

Now, write your soliloquy as your activated self:

- "I'm here because..."

- "This is what I'm afraid of..."

- "My body feels..."

- "What I wish I could say is..."

Let this voice be raw and unfiltered. Don't edit or analyze—just let it speak.

The Line of Activation

On the left side of the V is the path of activation—the fight-or-flight energy that rises when you feel threatened. This is where anger, defensiveness, and urgency live.

Write your soliloquy as you climb the line of activation:

- "I can feel the heat rising because..."

- "I want to fight/leave because..."

- "What I really need right now is..."

Pause at the top of this line and reflect: "What happens if I keep going this way?"

The Line of Shutdown

Return to the trigger point (X) and move up the right side of the V—the path of shutdown. This is the collapse, withdrawal, or numbness that happens when it feels too disturbing to stay engaged.

Write your soliloquy as you climb the line of shutdown:

- "I feel myself disappearing because..."

- "It feels safer to go quiet because..."

- "What I'm really afraid of is..."

Pause at the top of this line and reflect: "What happens if I keep going this way?"

The Line of Balance

Now imagine stepping onto the line of balance—the space connecting the two upper points of the V. This is where you feel grounded, present, and able to choose how to respond or not to respond.

Write your soliloquy as your wise, balanced self:

- "When I'm balanced, I can see . . ."

- "I notice what's mine and what's not mine to carry . . ."

- "I can choose to . . ."

Breathe deeply as you write and notice how this voice feels different in your body.

Why This Matters

When you were young, shutting down or holding back big emotions may have been the only way to survive. Now, those old patterns can surface in ways that don't serve your present life. Writing from these three perspectives allows you to see the inner dynamics clearly—and to practice responding with awareness rather than reaction.

Every time you pause and give voice to your inner world, you remind your nervous system: *I am not trapped in the past. I can hear these parts, and I can choose a new way forward.*

Exercise

Owning Your Side of a Conflict: Giving Voice to Your Activated Self

When we get triggered as adults, it's often not just about what's happening in the moment—it's about old wounds rising to the surface. Many of us learned as children to shut down our feelings in order to get through. Later, those long-buried emotions can erupt in ways that surprise even us—rage, withdrawal, overexplaining, or freezing.

This exercise helps you step into the perspective of your *activated self*—the part of you that reacts quickly and instinctively when you feel threatened—and then begin to engage with it from your *wise adult self*. By giving this part of you a voice without judgment, you can start to reclaim choice in how you respond.

Write as Your Activated Self

In your journal, let the activated part of you speak freely. Don't filter or edit—this is about listening deeply to the voice that often gets buried or bursts out under pressure.

- "My name is . . ." Give this part of you a name or image. It could be "Little Me," "the Protector," "the Fighter," or simply your own name.

- "I'm triggered when . . ." Describe the situation, person, or behavior that sets off this reaction.

- "When this happens, my body feels . . ." Do you clench your fists? Freeze? Feel heat rising in your chest? Sense your heart pounding? Describe it in detail.

- "The emotions under the surface are . . ." Even if anger is loud or withdrawal/shutdown is intense, what's underneath? Fear? Grief? Loneliness? A sense of helplessness?

- "The first time I remember feeling this way was . . ." When, as a child, did you have to silence your anger or sadness to keep the peace?

- "Back then, I wasn't allowed to say or do . . ." What words, feelings, or actions weren't safe for you to express?

- "Now, as an adult, this part of me reacts by . . ." Do you lash out? Shut down? Overthink? Try to control? Numb out?

- "What I wish others understood about me in these moments is . . ." What's the vulnerable truth underneath this reaction?

- "If someone could truly see the real me, I'd want them to . . ." Describe the kind of support you long for.

- "What I most need from myself in these moments is . . ." Comfort? Boundaries? A pause? Reassurance?

After writing, pause and read your entry. How did it feel to give this part of yourself a voice? Did anything surprise you? What is one thing you can take from this journaling exercise into your daily life?

When you feel triggered in a conflict, it can feel like your body and mind are hijacked. You might say or do things you later regret—or shut down and abandon your own needs entirely. This exercise is about slowing down the moment, listening to the younger part of you that's still trying to protect itself, and rewriting the story in real time.

Replay the Moment

Think of a recent time when you got highly activated in a conflict. Close your eyes and visualize the scene like a movie. Notice:

- Who was there? What was said?

- What sensations arose in your body? (Tightness in your chest? Heat in your face? A frozen stillness?)

- What did you do in response? (Shout? Leave? Overexplain? Go quiet?)

Now, journal for two or three sentences from these prompts:

- "When this happened, I felt . . ."

- "I reacted by . . ."

Meet the Younger Part

Imagine the younger version of yourself—the child who learned to shut down or hold back feelings to stay safe—standing in that moment. Consider:

- How old does this part feel?

- What does their face look like?

- What do they most want or fear?

In your journal, complete these prompts as your younger self:

- "When conflict happens, I feel . . ."

- "Back then, I learned to get through the moment by . . ."

- "What I really needed but didn't get was . . ."

Take a breath and thank this part of you for trying to keep you safe all these years.

Pivot into a New Pattern

Now imagine your wise adult self stepping into the scene. This part of you is calm, feels grounded, and has choices your younger self may not have had.

Ask yourself:

- What would it look like to stay present here without shutting down or lashing out?

- What could I say or do to take care of myself and keep the connection alive?

- How might I slow the moment with a pause, breath, or boundary?

Now, write to these prompts:

- "Next time, when I feel triggered, I want to try..."

- "To support myself in these moments, I will..."

Why This Practice Works

Each time you pause and listen to the younger part of you, you help your nervous system learn it's safe now. And every time you pivot into a more intentional response, you strengthen new neural pathways for self-regulation and connection. Over time, this process becomes less about managing triggers and more about healing the parts of you that were never heard before.

If you're in a partnership, once you learn to own your side, you'll have the capacity to see if your partner is owning theirs. If they are not, consider getting some professional help or finding a couples support group. Keep in mind that healing is messy and can take a long time, so don't be discouraged if this process doesn't go smoothly—it often doesn't. The trick isn't to be perfect; it's to take a deep breath, recognize the pattern, and step back together.

In the next chapter, we'll explore the many ways we try to outrun pain—through distraction, denial, numbing, and other process addictions. Then we'll examine how to turn toward this hidden pain that's still vibrating under the surface and driving our addictions, and we will learn how to grieve it.

7

Process Addictions

Why Can't I Stop Doing This?

When we can't manage what is activating us, we want to make it go away, to medicate it, to get the uncomfortable sensations in our bodies and feelings that erupt from them to stop! And that's where process addictions come in.

Simply put, process addictions are the hiding places for unprocessed pain. They are the seemingly ordinary, everyday, repeated behaviors or habits that we use compulsively to numb pain that is slowly becoming big on the inside. If it had a voice, our unprocessed anxiety or painmight say, "This feels like too much for me to manage. I want relief from what's going on inside of me, and I know how to get it." The arm that automatically reaches out for something sugary or starchy, the body that can't stop exercising, the shopper who can't say, "Maybe another time"—all are looking (frantically) for temporary relief from feelings that they believe they can't manage on their own. What makes process addictions so insidious is how easily they weave themselves into the fabric of daily life, masquerading as habits or even personality traits.

How Process Addictions Come to Have a Life of Their Own

We often assume that addiction is about chasing pleasure—the high, the buzz, the relief. But neuroscience tells a more nuanced story. According to the work of Kent Berridge and Terry Robinson, dopamine—the brain chemical long thought to signal pleasure—isn't only about liking; it's also about wanting.[1] Neuroscience has discovered something counterintuitive but crucial: dopamine doesn't actually surge when we get the reward; it surges when we anticipate it. This means the brain isn't fixated on the substance or behavior because it feels good—it's fixated because it once did and we think it will again. The anticipation itself, the promise of relief or pleasure, can feel intoxicating—like a kind of *dry high*.

But once you overeat, or engage in an affair, or overbuy, shame and regret kick in pretty fast. So it's the memory of that early feel-good experience that happens on the first few bites, or as you make plans to hook up, engage in sex, or go shopping that lights up the reward circuitry. And the surrounding cues also get wired in—a bar stool, a smell, paraphernalia, lighting up a cigarette or joint, being hearted on social media or the ding of a phone or slot machine—become magnetic. So we start to crave the cue, the promise, not even the reward itself.

You might find yourself going back to the gym for a second workout, even when your body is aching and exhausted. Or staying up past midnight to get to the next level of a video game or clicking "add to cart," knowing full well that the rush will fade by morning. Or returning again and again to a relationship or even relational dynamics that leave you raw and unraveling. And somewhere inside, you're asking yourself the same question: Why do I keep doing this, even when it makes me feel bad later or doesn't even make me feel that good for long?

This is the painful, confusing loop of a **process addiction**—when the thing you feel compelled to do isn't a substance, but a behavior that promises relief. Shopping, restricting food, bingeing, working, scrolling, exercising, gambling, seeking sex or attention—these aren't inherently harmful. In fact, they often start as coping tools, or even sources of strength or resilience. But when you start to feel like you can't not do them—when stopping floods you with anxiety, shame, or emptiness—you may be caught in a pattern that's bigger than willpower.

That little thrill you feel right before you check your phone, walk into a store, or step on the scale? That's the *dry high* in action—your brain lighting up in response to a cue it's learned to associate with relief, reward, or escape. Over time, the brain tags these cues as intensely desirable—even if the reward itself is disappointing or short-lived. We start chasing the cue, not the outcome. This is called **incentive salience** a neuroscience term describing how the brain assigns **motivational importance**—the "wanting"—to certain cues or experiences. It's the process by which something neutral or ordinary (a sight, sound, smell, or thought) becomes powerfully attention-grabbing and emotionally charged because it has been linked to reward or relief in the past.[2]

But there's another layer: the more you repeat the behavior, the more the brain adjusts. It adapts by **downregulating**—dulling your dopamine receptors and releasing less dopamine in response to the same cue. This means the behavior that once felt thrilling now barely registers. And yet, you may feel even more compelled to do it, just to feel something or to give you relief from an emotion that you don't want to experience. It becomes less about seeking pleasure and more about avoiding anxiety or emptiness. What once gave you a lift now just helps you not fall apart.

That's what makes process addictions so hard to spot—and even harder to explain. There's no chemical dependency in the usual sense. Often, there's no dramatic "bottom." On the outside, you might look great. People might even praise you for your discipline, your drive, your beauty. But inside, you feel stuck in a self-sabotaging loop. You keep doing the thing—working, restricting, spending, scrolling—but it doesn't work anymore. The soothing doesn't soothe. The thrill is gone. Yet the pull is still there.

Trauma complicates this. If you grew up in chaos, neglect, or emotional unpredictability, your nervous system may have adapted by looking outside yourself to calm what was happening inside. Maybe work made you feel safe. Maybe restricting food gave you a sense of control. Maybe compulsive sex carried the promise of intimate connection and shared pleasure.

And to add another layer to this cycle, just when you need relief the most, downregulation kicks in. The brain, overstimulated by the same reward loop, starts to go numb. The behavior no longer gives the high it once did—and neither does anything else. Joy, rest, intimacy . . . it all goes flat. Life loses color. The very behavior that's draining you starts to feel like the only thing that might bring you back to life. It doesn't. But the memory of the hit—the hope that it might—keeps you coming back.

This is the heartbreak of process addiction. That if only you had more willpower, more gratitude, more self-control, you could stop. But what you're caught in isn't a failure of character. It's a loop—wired by unresolved or self-medicated pain, reinforced by brain chemistry, and powered by the very human need to feel okay inside your own skin.

Getting out of that loop doesn't start with discipline alone. It starts with understanding. It starts with compassion—for the part of you that latched onto something, anything, that made the chaos quiet down. You can begin to ask, gently: *What is this behavior trying to manage? What part of me still calls out for safety, care, or connection?*

And when you start to listen, instead of override or shame, something begins to shift. You stop fighting yourself. You stop chasing a feeling that never quite lands. And you start to find new ways to regulate—ways that leave you feeling more whole, not less.

Here are some of the most common process addictions I have seen over my years working with relational trauma and addiction:

- **Overeating**: Using food, particularly binge eating or emotional overeating, to numb distress, self-soothe, or regulate emotions rather than or in addition to physical nourishment and enjoyment.

- **Food restriction and dieting**: Compulsively restricting food intake, obsessing over "clean" or "healthy" eating (orthorexia), or engaging in cycles of yo-yo dieting to exert control, manage anxiety, or suppress deeper emotional pain.

- **Compulsive sex activities**: Engaging in compulsive sexual behaviors, such as excessive pornography use, affairs, or risky encounters, to escape painful emotions or trauma.

- **Workaholism**: Using excessive work, long hours, or professional achievements to avoid emotional discomfort, personal struggles, or relational difficulties.

- **Compulsive exercise**: Exercising obsessively to regulate emotions, gain control, or numb distress, sometimes at the expense of physical well-being and relationships.

- **Shopping/compulsive buying**: Engaging in impulsive or excessive shopping to relieve anxiety, boost mood, or fill an emotional void, often leading to financial and relational strain.

- **Compulsive screen use**: Excessive use of digital devices, including social media, gaming, and/or streaming, to feel good, self-medicate, or avoid real-life emotions, responsibilities, or social interactions.

- **Compulsive gambling**: Repeatedly engaging in gambling despite financial and emotional consequences; chasing dopamine highs to escape deeper pain and shame.

- **Compulsive self-harm**: Self-harm becomes a silent cry for relief. The cycle is heartbreakingly familiar: Tension builds, action is taken, and emotional release floods in, only to be followed by guilt, shame, and renewed tension.

- **Compulsive risk-taking**: High-risk behaviors provide an adrenaline rush that temporarily masks emotional pain. But as tolerance builds, the risks must grow bigger to deliver the same relief.

- **Compulsive love and fantasy**: Escaping into obsessive crushes or falling into cycles of infatuation and losing interest to avoid real intimacy, to cope with emotional pain, or to soothe unresolved attachment wounds. Fantasies of perfect love or obsessive infatuations offer escape routes from real vulnerability.

- **Compulsive raging**: Habitually using explosive anger, outbursts, or conflict to release emotional tension, suppress vulnerability, or feel temporarily powerful. Over time, rage becomes a dysfunctional form of emotional regulation, damaging relationships and increasing chronic stress.

- **Compulsive hoarding and withholding**: Accumulating excessive possessions and struggling to discard items because of emotional attachment, fear, or anxiety. Withholding can also manifest as compulsively keeping resources (money, love, information, or support) from others—or even from oneself—to feel in control, avoid vulnerability, or exert power in relationships. Both behaviors often stem from scarcity fears, attachment wounds, or deep insecurity.

One of the things that makes process addictions so familiar, seductive, and powerful is how they mimic the dynamics of your past. Gambling or spending, for instance, might recreate the unpredictability of living with an alcoholic or mentally ill parent. Workaholism could mirror the perfectionism you relied on to navigate a chaotic or critical household. In all cases, process addictions signal that we're chained to something, whether it's a feeling or a sense of closure that we can never quite attain.

The Clustering of ACEs and the Risk for Process Addictions

Robert Anda, co-investigator along with Dr. Vincent Felitti of the landmark Adverse Childhood Experiences (ACE) Study, tells us that ACEs rarely occur in isolation. "ACEs tend to cluster," he explains. "If a child is exposed to one form of adversity, it's very likely that other adversities are also present—such as neglect, abuse, household substance abuse, or mental illness."³ This clustering places an increasing burden on the developing emotional and physiological systems, leaving the child far more vulnerable to later difficulties—including process addictions. As ACEs accumulate, so does the likelihood of turning to compulsive behaviors to regulate emotions, soothe chronic stress, or escape unresolved pain.

Sexual abuse, in particular, is an adversity that often clusters with others—and its impact reverberates across emotional, relational, and behavioral domains. Children who experience sexual abuse frequently struggle with emotional dysregulation and a heightened sense of vulnerability. Over time, many turn to compulsive behaviors to soothe overwhelming feelings or reclaim a sense of control.

Sexual abuse is sadly all too common in families where addiction is present. When alcohol and drugs enter the picture, they don't just impair judgment—they dissolve the natural boundaries that are supposed to keep children safe. In these homes, the usual emotional and physical safeguards often aren't there, and the people children should be able to trust can become sources of harm. Sexual abuse is frequently unspoken, deeply buried, and tragically underreported. The ACE study revealed just how widespread this is. Originally, Felitti hadn't set out to study trauma; instead, he was running a weight loss clinic. But he noticed something unexpected: Numerous patients who successfully lost weight were suddenly dropping out. As he interviewed his patients to understand why they were dropping out, he discovered that many of them had histories of childhood sexual abuse.⁴ For them, extra weight gave a sense of protection, a shield, a way to feel less exposed or vulnerable to attracting unwanted sexual attention. Once Anda heard about this, he recognized the need for further research, brought in the CDC and began the ACE study.

Case Study: Marisa and Speaking the Unspeakable

In one of my RTR groups, a woman named Marisa came in with a familiar mix of control and exhaustion. A mother of three and a highly competent professional, she described herself as "constantly on edge," as she thought about normal life pressures. Marisa talked about gaining twenty pounds "with each of my kids." She thought she should go on a diet sometime but saw herself as lacking the discipline. With a little exploration, I found she began using food to self-medicate when she was a child, and the habit slowly built when she became a wife and mother. She ate secretly, sometimes to reward herself for working so hard and making a lot of money, sometimes to soothe her stress. In traffic, her arm would mechanically reach over to a bag of marshmallows; she knew just the right "dose" that would calm her down. Sometimes her numbing substance was junk food from her favorite drive-by windows when she was on the road for work.

She came in one evening admitting, almost reluctantly, sharing that she'd exploded in anger when she had felt challenged and disrespected by her teenage daughter. Her daughter's grades were starting to drop, the school was asking questions, and Marisa was trying to talk to her about it. "She just rolls her eyes," Marisa said, "and something in me snaps. I hate it. I turn into someone I don't recognize."

While consuming white flour, junk food, and sugar gave Marisa the shot of dopamine or anticipation of relief she wanted, her rages gave her relief when her inner pain overwhelmed her. The rage state instantly flooded her body with adrenaline and helped her to fight off her urge to collapse into sadness and helplessness. It got rid of the emotions that were bursting inside of her. I wanted to help Marisa to get underneath the buried pain that was fueling her process addictions.

As we moved into the experiential part of the group, I invited Marisa to do a simple role-play using an empty chair. "Can you reverse roles, become your daughter and show us how she sits, what she might say?" I asked.

She mimed a stereotypical teenager rolling her eyes and making dismissive remarks. Clearly, she hadn't truly reversed roles and *become* her daughter. Rather, she was using role reversal to show us what a brat she felt she was, with little sense of a real person beneath the caricature. I asked her to reverse roles back into herself and respond to her daughter. She barely got a few words out before her voice rose sharply.

"Don't you walk away from me! You think you know everything, but you don't!" Her fists were clenched, her shoulders and neck were rigid, her face was red and blotchy. She was shaking—but not from the present-day scene. Her nervous system had dropped into something older, deeper.

"Can you pause for a moment and just notice what's happening in your body?" I asked.

She closed her eyes. "My whole chest is hot. I want to scream. I feel . . . out of control."

I asked if she could double for herself in this state.

She stood up behind her chair and said, "I couldn't do anything. I hated it."

What came out surprised even her. She then turned to a second empty chair and began to speak, as if to someone from long ago who had just moved from the background to the foreground of her mind.

"You don't get to look at me like that. Don't come in my room. Don't touch me. Don't act like I owe you anything." As her deep anger surfaced, the room went still and tears streamed down her face. Her voice dropped to a whisper, "It was my uncle. He lived with us. No one ever knew. I've never said it out loud before."

She was six when the fondling and molestations started, and they went on until she was old enough to leave home. Her body had carried it all these years—this searing memory hidden beneath layers of competence and control. Suddenly, she realized that her rage wasn't just about her daughter. It was about the helplessness she'd never been allowed to feel, the betrayal that had gone unacknowledged, and the unspeakable that had made itself survivable by going underground. This is what her overeating was about as well. She was using food to numb her unconscious pain and her weight as a shield from a kind of attention she didn't want to attract. Because she was a child when the abuse started, she didn't realize that she wasn't complicit in attracting her uncle's attention. Besides, her uncle kept telling her how beautiful and alluring she was and making lewd and frightening comments like, "I know you like this."

The fact that she had brought her uncle in spontaneously signaled that she was ready to meet him on stage. She had been in group therapy for two years; she'd witnessed countless psychodramas, participated in them, and developed trusting relationships. That evening, she felt a pressing need to go deeper. We let her lead the way.

Over the next many months, Marisa went back into her history. She did many psychodramas, pouring out her feelings to her mother. A typical one: "You let him use our house like his place to flop. He'd come home drunk or high, and you just let him stay here, and this is what happened. Your father was an alcoholic, your brother was an alcoholic, and you pushed it all under the carpet and stuffed yourself with food and taught me to do the same. Food was comfort, it was love, it was caring, escape, companionship . . . everything. You fed him like he was your little boy. You were so nice to him, and look what he did! Why didn't you ever see what was going on?" After she finished, she turned back to the chair representing herself as a girl and said, "You've been scared all your life." She made friends with the frightened child in her who felt so unprotected and alone. We did many dramas like this, with Marisa talking to her inner child and gradually building a relationship with that younger part. Whenever she reversed roles and spoke as the younger girl back to her adult self, more truth poured out. We watched as she became more whole, stable, and integrated.

Over time, she learned to recognize when she was being pulled into the past and to differentiate between her child's defiance and her own buried terror. She brought these moments into therapy and unpacked them rather than acting out. She used therapy beautifully to explore her triggers. She woke up and became conscious of who she was, using what triggered her most as a window into her unconscious.

Slowly, her initial rage became something else—an invitation to listen, to honor, to protect. One evening, she asked to put three empty chairs on stage: one for her and two facing her, for her daughter and her inner child. She made a point of creating a significant space between the chairs. She talked to both of them at first: "I have been confusing you with each other. I couldn't tell you apart. You were swimming around the same wound inside of me, all black and blue and sore."

Next, she talked to her daughter. "I am so, so sorry for taking out the rage inside of me, her rage"—she pointed to her inner child—"on you. If I could take it all back, I would. It wasn't about you; it was about her, about me. Can you ever forgive me?"

Then she talked to her inner child: "I will protect you, I will protect you, I will protect you. I won't put you in situations that scare you. You don't have to stuff your pain down anymore. You don't have to feed your feelings. You can feel them, and I will pay attention. I will hear you, and we will change together."

For the first time in decades, that little girl inside her exhaled.

Grandchildren of Addicts and Intergenerational Dysfunction

I've always questioned the phrase "Addiction skips a generation." It never felt true to what I've seen in families. Trauma doesn't skip anything. The pain tied to addiction doesn't simply vanish when the substances are removed; it transforms. It *evolves into different coping mechanisms*. And process addictions offer many forms through which that pain finds voice and expression.

The focus on visible addictions like alcohol or drugs makes it easy to believe that abstaining from substances breaks the cycle. But the legacy of trauma doesn't disappear when the bottles are put away. Even in families where addiction isn't outwardly present, the emotional and physiological residue remains, often driving unconscious acting out in subtler but equally damaging ways.

It should come as no surprise, then, that research on grandchildren of addicts (GCoAs) suggests they often exhibit patterns similar to those of adult children of alcoholics (ACAs)—even when their parents never struggled with addiction. Psychologist Alan Berkowitz and sociologist H. Wesley Perkins found that late adolescents and young adults with alcoholic grandparents but nonalcoholic parents displayed personality traits often associated with ACAs, such as difficulty forming secure attachments, struggles with emotional regulation, and heightened anxiety or depression.

This generational ripple is further illuminated by the work of researcher Tricia Neppl, whose studies show that substance use and related problem behaviors can transmit across three generations. She found that grandparental alcohol problems and harsh parenting were linked to increased aggression and emotional dysregulation in grandchildren. Process addictions, in particular, create a cascading effect—subtly reinforcing addiction-related behaviors and emotional turmoil throughout family lineages.

As Dr. Aimie Apigian writes in *The Biology of Trauma*:

> Unresolved attachment wounds create an enduring sense of incompleteness, as though a vital part of you is always just out of reach. This inner restlessness and lack of closure trap your nervous system in a feedback loop of searching—always yearning for safety, connection, and resolution that seem unattainable. So when you discover something—a behavior, substance, or habit—that quiets this ache even for a little while, it feels like a lifeline. Addiction, whether to substances or compulsive, self-medicating behaviors, becomes your body and brain's frantic attempt to close the loop. It mimics the feeling of completion you've been longing for, tricking your system into thinking, "Ahhh, this is the feeling I've been looking for. This is what I've needed."[5]

If you're a grandchild in this lineage, the legacy of addiction doesn't disappear—it shape-shifts. With no language for what went wrong and no repair modeled, you may unconsciously inherit the same emotional chaos as your parents, though it shows up differently. Perhaps you turn to work, food, shopping, or relationships to soothe yourself. Perhaps you wrestle with depression, anxiety, or patterns of emotional volatility. Without intervention, these unhealed wounds can echo louder through each generation—until someone finally names the pain and begins the slow, courageous work of repair.

Intergenerational Impact: A Case of Untreated Process Addictions

Take Rachel, a thirty-two-year-old therapist I worked with who never struggled with substance use but found herself compulsively overworking to the point of exhaustion. Raised by a mother who carried her emotional dysregulation and cognitive distortions into her parenting style, Rachael learned to put her mother's needs first and instinctively took care of the wounded child that lived within her parent. Her mother's parenting could swing between cloying closeness, hurtful manipulation, and meanness. Now, as an adult, whenever Rachael tried to slow down, she felt an overwhelming sense of restlessness and dread. What she didn't realize was that her nervous system had inherited the survival responses of past generations. Her grandmother had been an alcoholic, and her mother had coped by controlling everything in sight. Rachel's overworking wasn't just ambition; it was her body's way of trying to outrun her mother's unspoken fear, chaos, and loss.

Her recovery began the moment she recognized the pattern in her body—the way her chest tightened before she pushed through exhaustion and the buzzing energy of hyperarousal she felt when she tried to rest. For GCoAs, the addiction isn't always obvious, but the nervous system always tells the story. Healing begins with listening inside.

Somatic Connections: The Body's Role in Process Addictions

As Peter Levine's work in trauma healing reveals, when the nervous system becomes stuck in a freeze state from a survival response to past trauma, compulsive behaviors can feel like a way to create movement or regain control.[6] He describes that when the body is unable to complete its natural fight-or-flight response during a traumatic event or when it's triggered later, the energy mobilized for action becomes trapped. It's like a car engine revving at full speed while the brakes are being slammed on. That's when engaging in a compulsive behavior of some kind can serve as an unconscious attempt to discharge the unresolved arousal and regain a sense of control. The thrill of gambling, the endless busyness of overworking, the repetitive scrolling on a device—these actions mimic resolution, even as they deepen the sense of stuckness. They provide an illusion of relief while leaving the underlying pain unaddressed.

Levine often describes trauma as "unfinished survival energy" that has been locked inside the nervous system.[7] If that energy doesn't get discharged (through safe movement or completion of defensive actions), it can live on in the body indefinitely, showing up as anxiety, compulsions, panic attacks, somatic pain, restlessness, emotional flooding . . . or an urge to engage in a process addiction.

Later in this chapter, we'll discuss healthy alternatives to process addictions, but as a quick hack, next time you notice your nervous system reacting with that trapped feeling, stand up (if you're able) and move your body in whatever way feels best. You could jog in place for a moment, shake your arms and legs, or both. Movement like this tricks your body into thinking you're escaping a threat, so your nervous system can get rid of the chemicals it has mobilized.

How to Work with Your Body to Process Your Revved-Up Internal States

Understanding how process addictions operate opens a doorway to healing and reclaiming your agency, your connection to your body, and your ability to process rather than deaden your emotions. Tuning in to what your body is trying to tell you is where the real work begins.

The first step is learning to recognize when your nervous system is dysregulated—when you're caught in a loop of fight, flight, freeze, or fawn responses. The next step is to interrupt the urge to engage in your process addictions. When you don't use these behaviors to soothe yourself, you are left with the raw urge but no medicator. In these moments, the trapdoor flies open, and you can see and sense what you were trying not to feel. This is where a good support system is so important. You'll need a place to process the feelings that come forward as you remove your medicator. You can also explore the exercises in this chapter to gain insight on what is beneath the level of your day-to-day awareness. Without this awareness, compulsive behaviors take over as unconscious attempts to self-soothe.

Exercise

Exploring Your Process Addictions

Try this exercise to explore whether or not you have a process addiction and, if you do, to examine what might be driving it, what it gives you, and what it takes away.

What Does Your Process Addiction Do for You?

What process addictions on pages 165–167 do you identify with most? For each process you identify, answer these questions in your journal:

- What do I feel right before I engage in this behavior? Overwhelmed, anxious, lonely?

- What does this process addiction give me in the moment? Distraction, a sense of control, a numbing of my emotions?

- What is the story I tell myself about why I need to engage in this behavior? ("If I don't work hard enough, I'll fail," "It's the only way I feel good about myself.")

Uncovering How Your Process Addictions Hold You Back

Next, reflect on the potential downsides or limitations of this behavior. Ask yourself:

- How does this process addiction affect my relationships? ("I prioritize work over my family," "I avoid vulnerability with others.")

- How does it impact my mental, emotional, or physical health? ("It leaves me exhausted," "I'm disconnected from my emotions.")

- What do I avoid or miss out on by relying on this process? Deeper self-reflection, opportunities for genuine connection?

Your Relationship with the Process Addiction

Now that you've explored the supposed benefits and drawbacks of your process addiction, consider the following in your journal:

- What needs am I trying to meet through this process? Feeling safe, in control, loved? Calming my activations when I feel panicked or stressed?

- What feelings does my process addiction help me avoid? Shame, anger, loneliness, fear?

- Do I have memories or situations from my childhood that trigger these suppressed or denied feelings? ("When my parent was unpredictable," "When I felt abandoned," "When I was blamed for things.")

- How does my process addiction mirror the dynamics of my family? ("Overworking makes me feel like I'm in control, which I never felt as a child.")

Reframing, Gaining Perspective, and Growing

Finally, with the root of your process addiction a bit clearer, reflect on the following:

- How might facing these feelings help me grow? ("I could begin to loosen the automatic behaviors from my past," "I could create healthier patterns.")

- What healthier tools can I use to meet those needs or calm those activations? Journaling, taking a pause, breathing, becoming mindful of what's going on inside of me, taking a walk, engaging in a flow activity like playing music, talking to a trusted friend, going to a twelve-step meeting?

Walking and Movement as Medicine for a Traumatized Brain

I have always incorporated walking and exercise into my recommendations for clients who want to do a life reset that involves inner work and adopting new, healthy habits. The benefits are so life enhancing. For example, recent science is showing us that mindful movement—whether it's walking, yoga, or tai chi—does far more than soothe your body. It actually reshapes your brain. Simply engaging in these enjoyable activities boosts blood flow, reduces inflammation, and releases mood-lifting chemicals like dopamine, serotonin, and BDNF, all of which support emotional regulation and healing. These practices even promote neurogenesis in the hippocampus—the brain's center for memory and mood—which is often shrunken in people who've lived with chronic stress or trauma. "You're actually increasing the birth of new neurons within the brain," says Mazen Kheirbek, a professor in the Department of Psychiatry and Behavioral Sciences at the University of California, San Francisco.[8] Over time, this helps bring balance back to overstressed circuits and rebuilds the prefrontal cortex—the part of your brain that governs decision-making and self-regulation, which so often goes offline in trauma.

Research confirms these effects again and again. Regular aerobic exercise like walking has been shown to increase hippocampal volume and sustain mood improvements over time.[9] Similarly, yoga and tai chi combine gentle movement with breath and focused awareness to quiet an overactive stress response while increasing gray matter in the hippocampus and prefrontal cortex.[10] In one recent study, just twelve weeks of tai chi reduced anxiety and boosted theta brain wave activity—those slower, restorative patterns that reflect calm and emotional balance.[11]

In trauma recovery, these practices do more than offer temporary relief. They literally help repair the brain's architecture, allowing the nervous system to step out of survival mode and into a place where connection, safety, and self-awareness can take root. Every step, every breath, every mindful movement becomes a way of telling your body: *You're safe now. You can heal.*

Why Walking Works on So Many Levels

Walking, in particular, has a quiet kind of magic. It does more than soothe your nervous system; it reconnects you to your body and your environment. Walking with a friend adds another layer of healing by tapping into the power of connection. Sharing the experience boosts oxytocin—the bonding hormone that eases stress and strengthens emotional ties—and acts as a buffer against loneliness. The rhythm of your steps regulates your breath and calms overactive stress circuits in the brain, creating a sense of flow. (More about flow in a moment.)

Walking in nature magnifies these effects. Time spent in green spaces lowers cortisol, quiets brain regions tied to rumination, and fosters a calmer, more resilient nervous system. Even ten minutes among trees or along a quiet path can ease anxiety and depression, sharpen cognition, and bring emotional balance.

The Japanese practice of shinrin-yoku—or forest bathing—takes this even further. It invites you to slow down and immerse your senses in the natural world. Studies show it reduces blood pressure, strengthens immunity, and gently shifts the body out of survival states into deep restoration.[12]

Research consistently demonstrates that something as simple as walking can be just as effective as antidepressant medication for alleviating depression. In a 2000 study at Duke University, researchers found that thirty minutes of brisk walking three times a week produced symptom relief comparable to standard antidepressant treatment among older adults.[13] Complementing this, a comprehensive meta-analysis in 2018 reviewed dozens of trials and found that aerobic exercise—including walking—delivered antidepressant effects that rivaled those of pharmacotherapy.[14] These findings affirm that walking isn't merely a mood booster—it's a scientifically validated intervention for depression. This effect doesn't just occur during the workout; psychiatrist James Blumenthal adds that the benefits "sustain emotional balance long after the walk ends."[15]

In my Relational Trauma Repair model, I often use the simple act of walking as part of therapy. As people move around the room, making choices about what they feel and what they identify with, walking activates their limbic system—the part of the brain where sense memory and emotions are processed. This movement helps open the mind and body for deeper connection and engagement, much like how a walk with a trusted friend often leads to conversations that feel alive and authentic.

Find Your Flow State Activity

My next favorite mood regulator is the flow state. Flow is a psychological state where your sense of time, self-consciousness, and even bodily awareness seem to dissolve, leaving you fully absorbed in the task at hand. It's often described as being "in the zone." According to psychologist Mihaly Csikszentmihalyi, who pioneered flow research, this state arises when your skills are well matched to a meaningful challenge: stretching you just enough to stay engaged, but not so much that you feel overwhelmed.[16]

Activities that naturally invite flow include creative pursuits like painting, writing, playing music, and dancing, as well as physical activities like rock climbing, dancing, long-distance running, yoga, and even housework and woodworking. Even certain types of work, like coding, designing, or deep problem-solving, can evoke flow when approached with full presence and intrinsic motivation. The hallmark of flow is that it feels rewarding in itself—not because of an external payoff, but because being fully engaged feels enlivening, effortless, and deeply satisfying. You will find that you emerge from flow activities feeling calm and integrated. They will act as a building block in your new design for living!

You Can Do It: Accessing the Medicine Chest Inside of You

Too often, we see healing as just a matter of resolving old attachment wounds, but it's so much more than that. This book is not meant to replace recovery work; instead, it is your handbook to carry with you throughout your recovery process. What truly facilitates long-lasting recovery is an ongoing commitment to healing your attachment wounds, changing your habits, and creating a healthy support network. It's also about learning how to recalibrate your nervous system when you're activated, so you don't compulsively reach for unhealthy solutions, like process addictions, to calm down. Calming your nervous system and maintaining that calm throughout your day is always your first order of business. We need to learn how to use activities that activate the medicine chest nature has built inside of us to restore and enhance our sense of well-being.

Support Your Reset with Healthy Dopamine Hits

Once you stabilize your emotional state, you can replace old survival habits with nourishing, life-affirming ones. Feed your nervous system the right kind of reward:

- Move your body regularly. Dance, walk, stretch.

- Be in nature as often as possible.

- Rest deeply. Sleep well.

- Eat nourishing food.

- Connect with community. Connect with friends you can be yourself with.

- Work, play, create. Participate in the world meaningfully.

- Allow yourself leisure without guilt.

- Engage in a flow activity.

- Tend to your inner child with compassion.

- Seek therapy if it feels supportive.

- Attend a twelve-step meeting or support group.

- Let yourself enjoy ordinary pleasures rather than rushing past them.

The recovery journey doesn't end with abstinence; in many ways, that's where it begins. Support programs have long understood that emotional and physiological dysregulation is a primary driver of addictions of all kinds. When we can't regulate what's happening inside, we reach for something outside to soothe, distract, or numb. True healing asks more of us than abstaining. It asks us to turn inward, to learn how to sit with ourselves rather than escape. This is what Bill Wilson, cofounder of Alcoholics Anonymous, referred to as "emotional sobriety."

In my many years of treating adult children of addicts, I've learned something universal: We all need to actively grieve. Grief isn't a detour—it's the doorway. Without it, pain hardens in the body, numbing our senses and closing us off from life. To grieve is to let the frozen places soften and the broken places mend. It frees us from carrying the weight of unspoken sorrow. In this sacred work, grief clears a space inside us where joy, connection, and the quiet rhythm of life can return. That is the true miracle of recovery—not just what we leave behind, but who we become in the process.

8

The Healing Power of Grief
Giving Your Inner Child a Voice

In 1997 I wrote a book called *Heartwounds: The Impact of Unresolved Trauma and Grief on Relationships*. Until that point, people mostly talked about grief in relation to death, but I wanted to talk about grief in life. The kind that doesn't come with rituals or casseroles. The kind we bury in our bodies. As I recognized that those I worked with, including myself, needed to allow themselves to grieve in order to get better, to cry their frozen tears and allow their deep resentment to surface, I became fascinated with the subject of grief. I wondered what we could do with the kind of inner death that happens in life, the kind that goes unacknowledged and too often unseen—that ephemeral sense of loss that pressed on me from the inside and that virtually all of my ACA clients, relatives, and friends carried in one way or another.

How do we mourn someone we lose while they are still living? How do we grieve the loss of half a parent, two-thirds of a family, and years of our childhood spent carrying worries we pretended weren't there? How do we grieve the parent we both hate and love, the drunk who haunts the shadows of our memory, sometimes whole and happy, sometimes sick and disturbing? A parent who is two very different people, depending on whether they are high or sober? A family that became dysregulated and internalized the behaviors that mirror drunkenness and dysregulation right alongside the addict who modeled them?

People expect you to grieve loss in a tangible and final way. But unlike the grief that follows a singular, identifiable loss, your grief as an ACA is cumulative. It builds over years, often unnoticed, as you learn to adapt to an unpredictable world. Maybe you grew up convinced that if you just worked harder, behaved better, believed more fervently, or stayed quieter, things would improve. And when they didn't, you may have turned that pain inward, thinking you just were incapable of being right or doing right. Grieving this experience is about not only acknowledging what happened but also allowing yourself to feel the sadness of what didn't. It is about naming the void—the birthday parties that went uncelebrated; the comforting hugs that never came or came only when it was your parent who needed them; the good talks to clear the air that blew up instead; the abuse that everyone colluded in keeping hidden; the protection you needed but didn't receive. For ACAs, grief is layered and complex. It's not only about mourning a loss but also about coming to terms with what can't be changed: the loss of what *could have been*. It's a vague sense of longing for something you can't quite name, a life that could have unfolded differently.

But the other reason I wanted to write *Heartwounds* was to describe a way out of this buried pain—the miracles I was seeing happening over and over again, when clients finally just let themselves cry and give in to their grief. So many resist this surrender, afraid of what they will feel or fearing they will never come out of it. But in my experience, grief offers the shortest way through; resisting it is what makes sadness and regret feel endless.

I witnessed this giving into grief happening when clients stopped talking *about* their pain and anger and began to talk *to* them. When they finally let their hurt have a voice: "Where were you? I loved you. Why couldn't you stop using? Why couldn't you turn around and choose me, not a drug? Wasn't I enough to get sober for?" These were the moments when the child inside of them fought its way past clenched jaws and choked voices, and decades of old pain came pouring out. When they finally dared to express their rage and indignation for being dropped midair and abused when they tripped into the blast radius of their parent's drunkenness or their family member's hidden pain and rage. When they risked expressing the love they normally had to hold back because they didn't feel safe expressing it.

During our psychodrama sessions, I watched as my clients time traveled back to their childhood, grabbed their own hand, and pulled until they released their inner child from the grip of frozen family pain, recovering their own innocence and hope. In volume 1 of *Psychodrama*, psychiatrist J. L. Moreno recounted a chance meeting when Sigmund Freud asked him about the work he was doing. He gave this description of the power of embodiment over words: "Well, Dr. Freud, I start where you leave off. You meet people in the artificial setting of your office. I meet them on the street and in their homes, in their natural surroundings. . . . You analyze and tear them apart. I let them act out their conflicting roles and help them to put the parts back together again. You analyze their dreams. I give them the courage to dream again."[1]

Sometimes trauma leaves us feeling like we've been shattered into pieces, living in fragments instead of feeling whole. Psychodrama helps you gently reenter those frozen, broken places, not just by talking *about* the past, but by *experiencing* it in a safe, supportive setting. When you step into a role—as, for example, your younger self, a parent, or what internal family systems (IFS) therapy calls a "part"—you bring implicit memory into conscious awareness. You begin to *see* and *feel* the inner life of the part or role in a new way; you are then able to experience and bring a kind of closure or what feels like a new ending. Psychodrama engages both hemispheres of the brain by weaving together verbal and nonverbal processing. The left hemisphere, responsible for language and logic, is activated as participants tell their stories, name roles, and reflect on insights. The right hemisphere, which holds emotion, imagery, and sensory memory, comes alive through movement, enactment, and embodied expression. This integration allows implicit, often wordless experiences to surface and be organized into a coherent recollection bridging the gap between feeling and understanding. In doing so, psychodrama supports whole-brain healing, helping participants process unresolved trauma and create new relational patterns. Healing is both bottom-up and top-down—meaning it works through the body's felt experience as well as the mind's capacity to make sense of that experience.

In his endorsement of my 2023 book *Treating Adult Children of Relational Trauma*, Bessel van der Kolk, the groundbreaking PTSD researcher and author of the bestseller *The Body Keeps the Score*, wrote about the value of this modality:

> Psychodrama is one of the most effective treatments of PTSD and developmental trauma that I am familiar with. . . . Psychodrama helps to make our inner world visible and manifest what we struggle with, not so much by words, but by actions, making the invisible observable and measurable. Operating in a space where important people from our past are recreated in the living present, and where we can experience and manifest our confused inner world, we can finally say the words that were never spoken, and allow feelings to emerge that could not be expressed back then. Working with others in three-dimensional space, as psychodrama does, can not only uniquely create a timeless experience where past and present can merge to help us reconfigure our mental alignment, but also provide profound reparative experiences.

As you read this chapter, I hope you will become more comfortable feeling your grief, knowing that as you do, you will also open your capacity for joy. Many ACAs fear that their grief might overwhelm them, but they are often pleasantly surprised, as I hope you'll be too, to discover that honestly expressing your grief allows you to lift the decades of burden, pain, and anxiety off your shoulders, one tear at a time. Grieving allows you to let go of the belief that it was your job to save your family. Admitting that the task was just too big can be a path toward liberating yourself from a job that should never have been yours in the first place. The exercises throughout this chapter will guide you to begin this journey for yourself.

Why Grief for ACAs Is Different

What makes ACA grief so hard to get to is that it is often steeped in denial, forced to hide under layers of survival strategies and defenses. You may have learned to push your pain aside or to numb it. You forget it, remember it, then forget it all over again. You think you've left it behind, only to have it resurface in unexpected ways and at odd moments: as a sudden wave of sadness while watching a tender family scene on TV or hearing a familiar song, as an ache in your chest rises when a friend speaks lovingly about their family. That's because unacknowledged grief doesn't disappear; it waits in an empty room inside of you. It lives in the shadows.

It slowly forms hidden pools of pain that get triggered when you least expect it, shooting to the surface and getting projected at the wrong person, in the wrong place, and at the wrong time. Without acknowledgment, this grief can go unidentified, or what Dr. Kenneth J. Doka called "disenfranchised" in his book *Disenfranchised Grief: Recognizing Hidden Sorrow*. When this disenfranchised grief surfaces, you might feel like you're careening back and forth between two worlds—the present and the past—trying to fend off something intangible and unknowable, unable to reconcile the dissonant realities of your past or get them to fit together into one coherent whole. You may wrestle with the grip that old patterns of thinking, feeling, and acting have on you, only to realize that the fight isn't just with the ghosts themselves but with the way they've taken up residence inside of you. True healing begins when you stop careening, turn toward those shadowy parts and become willing to know what's in there.

Disenfranchised loss refers to grief that isn't openly recognized, validated, or supported by society—the kind of loss that falls outside cultural norms. Many forms of disenfranchised loss are common among ACAs. Here are some that I see most often.

- **Loss of connection to self**: Growing up in the confusion of addiction and trauma can cause you to shut down, dissociate, or repress emotions that threaten to overtake you. If you don't return to these, feel them, and understand them, they may remain unavailable to you. If this happens over and over again, you can lose touch with what you feel about significant chunks of your life. While this may have been a necessary survival strategy, recovery asks us to open to these inner parts (to use IFS language) and hear what they have to tell us, to feel what we've shut down.

- **Loss of the addict to their substance**: You may need to grieve the loss of who your addicted parent was before substances took hold and left them feeling like a stranger to you. And if they're sober today, it's just as important to grieve the parent you had growing up, so you can meet them in the present without carrying the weight of unresolved childhood emotions. Psychodrama gives you the chance to speak to the parent you had *then*, from the perspective of the child you were *then*.

- **Grief of your inner child**: You may grieve that your parent's addiction meant that they came and went, that as a child you lived cycling between anxious hope and bitter disappointment as they moved in and out of their strange and dissociated world of addiction. That inner child may still carry the confusion of having warm connection given and taken away repeatedly.

- **Loss of a safe, unencumbered childhood**: Your childhood may also have been filled with adult burdens that made you feel different from your friends. You likely grew up too soon, carrying the pain that the family wanted to pretend wasn't there. You also saw a side of life modeled that was demeaning, mortifying, and may have made you feel a sense of shame about your family or yourself.

- **Loss of a functional family system**: In homes where one or both parents are consumed by addiction, illness, or emotional absence, siblings often become each other's primary caregivers—or, at times, each other's caretaking burdens. You may have been thrust into a parental role far too young, tending to younger siblings while quietly burying your own needs. Or perhaps you were placed in the care of an older sibling whose ability to nurture was complicated by their own unmet needs for safety, sometimes protecting you with tenderness, other times lashing out and repeating the patterns they had endured. Maybe you sought love and belonging by fostering dependence in a younger sibling. Or perhaps you were the younger one, sacrificing your own autonomy to hold onto their love.

In these systems, the absence of a consistently attuned parent creates fertile ground for rivalry, confusion, and longing. Siblings become stand-ins for the love that's missing, sparking a fragile blend of competition, envy, and misplaced loyalty. Without a stable adult to mediate or model healthy dynamics, children often internalize power struggles rather than learning the mutuality and trust that define healthy peer relationships.

- **Loss of innocence or potential**: Living with addiction can steal your innocence. Your ability to trust intimacy, to let go and have fun, to relax and be yourself can become sorely compromised while living with the frightening and distressing chaos that surrounds addiction. You may feel somehow dirty, tarred by the same shame brush that the addict feels painted with. Addiction steals time, relationships, and dreams. You might mourn the opportunities and versions of yourself that you didn't get to explore or become.

- **Loss of a beloved pet**: Pets offer unconditional love and companionship, often serving as a refuge in a chaotic home. Many ACAs turned to their childhood pets as sources of love and support. Losing a pet can resurface childhood grief, reminding you of moments when a childhood pet was an important source of comfort, love, or safety.

- **Loss due to abuse**: Abuse, whether sexual, physical, or emotional, isn't just about what was done to you. It's also about what was taken away: trust, security, the freedom to simply be a child. To get through, you may have pushed down your fear, swallowed your anger, split off from your own body. You learned not to feel, because feeling was dangerous. But now, as you begin to unfreeze, the grief may come rushing in, as well as the rage buried beneath experiences of helplessness and collapse.

- **Grief from neglect—the invisible wound**: Neglect is a wound without a headline, but not without consequence. It leaves no bruises, no dramatic stories to recount, just a quiet ache that seeps into the spaces where connection should have lived. You may struggle to name what hurt, because there was so little to point to.

  You may grieve the feeling of being unseen, the meals you prepared for yourself, the questions no one asked about your day. And now, perhaps without realizing it, you carry that same template into adulthood, apologizing for having needs, not quite believing you're worth someone's care.

- **Loss due to divorce or abandonment**: A parental separation or custody change can leave a child feeling displaced, rejected, or split between two worlds. If this occurs on top of addiction, it can intensify the impact of family dysfunction. While divorce or separation may be part of a solution and best in the long run, you may have lost access to a parent or struggled with the mixed grief of longing for them while also knowing they weren't safe to be around.

Exercise

Recognizing and Voicing Disenfranchised Loss or Grief

Noticing your grief is the first step toward integration, and giving it space allows it to move rather than stay stuck. Take a moment to reflect on the following prompts in your journal:

- Read over the descriptions of disenfranchised losses above. Do any stand out to you as something you experienced?

- Which form of disenfranchised loss or grief resonates with you the most?

- Have you given yourself permission to grieve this loss, or has it remained unspoken?

- If that part of you had a voice, what would it say to you today? What would you say back as the person you are today?

- Is there anything you notice as you unwind your emotions through role-based journaling? If so, what?

Signs and Symptoms of Unresolved Grief

I look at behaviors to understand how disenfranchised grief might be showing up. Here are some of the disguised ways unacknowledged grief may surface:

- **Sudden angry outbursts or bouts of rage**: You may find yourself snapping or exploding over things that seem minor, because your anger is carrying older, deeper pain that hasn't yet found words.

- **Caretaking, fawning, and placating behavior (codependency)**: You might automatically rush to soothe, fix, or please others, sacrificing your own needs to make your real feelings known just to feel safe, valued, connected, or in control.

- **Constant resentment, victim mindset**: You may feel trapped in cycles of unfairness, convinced that no matter how hard you try, you're always overlooked, taken advantage of, or left with the short end of the stick.

- **Chronic negativity, rumination on the past, or preoccupation with dark subjects**: You might find yourself mentally looping through old wounds, drawn to heavily negative subjects as a way to release hidden pain and resentment.

- **Easily triggered into overly intense emotional reactions or shutting down entirely**: You may struggle to regulate emotions, exploding or imploding, having outbursts of rage or tears or going numb, or shutting down and disappearing inside.

- **Chronic low mood, recurring or long-lasting depression**: You may carry a quiet heaviness or sadness that lingers in the background, a kind of emotional gravity that feels like your baseline.

- **Excessive or chronic anxiety, hyperreactivity, or chronic hypervigilance**: Your nervous system may live in a state of overalertness, always scanning for what could go wrong, even when things are objectively okay.

- **Somatization such as body aches, pains, or unexplained health issues**: Your body may be expressing what your mind learned to suppress. Grief, stress, and fear might show up as stiffness, tightness, fatigue, headaches, or physical symptoms that are hard to pin down.

- **Self-harming behaviors**: You may turn your pain inward, using physical harm as a way to express or manage emotions you can't otherwise release.

- **Excessive guilt, shame, and feeling needy**: You might feel overwhelmed by self-blame or believe you're fundamentally "bad," "too needy," or "wrong," even when you've done nothing to deserve it.

- **Constant crying or feeling perpetually weepy**: Tears may come easily and often, even when you can't clearly name what you're grieving.

- **Emotional numbness or dissociation**: You may feel detached from your feelings altogether, like you're living behind a glass wall where nothing fully reaches you.

- **Persistent desire to self-medicate with food, alcohol, drugs, sex, or screens**: You might find yourself compulsively reaching for something, anything, to numb out, escape, or create a temporary sense of relief.

Exercise

What Is My Behavior Trying to Tell Me?

Use these prompts to explore what comes up in your journal. Approach the questions with curiosity and self-compassion.

- Which signs or symptoms of unresolved grief do you recognize in yourself?

- How do you feel, emotionally or physically, when you experience this state or engage in this behavior?

- What parts of yourself or your story might this behavior be trying to keep hidden?

- What might it be trying to reveal to you about grief you haven't yet been able to name or feel?

- Does it surprise you to realize that long-buried pain may still be quietly affecting you?

- What do you need to build into your life or yourself to feel safe enough to feel your grief?

It's Okay to Let Yourself "Know"

If triggers for ACAs are about managing inner dysregulation and activation, grief is about coming to terms with the cumulative losses and unresolved pain that become the jet propulsion for those very triggers. Each time you let yourself grieve rather than stuff your emotions, you drain the fuel tank that powers your activations and triggers. Grief for ACAs isn't just sadness; it's a reckoning. It's facing the emotional debris left behind by years of trying to make sense of chaos, soothe a parent's pain, or pretend everything was fine when it wasn't.

But here's the big problem: Many ACAs desperately want to fix their pain rather than feel it, to *think* themselves out of it so they can avoid the vulnerability of their own inner world. But just because you think you know something doesn't mean your dysregulated nervous system got the message. ACAs often don't know that they don't know. They believe what they tell themselves. This is why psychologist Janet Woititz used to say, "ACAs don't have relationships; we take hostages."[2] And the first hostage you take is your inner child. This is why I look at behavior rather than listening to words. Words can lie, but behavior and the way our nervous systems handle moments of activation tell the real story. When ACAs let themselves feel the pain that's turbocharging their activation before they act it out or make it about someone or something else, they can see the confusion, helplessness, rage, and hurt their inner child or other parts of them may still be carrying.

In essence, grieving helps you bridge the gap between the trauma of your past and the potential safety of your present. It allows your nervous system to move from a state of survival to a state of calmness and aliveness. You become better equipped to face your emotions, process them as they arise in you, and live from a grounded place.

Reawakening Inside: Recognizing, Feeling, and Healing Grief

Grief may seem like the last thing you want to feel, but when you allow it, even in small doses, it often becomes the most direct path through the pain. Avoiding grief, on the other hand, can stretch across a lifetime, pulling at you like an undertow every time you try to move forward. Sometimes the most radical step you can take is to stop running and sit with what's already inside you.

It might feel like your grief could swallow you whole, but grief, when you let yourself feel it, becomes a gateway. In mourning what was lost, you begin to reclaim what's still possible. The wound breaks open, yes, but in breaking, it makes room. Little by little, your pain is metabolized. Your story integrates. And something more whole and true begins to take shape in its place.

Exercise

Gathering the Pieces of My Story

Find some photographs from any time in your life of yourself, your family, scenes that are significant to you, or any other images that draw you. Now, respond to these prompts in your mind or in your journal, taking your time with each image.

- What feelings arise in me as I look at this picture?

- If I could double for or speak the inner life of me or this person at this time, what would I say?

- What couldn't I say then that I can say now, to myself, members of my family, or the world?

- Now, from the perspective of where I am today, what would I like to say to myself or anyone else in this picture?

- What am I seeing differently now?

Age Correspondence Grief: Confusing Your Inner Child with the Child You're Raising

The *age correspondence grief reaction* is one of the most mysterious portals into our unconscious that I see. An age correspondence reaction is a phenomenon through which the age or stage of another person, commonly a child, stimulates that same age or stage within you. For example, you may find yourself worrying about or feeling protective of your seven-year-old child, convinced that they are struggling deeply if they report having some vulnerable feelings, because their age has stimulated the unprocessed wounds of the seven-year-old (or thereabouts) inside of you. Their normal problems or feelings of hurt or insecurity might be stirring up your unhealed childhood pain, but you don't make the connection. Instead, you try to fix in *them* what really needs fixing in *you*. You may dive in with "solutions" or, conversely, sort of collapse in the face of their neediness or hurt feelings; you may even alternate between distancing yourself from them and becoming controlling and codependent.

If an age or stage from your child's life is activating you, take a step back and ask yourself, "What was going on in my life at more or less this age or stage?" An age correspondence reaction isn't just remembering the past—it's reliving it through someone else. You unconsciously project your unhealed pain onto a child, student, or young person in your life, reacting as if their vulnerability is your own. You become activated, not because of what's happening to them, but because something unfinished in you is being stirred. You move to protect them with an urgency that really belongs to your own past, but you don't connect the dots. You think it's only about your child, young relative, or student today, when in truth, you're responding to your own unhealed wound.

For example, Andre, a devoted teacher in his early forties, noticed himself becoming uncharacteristically anxious whenever one of his quieter students, Jamal, seemed withdrawn. If Jamal didn't smile or speak up in class, Andre felt a knot in his stomach and an almost panicked need to fix Jamal, asking if he was okay, checking in repeatedly, and even staying after class with him. It wasn't until Andre reflected on his own childhood—growing up in a home where sadness was ignored and silence meant being invisible—that he realized what was happening. Jamal's quietness activated Andre's younger self. Andre's reaction wasn't only about Jamal; it was also about the boy inside him who once longed for someone to notice.

When he shared this in the group, I asked, "Who could play you as a boy, and what would you like to say to him as the grown man you are today?" By talking to his inner child, reversing roles and talking back to his adult self today, then coming back into his adult self and reassuring his inner child, he was able to integrate this neglected part of himself back into the fine man he had become.

Another client, Elena, a thirty-two-year-old new mother, couldn't understand why she struggled to bond with her newborn. She felt numb, uneasy, and had a hard time nursing. Other mothers seemed flooded with love, but she felt a mix of love and a need to have distance. She had no conscious memory of early trauma, no explanation for why caring for her baby triggered so many mixed emotions in her. But when I reminded her of her own life at that moment in time, it all became clear to her.

When she was eight months old, Elena's father left. Her mother, forced to work full-time, placed her in the care of others. Though she had no explicit memory of these events, her body remembered, associating infancy with loss, absence, and disconnection. Now, holding her own baby, that old imprint resurfaced.

For Elena, making the connection between her eight-month-old self and her difficulty bonding with the baby she was so excited and grateful to welcome into her life changed everything. It wasn't that she didn't love her child; it was that her nervous system was protecting her from a loss that had already happened, a loss in her own childhood. As she processed her past, she could allow herself to stay present, hold her daughter, and slowly feel and coregulate together. Healing began, not just in her relationship with her baby, but for the infant she had once been.

Remember that trauma causes significant changes in the brain, particularly in areas like the amygdala, hippocampus, and prefrontal cortex, which regulate fear, memory, and reasoning. These changes can make it difficult to distinguish between past and present, causing you to relive your old pain—in this case, through someone else. You're interpreting a child's perhaps normal pain through the traumatized lens of your wounded inner child.

And that's why healing, in this way, is not just a personal act; it's an act of transformation that frees the next generation.

Exercise

When Old Wounds Meet New Moments: Separating My Story from Theirs

Age correspondence reactions can happen without us realizing it, as our mind/body blends our own unmet needs as a child with the needs of the child in front of us. This exercise will help you gently separate the two, so you can respond with greater clarity, maturity, and calm.

Think of a recent moment when a child's behavior or emotion triggered a strong reaction in you. Ask yourself the following questions.

Recognize the Reaction

- What did I feel in my body?

- What story did I make up about the child's experience?

Trace It Back

- Does this reaction feel like it belongs to a younger part of me?

- If so, how old do I feel in this moment?

- What was happening in my life at this age?

- What am I imagining this child is experiencing that may really be about my own unconscious and unresolved inner child pain?

Separate Past from Present

- How is the child in front of me different from the child I once was?

- What support does this child have that I didn't? (Including me as an adult.)

- What does my child self need to say to me now? What things do I need to say to the wounded child in me that they have longed to hear? Say them now and say them fully.

Reparent Through Presence

- What wounds from my own childhood am I layering onto the child I am parenting, teaching, or loving today?

- What do I need to do for my inner child so I can become healthier and more healed?

- What do I see now that I couldn't see before?

Healing isn't about achieving perfection; it's about learning how to live with grace in the presence of what's broken, mending what you can mend, and making peace inside yourself by accepting what you cannot change. It doesn't have to mean erasing the past or getting over the pain; it means acknowledging what was lost and honoring it. Facing your inner demons in this way can give you a kind of fearlessness and confidence. You've done the work to wrestle them to the ground, and you have won the battle, not by fighting it to a bloody finish, but by embracing it and making room for all of it, including all aspects of you. Over time, as you mourn, your pain will loosen its grip, and you will find a way to use it as motivation to build a life filled with meaning, connection, and purpose.

As you turn toward your grief and the parts of yourself left waiting for care, you may discover that what you've called boundaries were sometimes born of fear rather than choice. Perhaps you learned to seek safety by overgiving, or vanishing, because saying no felt unsafe. Or perhaps you braced yourself behind rigid defenses that may have left you lonely. This is the ground we'll walk next, to learn boundaries that feel organic, that protect you but allow you to comfortably connect as well.

9

A Sanctuary for Self

Building Boundaries That Honor Connection

It can be helpful to think of boundaries as bridges rather than barriers—a meeting point where your need to maintain your sense of self exists alongside your natural desire for connection. Healthy boundaries make room for both autonomy and relationship. When they come from a place of regulation rather than dysregulation, they allow you to separate without cutting off and to connect without losing yourself in someone else's experience.

As Daniel Siegel, founder of interpersonal neurobiology, explains, "Integration is defined quite simply as 'the linkage of differentiated parts.' With integration emerges coherence and harmony; when integration is impaired, chaos or rigidity ensues." In this sense, healthy boundaries reflect that integration in action: the capacity to stay anchored in your own emotions, needs, and values while remaining open and attuned to others. This balance depends on a well-regulated nervous system; when we feel safe, the brain can hold both self-awareness and empathy at the same time.[1]

But in families shaped by addiction or trauma, this integration is often disrupted. Boundaries tend to swing to extremes, either hardening into walls or dissolving into enmeshment and identity blending. In both cases, our capacity for authentic connection erodes, and emotional safety becomes harder to access.

As a child, the denial, gaslighting, and fear surrounding addiction may have messed with your fledgling attempts to have boundaries. You may have assumed that you had no right to them, or you learned to override your inner signals to withdraw in order to gain a sense of space or to placate and fawn in order to belong. So now, as an adult, when you try to manage your margins, it can feel like you're thrown back into a younger, more vulnerable version of yourself. Your voice feels small, and you may even question if it's okay to have boundaries at all.

The good news is, as an adult, you have the power to shift these patterns. Your brain's natural neuroplasticity, its ability to rewire and form new pathways, makes it possible to move beyond the survival strategies of your past. The patterns you learned in childhood are not permanent; you can grow and change if you want to and are willing to learn.

Each time you set the kinds of boundaries that respect both your own needs and those of others, rather than the kind that just perpetuate pain, you're literally laying the groundwork for slowly rewiring your brain to respond from your adult mind, the grounded, wise part of you, instead of the reactive wounded child mind. Over time, this process becomes a powerful act of reparenting, of self-respect and self-love, building not just healthier boundaries but also a deep sense of resilience. And as you strengthen these new patterns, you're creating a ripple effect in your relationships, fostering healthier, more fulfilling connections and paving the way for lasting change.

This chapter will guide you through the process of growing up your boundaries, helping you create ones that are more mature, flexible, and aligned with who you are today. By doing the inner work to repair what got in the way of your sense of wholeness and safety in your relationships, you create the possibility for you to take care of yourself while also creating space for others to do the same.

Listen to Your Body: How the Body Says, "NO!" When You Can't

When your boundaries are impinged upon, does your body sometimes register it before you do? Maybe you get a sinking in your stomach, tightness in your chest or shoulders, or heat rising to your face? Maybe your heart starts pounding or your breath gets shallow?

If so, your nervous system may be sending a signal saying, *Something isn't feeling right for me.* Even if your mind tries to brush it off, your nervous system still registers some sense of intrusion.

The most challenging part? If you've grown up in a family where your boundaries were often ignored or disrespected, this physical reaction might feel normal or, worse, invisible. In these cases, the body sometimes becomes the last truth teller. When we cannot let ourselves have boundaries—whether around the demands of others, the pressures we place upon ourselves, or the unspoken expectations buried in our early relationships—our bodies may eventually say no for us. As Gabor Maté describes in his book *When the Body Says No*, suppressed emotions, chronic stress, and disowned needs don't simply vanish; they embed themselves deep within the nervous system and the cells of the body, quietly eroding our health over time. Then illness can, paradoxically, emerge as both a crisis and a messenger—a forced pause, a threshold we cannot cross without reckoning with the deeper truths we've neglected. Similarly, a nervous system meltdown—a collapse into exhaustion, anxiety, or emotional overwhelm—may be not just a breakdown but a breakthrough: the body's urgent call to recognize the cost of self-abandonment and to reclaim the need for inner safety we were once taught to override. When seen through this lens, both illness and nervous system dysregulation can become unlikely gifts, painful but profound invitations to heal not only your body but your life.

Shadow Boundaries: How Dysfunctional Families Collude to Say No

ACAs often perceive themselves as having no boundaries, but I don't believe that's entirely accurate. It's not that we lack boundaries; it's that we weren't supported in developing boundaries that feel authentic and right *for us*. Instead, we were co-opted and controlled by a hidden set of what I call *shadow boundaries*, designed to obscure addiction and dysfunction within our family system and control the behavior of family members.

In addicted or dysfunctional family systems, boundaries are rarely the result of mutual, thoughtful negotiation. Instead, the chaos introduced by an addict's behavior often compels other members to seize control in a bid for order. This reactive process leads to constantly shifting boundaries established not from a calm, considered place, but from a state of sympathetic nervous system arousal. In this state of sympathetic arousal—marked by hypervigilance, stress, and a drive to protect both oneself and the family's unspoken secrets—boundaries are reactive rather than intentional, shaped by survival instincts rather than thoughtful choice.

An addict's need to protect and sustain their addiction becomes ground zero for creating dysfunctional family boundaries. These boundaries, if they can even be called that, are entirely dictated by the addict's needs, not the family's. They often revolve around maintaining secrecy, control, and access to their substance, behavior of choice, or hidden dysfunction. Messages like "Don't ever confront me about my use," "Keep family secrets; don't talk about my addiction(s) to anyone," or even "Don't make noise in the morning or need anything right now" grow into unspoken rules that govern the household. These boundaries are narcissistic in nature, designed solely to preserve the addict's supply and prevent accountability rather than foster mutual respect or connection.

In essence, the addict's skewed and self-serving boundaries distort the entire family's understanding of what boundaries are meant to be, creating confusion and emotional harm for everyone involved. The family absorbs these dysfunctional and dysregulated boundaries and comes up with their own variations, variations that are designed to maintain a sense of safety even as family members feel like they're constantly warding off potential problems.

Codependency and Boundaries: How the Body Remembers the Cost of Connection

Codependency is not simply a pattern of putting others first: It is a survival strategy embedded in the nervous system. When your safety often depended on vigilance, fawning, caretaking, or emotional invisibility, your body adapted accordingly. Over time, prioritizing the needs, emotions, and problems of others became a conditioned reflex, a way to maintain connection and avoid punishment or rejection.

The problem is that what once gave you a way to stay connected as a child—even when it included self-abandonment, hypervigilance, or compulsive caretaking—can keep you from being able to know how to take care of yourself as an adult. You may exhaust yourself with people-pleasing behaviors, push yourself through when you need to rest, and override your own boundaries before you are even asked to. And, equally, you may have little sense of when you cross the boundaries of others, because you lack a felt sense of how it feels to have healthy boundaries of your own.

I find that addicted family systems often set boundaries from a state of inner panic, so they can feel controlling, competitive, and even bullying. This is what I am calling shadow boundaries. Shadow boundaries are covert, crafted to normalize the increasingly unhealthy behavior of family members and hide that anything threatening is happening. But something threatening *is* happening. These boundaries, then, have to exert their powerful control in secret, in the dark shadows of the family's increasingly hidden world.

Despite being unspoken, shadow boundaries still hold significant influence and control, often perpetuating the trauma-based patterns of all-or-nothing thinking into the next generation. When we stay entangled in the shadow boundaries of our past, we often carry those same dysfunctional patterns into our adult relationships and the families we build. They become a kind of portable dysfunction, shaping both our inner world and how we connect with others. We cling to them as if our very survival depends on it. Breaking the cycle starts with tending to your own attachment wounds and calming a nervous system stuck in old survival states.

Let's take a look at some of the most common shadow boundaries I see in my practice. I have broken them into categories and given them names so you can more easily identify the ones your family used when you were growing up. You may recognize that you are unknowingly still recreating them today. Buckle up—here goes!

Proxy Boundaries

- **Definition**: Proxy boundaries occur when one person—often an addicted parent or enabling coparent—sets the boundaries for the entire family, creating power imbalances. Parents may even favor children who go along with these boundaries because it helps keep the family's fragile system intact.

- **Example**: A dominant parent decides who's allowed to speak, what topics are off-limits, and how emotions should (or shouldn't) be expressed—leaving you with little room for your own voice. Sometimes these rules take the form of "shadow loyalty" boundaries, where unquestioning agreement and allegiance are valued over individuality and truth.

- **Impact**: Growing up this way can chip away at your autonomy and leave you anxious about challenging authority, even as an adult.

Pretend Normal Boundaries

- **Definition**: Pretend normal boundaries enforce the appearance of normalcy while denying underlying dysfunction. They can involve getting family members to act as though everything is fine, regardless of the underlying reality; using denial and rewriting reality to hide behind; or bending normal to create a false front. Phrases like "We don't talk about that outside this house" may be commonplace, or family members may be required to keep secrets to uphold the family's public image or adopt survival roles designed to support the looking-good family.

- **Example**: Insisting that "everything is fine" despite clear evidence of dysfunction; silencing dissent to maintain the family's façade.

- **Impact**: The sad thing about pressure to look good is that it can increase a feeling of emptiness. The gap between the family façade and the pain that is being denied becomes wider, and your disconnection to your genuine inner world grows accordingly, until it becomes hard to know who you are and what you want.

  You might find yourself brushing off your problems, saying, "It's no big deal" even when you feel deeply, because pretending feels safer than confronting the truth. And keep in mind that physical, emotional, and sexual abuse may be part of the picture in an addicted family system, which raises the stakes on what the family is hiding.

Withholding: Silent Control

- **Definition**: Silent control occurs when family members withhold affection, attention, time, support, communication, or inclusion as a way to punish, control, or coerce. If you received the silent treatment, experienced emotional withdrawal, or were left out of certain activities, you may know what I'm talking about here.

- **Example**: Imagine you express a differing opinion from or challenge the dysfunctional norms within your family. Instead of engaging in dialogue, a parent or sibling may shut down, lean back, cross their arms, refuse to engage with you, or dismiss your perspective entirely. This pattern can escalate to exclusion from family events or decisions, all done as a form of punishment or manipulation.

- **Impact**: The withholding and stonewalling inherent in silent control often foster a deep sense of rejection or fear of abandonment. These emotional wounds can compel you to prioritize others' expectations over your own authenticity to avoid their withdrawal. Over time, this dynamic can affect your sense of self-worth or increase your need to please in order not to be rejected.

Gaslighting

- **Definition**: Gaslighting happens when someone makes you doubt your own memories, feelings, or reality—often to avoid responsibility or keep control.

- **Example**: You try to explain how a boundary was crossed, and they reply, "You're overreacting" or "That never happened."

- **Impact**: Growing up with gaslighting can leave you second-guessing yourself and your instincts. You may hesitate to speak up or set boundaries now, unsure if your perspective is valid or if you're just "too sensitive."

Emotional Blackmail or Secrecy

- **Definition**: Emotional blackmail uses guilt, fear, or obligation to pressure you into compliance and keep family norms intact. Or you may be asked to keep a parent's or sibling's secrets so you "won't get them into trouble."

- **Example**: Comments like, "If you really loved me, you wouldn't question this" or "After all I've done for you, how could you say no?" are used to manipulate your emotions to gain control.

- **Impact**: Emotional blackmail undermines your right to say no or act on your own behalf. It fosters guilt, resentment, and powerlessness, making it difficult for you to prioritize your needs without the weight of someone else's expectations.

Weaponized Boundaries

- **Definition**: Boundaries are used to manipulate, punish, or control rather than foster mutual respect. Instead of promoting safety, they create confusion, fear, and power imbalances.

- **Example**: A family member who often dismisses your feelings suddenly declares, "I need to set some boundaries around this subject" not as genuine self-care, but to shut down hard conversations or dodge accountability.

- **Impact**: These boundaries can make you question your needs for connection and resolution, creating emotional confusion where boundaries feel like tools of control. Over time, trust erodes, leaving you feeling isolated, dismissed, or reluctant to set your own limits.

Boundary Enforcement Through Fear, Punishment, or Abuse

- **Definition**: When someone uses threats, intimidation, or harsh consequences to force you to comply with their boundaries while dismissing your own. This dynamic can include physical, sexual, or emotional abuse.

- **Example**: You might experience physical harm, belittlement, or pressure to act against your comfort. For instance, a partner might say, "If you leave me, you'll regret it," or a parent might react violently or put you in compromising situations when you express your emotions. Or a parent or sibling might belittle or abuse you to control you.

- **Impact**: Over time, this enforcement makes you feel trapped, leading you to prioritize others' boundaries over your own well-being. You may become anxious about expressing your needs, believing it's safer to comply than to risk conflict or abandonment. Eventually, you hardly know what your needs are anymore, because you're so used to reading the room and doing what you're told.

Boundary Evasion Through Humor, Deflection, or Shame

- **Definition**: Using jokes, sarcasm, shaming, or changing the subject to avoid addressing emotional truths.

- **Example**: When you tried to set a boundary, you may have heard, "Oh, don't be so serious!" or "You can't take a joke."

- **Impact**: This dismissed important conversations and may have created confusion in you about whether your concerns were valid or worth addressing. Humor can be a wonderful way to provide relief or even an alternative path for connection, but when it's used to manipulate, it's controlling behavior. And shaming can make you feel that you are the problem.

Role-Based Boundaries: False-Self Functioning

- **Definition**: These boundaries are built around what the family needs, not what each person actually feels or wants. You may adopt a survival role—like the hero, scapegoat, or caretaker (see chapter 4)—or develop a false self that wins approval by hiding your real emotions and needs. Psychologists call this *false-self functioning*. Over time, the role becomes a protective boundary, but it disconnects you from who you truly are beneath the mask.

- **Example**: You take on a role because it feels safer than showing your authentic self. The role also keeps the family system going: The hero leads, the lost child disappears, the mascot uses humor to diffuse tension, and the scapegoat absorbs blame so the parents don't have to.

- **Impact**: These roles limit your individuality, asking you to trade authenticity for belonging. Over time, this can lead to identity confusion and make it harder to form genuine reciprocal relationships.

Exercise

How Shadow Boundaries Live On

Take a few moments to reflect on these prompts to see how shadow boundaries from your family system might still be influencing you today. In your journal, write about one or more of these patterns you recognize from childhood that may still play out in your adult relationships. How has it shaped the way you connect—or disconnect—from others? What might a healthier boundary look like for you now?

Proxy Boundaries

- Did someone in your family dictate the rules for everyone else—deciding who could speak, what could be discussed, or how emotions were expressed?

- As an adult, do you notice yourself waiting for others to set the tone or fearing the consequences of speaking up?

Pretend Normal Boundaries

- Were you expected to act like everything was fine, even when it wasn't?

- Do you now find yourself downplaying your own pain ("It's no big deal") or avoiding hard truths to keep the peace?

Withholding: Silent Control

- Did you experience affection, attention, or inclusion being withheld as punishment?

- Do you now silence your needs or overaccommodate others to avoid rejection?

Gaslighting

- Were you ever made to doubt your feelings or memories ("That never happened")?

- Do you struggle to trust your instincts today or second-guess your perception of reality?

Weaponized Boundaries

- Did someone in your family use boundaries as a way to shut you out or avoid accountability?

- Do you ever use boundaries as weapons? If so, how?

- Do you find yourself afraid that setting boundaries will make you seem cold or controlling?

Boundaries That Use Secrecy, Fear, Punishment, or Abuse

- Growing up, what were the consequences of saying no or asserting yourself?

- Do you notice yourself avoiding conflict now, even at the cost of your own needs?

Boundaries That Use Secrecy, Humor, or Deflection

- Were you asked to keep secrets for a parent, a sibling, or the family? Do you still fear reprisal if you talk about them?

- Are you still holding secrets that affect the way you feel about yourself or others?

- Did your family use humor or sarcasm when things got tense?

- Today, do you find yourself laughing off your own discomfort or using sarcasm instead of addressing it?

Role-Based Boundaries: False-Self Functioning

- Did you adopt a family role (hero, caretaker, scapegoat, et cetera) as a way to belong?

- Do you still feel like you have to "perform" for acceptance, even at the cost of your real feelings?

What Are Healthy Boundaries?

Boundaries are the unsung heroes of a well-lived life. They help you own what's yours—your feelings, needs, and values—and recognize what belongs to others. When you set clear boundaries, you create a safe space where your voice matters, your energy is protected, and your sense of self can thrive. Boundaries aren't selfish; they're an act of love, both for yourself and for the people around you. They allow you to show up with and model balance, because you're not giving more than you can or tolerating what doesn't align with your sense of self. Healthy boundaries also make relationships easier to live in because both people get to have their autonomy respected without fearing punishment or rejection, which makes connection feel safe.

Sometimes boundaries are easier to build and implement with physical distance. In their seminal research on ACAs, Drs. Sybil and Steven Wolin observed that ACAs who thrive as adults often live two hundred or more miles away from the family center, what the Wolins call "the magic two-hundred-mile radius."[2] This distance creates built-in boundaries, allowing them to participate in key holidays or ceremonies while still building lives on their own terms. Importantly, these individuals learn that they don't always need to explain their choices to their families, who might not understand or might even hold their preferences against them. They simply have used distance as a way to be separate but still connected. They love their families but find that they're happier when they have some distance from the daily fray of the legacy that dysfunction creates.

A word of caution as you learn to set healthier boundaries: Try to stay out of cognitive distortions like all-or-nothing thinking ("My boundary is that I never want to see you again!") or emotional reasoning ("I feel you have crossed my boundaries and because I really, really feel it! I am right!"). These would be boundaries set from the perspective of your wounded inner child mind. And another word of advice: Learn to say, "I'm sorry." Other people's feelings matter to them as much as yours matter to you. As you recalibrate your boundaries, you may overcorrect. If you do, saying a simple, "I'm sorry if I came on too strong there" can help someone stay open to a connection with you.

Inner Child Safety

Boundaries aren't just for the adult version of you; they are a lifeline for your inner child, the part of you that still carries the wounds of a past where boundaries may have been ignored, violated, or blurred. To work with this, ask yourself, *What are the hardest boundaries for me to set or live within?* Then, consider, *What would have happened to me if I'd tried to set that boundary as a child or if I'd even allowed myself to know I needed that care, space, or sense of autonomy?*

Learning how to set healthy boundaries now is an act of reparenting, a way of giving that younger part of you the protection and care they didn't receive.

And the first person you're letting your inner child connect with is *you*. The adult you can be that calm presence that you longed for. *You* can be there to listen to the needs of your inner child, understand if they are creating boundaries from a wounded state, and help that child in you heal before you set new boundaries.

When your wounded inner child is the one setting boundaries, you're making it another person's responsibility to understand and heal you, and you risk creating more distance than cooperation. While you may displease someone by setting a boundary, there is no need to use boundaries as weapons. Ultimately, good boundaries most often make relationships safer and stronger.

Reparenting Your Inner Child

Exploring your boundaries and listening invites you to peel back layers of old defenses, automatic reactions, and deeply ingrained patterns, a process that ultimately helps you reparent your inner child.

Consider Mei, a client of mine who was raised in a traditional family, where fulfilling expectations and maintaining harmony were paramount. For years, Mei found herself saying yes to every obligation—whether it was family gatherings or professional requests—even when it left her feeling overwhelmed and drained. Over time, she began noticing physical signs of stress and a subtle inner resistance, signals that her body was urging her to honor her needs—to breathe, slow down, and read the signals coming from the child within her instead of automatically complying. As she did this, she recalled scene after scene of being valued and loved when she complied with the family's unspoken expectations and punished with disapproving looks and withheld attention and love when she did not comply.

As a result, as a grown woman, no one even had to ask her to comply; she did it automatically. It was her way of "earning her place" and being valued and accepted. Unpacking this pattern and coming to understand her childhood with more distance and compassion gave her the courage she needed to take the next baby step: setting a small boundary she could test the waters with. In doing so, she was able to realize that not everyone in her life wanted her to play small and ignore her own needs.

Boundaries allow you to engage in relationships without losing yourself. When used to foster understanding and trust, not distance or control, boundaries become a form of reparenting. You're giving your inner child the structure and safety they didn't have, and in doing so, you're helping them grow into a mature, self-respecting adult.

The Five Stages of Learning to Set Boundaries

Boundaries don't arrive fully formed; they unfold as part of a deeper developmental arc. Cultivating them is a process, and it takes the time it takes! They can be messy, uneven, or lopsided at first, and that's okay. If you find yourself using your new boundaries to control others or manipulate situations, though, check back in with yourself and recalibrate so you can set boundaries from a state of inner calm rather than from an activated one.

In working with clients over the years, I've observed a recognizable rhythm, a kind of emotional and relational unfolding in stages, that many people move through as they begin to set and sustain healthier, more balanced boundaries in recovery. It's not a straight line, and it's certainly not a one-size-fits-all process. But having a map, even a loose one, can be grounding when the terrain feels unfamiliar. Here I've outlined five typical stages. They aren't sacrosanct—just here to let you know it's a process, not an event.

Stage 1: When Setting a Boundary Feels Like a Betrayal

In the earliest phase, the idea of setting a boundary can feel almost transgressive, like you're violating an unspoken family contract. If your early family connectedness depended on attunement to others' needs at the expense of your own, any act of separation may feel scary to you. Keep in mind, your inner conflict is not merely cognitive; it is also somatic, rooted in your nervous system's historical fear of rupture or abandonment.

- **What it feels like**: Guilt, shame, anxiety before you've even spoken. A quiet fear that you're doing something wrong or that naming a need will cost you love.

- **What you're learning**: It's not selfish to take up space—it's human. Your needs matter as much as anyone else's.

- **What helps**: Naming your fear, and your body sensations, validating and witnessing them, and gently experimenting with microboundaries in low-stakes relationships.

- **Reflective prompts**: When did you first learn that saying no could cost you connection? What boundary would your younger self have liked to have had to feel like you mattered?

Stage 2: Rebellious Boundaries: When Your Voice Comes Out Louder Than Expected

As you begin to assert a separate self, your boundaries may swing toward being reactive, sharp edged, urgent, infused with the energy of long-repressed needs. There can be a sense of overcorrection here: Boundaries become a line in the sand, drawn with force. While this can feel empowering, it may still emerge from dysregulation and be more about protest than integration.

- **What it feels like**: Resentment, defensiveness, a heady mix of relief and regret.

- **What you're learning**: That you can express yourself clearly (most times), that you don't always have to go along to get along, that you have a right to a boundary.

- **What helps**: Slowing down, finding the pause between stimulus and response. Remembering that boundaries are not ultimatums—they're invitations to real relationship.

- **Reflective prompts**: Think of a time when your boundary felt like a wall rather than a bridge. What fear or memory might have been fueling the intensity?

Stage 3: Shifting from Reaction to Reflection

In this stage, your boundaries shift from reaction to reflection: You're able to allow boundaries to grow out of your felt sense of safety rather than only constructing them in your head. You begin to take the other person's needs into account as well as yours. This is a phase of experimentation, testing where you end and another begins, without collapsing into fusion or swinging into rupture.

- **What it feels like**: Tentative clarity, more space to breathe, a growing sense of steadiness and mutuality.

- **What you're learning**: How to hold your own experience while staying open to someone else's.

- **What helps**: Noticing patterns in your body and nervous system—when you're overextending, when you're retreating, and when you feel you can experience your own separate sense of self while in connection with others.

- **Reflective prompts**: Where in your life are you discovering you have bottom lines, limits, edges? Where do you feel inner spaces in which you can remain present with yourself and others at the same time?

Stage 4: It Gets Real: When Boundaries Stop Being a Decision and Become a Way of Being

By now, your boundaries become less effortful, more embodied. They are no longer a task to perform but have become an expression of your integrated self. Saying, "No," "Later," "Maybe," or "Sure" is neither a crisis nor a performance: It is simply an honest response, given with clarity and increasing comfort. Your nervous system has learned that connection and autonomy are not mutually exclusive.

- **What it feels like**: Calm, congruent, grounded. You're in your body. You're in your experience.

- **What you're learning**: That you can be both kind and clear, both connected and whole. That you can respect your needs and someone else's with trust that it's okay.

- **What helps**: Letting your yes, your no, and everything in between rise from your inner mind/body state, from the present and not the past.

- **Reflective prompts**: When was the last time you set a boundary without guilt or an emotional backlash? What allowed you to trust that boundary?

Stage 5: The Boundary as Relational Maturity: The Boundary Becomes Part of the Relationship

In its most evolved form, boundary setting becomes not just an act of self-care but a part of the relationship itself. You set boundaries both to protect yourself and to preserve the quality of the connection. You begin to understand that love without clarity is sentimentality and clarity without empathy is control. True relational maturity lives in the integration of both.

- **What it feels like**: Ease. Mutual respect. The grace of being known and of knowing yourself.

- **What you're learning**: That your needs and theirs can both belong in the room. To sense your oneness with humanity while owning your individuality.

- **What helps**: Embracing complexity. Letting boundaries be relational, not just protective. Letting difference coexist with love.

- **Reflective prompts**: How does it feel to feel seen as yourself and loved as yourself and to offer someone else the same? How does it feel to know someone deeply and care about their well-being and your own at the same time?

Boundaries Without Walls: How to Stay Open Without Losing Yourself

Boundaries allow us to be in connection *and* in self, to show up with presence without disappearing into someone else. In this next section, we'll explore how boundaries shape our relationships across the many domains of daily life: work, friendship, intimacy, and parenting. Each context brings its own challenges, but the underlying principle is the same: Boundaries don't push others away; they allow us to be in connection while retaining our sense of self.

Boundaries in the Workplace

For ACAs, who often grew up overfunctioning or people-pleasing, setting limits at work can feel awkward or even guilt inducing. At work, boundaries aren't just about managing tasks; they're about managing your energy, self-worth, voice, and relationships. Clear communication is the cornerstone of workplace boundaries. For instance, instead of automatically accepting any and all tasks your boss or teammates request of you without regard for your bandwidth, you might say, "I'm unable to do this right now. But I'd love to help, and I'm happy to revisit this when my workload lightens," or sometimes "Sorry, I'm on total overload and not even sure I can manage what's on my own desk." These statements assert your limits while maintaining a collaborative tone.

In today's digital world, many people use *silence* as a boundary, by not replying to a message or ghosting the message sender. If that's your go-to, ask yourself: *What message am I sending by going silent? Am I okay with that message?* If not, a simple statement like, "Please don't take it personally if I go quiet, I'm working hard to manage my time" can preserve both clarity and connection. Healthy boundaries at work make you easier to collaborate with, not harder, because people know they can trust you to be real, responsive, and respectful.

Boundaries in Friendships

Friendships thrive on mutual care, not on one person absorbing all the weight of the relationship. For ACAs or codependents, who may be used to blurry lines and unspoken contracts, setting boundaries in friendships can feel risky, like saying no will make the other person walk away. But the truth is that healthy limits make real friendship possible.

Boundaries in friendships don't diminish connection; they sustain it. Saying, "No," "Later," or "Can we find a time that works for both of us?" is not rejection but an act of respect for the relationship. If you can't negotiate these mutual needs, you will wind up pulling away to set the boundary or sending confusing or distancing messages. For example, if your friend comes looking to vent and you've just had a long day, you can say something like, "I'd love to listen, but I need to recharge first" or "At the moment I am really stretched and have low bandwidth, but I'd love to get together as soon as things feel more manageable." These honest exchanges honor your limits while preserving the depth of the bond. A true friendship is a reciprocal dance, one where both people feel valued and seen.

Boundaries also involve respecting your friend's limits. When both people feel heard and respected, the friendship becomes a safe space for mutual growth rather than a source of obligation or resentment. Ultimately, setting and honoring boundaries allows friendships to flourish in a way that feels supportive and nourishing rather than draining.

Boundaries in Intimate Relationships

In romantic relationships, boundaries are one of the things that permit trust and intimacy to grow, allowing you to feel secure in yourself while creating a safe space for your partner to do the same. For those who grew up in chaotic, enmeshed, or emotionally volatile homes, this can feel counterintuitive. You may fear that asserting your needs will create distance, but in truth, boundaries create the *safety* that makes closeness possible. This is one of the reasons why relationships can be so healing for ACAs as we learn to do things differently.

Setting boundaries doesn't have to be about rejecting or withdrawing; it's about creating clarity and trust. For example, saying, "I really want to have this conversation, but I need a little time to gather my thoughts first so I can give it my best" or "I love being together and always prioritize time with you, of course, but I just need some inner quiet to recharge right now" communicates respect for both yourself and your partner. By tuning in to your emotions and needs and responding honestly, you foster an environment where both of you can feel free to be yourselves.

When you can get yourself to share your limits without shame or anger, you invite your partner to do the same. That's when intimacy deepens, because you're relating as two whole people, not fused parts of a fragile system.

Boundaries in Parenting

Boundaries in parenting are essential for creating a home environment where both you and your children feel secure, seen, and valued. They teach children that it's okay to have and state needs, say no, and express feelings while also showing them how to respect others' limits. As a parent, modeling healthy boundaries helps your children develop an inner sense of where they leave off and others begin, a part of emotional intelligence, relational intelligence, and social-emotional skill building that will serve them for a lifetime.

For instance, you might say, "Sweetie, I want to hear all about your day. I just can't be a good listener right now because I'm finishing something important, but I'd love to talk all about it in fifteen minutes." This communicates both your love and your needs while reinforcing your attunement and availability. However, if your child is too young to understand this postponement of their need, or if they're a teenager who tends to open up only on their own schedule, consider taking a break in your task and simply sitting down with attention and presence, knowing you'll get back to your task soon enough.

Boundaries create a balanced dynamic where love and respect flow both ways. Letting your children set boundaries with you, like saying no to a hug they don't want or "In fifteen minutes" about a task you ask them to take on, empowers them to trust their instincts and feel confident in their personal autonomy. Do keep in mind that early parenting will feel lopsided, as your young children will long for your full attention and you may not always be available to give it to them. In these moments, try to find ways to include them so they can feel part of what you're doing rather than on the outside looking in.

For example, when my daughter was little, she had her own little table and chair in the kitchen. When I prepared meals, I always gave her a job that mattered and was age appropriate, beginning with slicing bananas with a plastic knife. My son wasn't so interested in these activities, so we did other things that were more in alignment with his preferences and allowed him to participate. He liked lifting and carrying things, so I gave him tasks like that to help with. He also loved fantasy play, so I put a pegboard on his wall with his favorite outfits and hats. He dressed up often for dinner, sometimes as Davy Crockett, sometimes as Superman. Including them in ways that they had preferences around taught them that they were welcome as themselves.

In our final chapter together, we'll reflect on the deeper transformations that become possible when we commit to the inner work—not just as a phase of healing, but as a way of living. What begins as emotional and relational repair can evolve into something profoundly spiritual: a new relationship with your inner being, with others, and with the world around you. To close, we'll explore both the practical aspects of setting up your recovery network and the quiet miracles that unfold when you keep showing up, rooted, present, open, and willing to grow when you "don't quit before the miracle."

10

Spiritual Transformation and Post-Traumatic Growth

As an ACA myself, I am convinced that we need recovery as much as addicts do. And as a professional in the addictions field, I've learned that many addicts are themselves ACAs, and many ACAs become addicts. Addicts need recovery to stay sober and stay alive. And ACAs need recovery to stay emotionally sober and emotionally alive. If we don't attend to our deep attachment wounds, our lives will show it. And if we do, our lives will show it.

You didn't deserve the problems that got foisted on you in childhood, and your children and other loved ones don't deserve them either. By the time you pass your unexamined cognitive distortions and attachment wounds down to your kids, it will be even more confusing for them. You'll be unconsciously asking them to absorb your unresolved pain through the way you parent, while at the same time sending them the message that they are "luckier" than you were because you're parenting sober. But if you're not emotionally sober, *you're not sober*. Your children are being told they have it better, but depending on where you are in your own recovery, it may not always feel better to them. And they don't even have parental addiction to point to, so they end up carrying the burden of your hidden legacy wounds and trying to fill the chasm left in you by your unmet childhood needs. But because you're still stuck in your own pain, you cannot see theirs. This is how trauma gets passed down. But it doesn't have to be that way.

I wrote this book to offer you a clearer view of the path that intergenerational pain can follow, to trace how it weaves its way through family after family, recreating pain through unexamined cognitive distortions, unprocessed or disowned attachment wounds, and unconscious age correspondence reactions, projections, and transferences. These patterns didn't begin with us, but you can be the beginning of meaningful change.

You don't have to do this alone, nor should you. I've outlined a framework for building your recovery network, the kind I've seen sustain long-term inner growth. My deepest hope is that you'll feel empowered to engage in your own recovery, starting now, or to continue on the path you're already walking. That you'll take your healing seriously, not just for your sake, but for your children's. Because every step you take to repair what was ruptured in you clears space for something whole to grow. Remember that the person to change is you. Through healing your history as it sits inside of you and manifests in your relationships, you create intergenerational healing. You leave your personal world better than you found it.

Post-Traumatic Growth: Seeing the Glass as Half Full

Recovery holds the potential to transform the most vital relationship you'll ever have: the one with your own inner being. When we first turn back to look at our childhood, our eyes often fall on the ruptures—the places where love missed its mark, where needs went unanswered, where we were forced to grow up too soon. We see our wounds as evidence of damage, as proof that something was broken in us or in those who were meant to care for us.

But that doesn't tell the full story; we need to see another kind of truth. We need to recognize and respect the power of our inborn connection with life that's coded into our DNA, to own our strengths, and to value who we've become through meeting the challenges of our life. When we see the glass as half full, something shifts. We see the same life through different eyes. We begin to sense our resilience and recognize openness and vulnerability as the kinds of inner strengths that can allow us to live a fuller, more satisfying life. It's a choice to look on the bright side and place an emphasis on what is beautiful. When that becomes a habit of mind, what is beautiful seems to mysteriously multiply.

Psychologists R. G. Tedeschi and L. G. Calhoun describe "post-traumatic growth" as our innate capacity to turn suffering into something meaningful, something life-giving.[1] Your past isn't just a story of pain; it's a nervous system blueprint laid down by the very personal and interpersonal experiences that have shaped you. Yes, it holds the patterns of disconnection and the moments you had to shut down, shrink, or overfunction just to feel safe. But it also holds your experiences of love, faith, and the warmth and fulfillment of human connection.

The point of this recovery journey isn't to arrive at some perfect, healed version of yourself. It's to develop the skills to *process as you go*, to learn the art of living so that when you lose your balance you can find it again, to learn you can stumble and then rebuild your resilience. When you process pain as you go, it doesn't become a permanent part of you; it becomes fertilizer for inner growth. You are tilling the soil of your soul. You're not only repairing rupture, you're transmuting it into deeper wisdom and connection with self, others, and a higher source. This breaking and mending is what makes you human, and it is also what connects you to something divine. You don't need to have all the answers; you just need the courage to keep growing and believing in the mystery of the path unfolding before you. Your journey is not about perfection, but about presence. It's about developing emotional literacy and intelligence so you can feel, name, own, and reflect on your feelings rather than unconsciously acting them out through projections, blame, and transferences. Post-traumatic growth isn't about dismissing the reality of your suffering, but about how those very experiences have been a part of your becoming more.

This quiet awakening begins with a simple but radical act of allowing yourself to witness what's inside you without judgment or resistance. When you simply witness your tangled thoughts and emotions, letting them flow past your mind's eye like a current, through or past you, with no more notion of controlling them than of controlling the river, you observe the workings of your own mind. This gentle presence is, in itself, a nourishing state that can be sustaining and healing as you organically open to your deeper self.

Drs. Sybil and Steven Wolin introduced the Challenge Model, which reframes adversity as a pathway to resilience, showing that many ACAs develop inner strengths and coping skills that allow them to thrive in spite of the odds. Rather than being solely defined by hardship, or a "damage model," these ACAs report feeling something some soldiers say they have called "survivor's pride"—a deep sense of strength and self-worth that comes from overcoming difficult experiences.[2]

You can embrace this kind of possibility. You hold within you the potential to shift your perspective on any circumstance you find yourself in, to find the spiritual within the ordinary and meaning in what surrounds you, to use the circumstances of your life as the path to lead you home. Like Dorothy on her yellow brick road, you may discover that you've always carried the way home within you.

Blocks on Your Path: The Natural Negativity Bias

Something I see a lot in those of us who've grown up with addiction or relational trauma is an almost relentless pull toward focusing on what's wrong, ruminating on negative subjects, being attracted to drama, or bracing for the next letdown. You will be relieved to know that it's not just you. This tendency, known as the *negativity bias*, has deep evolutionary roots as a survival mechanism. Early humans who were hyperaware of threats, such as predators or food scarcity, were more likely to survive and pass on their genes. *Their* vigilance became part of *our* wiring.

Fear has an important purpose in signaling danger. But as ACAs, we need to be aware of how this bias toward expecting negative outcomes can keep us stuck in dark imaginings and hypervigilance. Our persistent expectation of harm can block the very thing we long for most: connection. Recovery asks a lot of us. It requires courage, vulnerability, and a willingness to face what's been buried—these are the qualities that let us begin to relate to our past, not as something to erase, but as something to transform.

Social neuroscientist Matthew Lieberman, in his book *Social: Why Our Brains Are Wired to Connect*, describes how the brain's default mode—its resting state when not focused on a specific task—is to think about people, relationships, and social belonging. His fMRI research revealed that our brains are literally wired for connection. He also found that social pain and physical pain light up the same neural pathways. In other words, disconnection doesn't just hurt metaphorically; it hurts in ways the body recognizes as real. And connection, when we allow it, soothes us just as deeply.

This is why role-play in psychodrama and RTR feels so real and alive. We are not merely reenacting; we are resurrecting and experiencing visceral connections—to attachment figures, to ourselves, to moments of rupture that have remained frozen in time. Even an empty chair can offer a middle space, a stage, where we can finally externalize and talk to these relational wounds. Our imagination conjures up a parent, a part of self, our inner child, and by putting these parts and people "out there," they cease taking up residence only inside of our minds. We can speak to the ghosts of our past, the pain of our present, and the tender possibilities of an imagined future self. We say the words we couldn't say then, thaw emotions held in silence, and bring them into the open. As the pain releases, something else emerges: a memory of the love that once lived beneath the hurt. We remember what it felt like to trust, to reach out without shame, to need and be met with care. We come alive again inside.

As Lieberman writes, "Our need to connect is as fundamental as our need for food and water."[3] Recovery asks us to honor that truth—to dare to connect first with ourselves, and then with others walking the same path. It asks us to stop running from our own vulnerability, to let ourselves be seen, and to discover the deep sense of aliveness that comes with sharing a fuller sense of connection.

Exercise

The V of Choice: Play It Through to the End

This exercise invites you to explore two possible futures: one in which you embrace healing and recovery and one in which you avoid it. By journaling from the perspective of two future points in time, you'll begin to feel into the emotional, mental, and relational impact of each path. Take a little journey into your future and see what comes up!

Set Up Your Page

On a blank journal page, draw a large V shape. At the top left side, write, "Where will my life be if I avoid healing?" At the top right side, write, "Where will my life be if I embrace healing and recovery?"

Along each leg of the V, mark three time points:

- One year from now

- Three years from now

- Seven years from now

You'll journal from the perspective of your future self at each point in time, imagining how your life has unfolded along each path.

Your Journaling Prompts

For each time point on both sides of the V, write a journal entry starting with:

- "It's one/three/five year(s) out, and I feel..."

- "I am doing/feeling/expressing /experiencing..."

- "My life looks like..."

- "What I want you to know about me is..."

Speak honestly from that imagined future self. Let your words come freely. Try to feel the texture of that life—the emotional landscape, relationships, rhythms, and daily experiences. Be specific. You might write something like this:

It's one year out, and I feel flat and disconnected. I'm still stuck in the same patterns, and while I've managed to get by, I still feel that ache underneath. My life looks controlled on the outside, but I know how much I'm holding in. I want you to know I wish I had made different choices sooner.

or

It's three years out, and I feel grounded. Life isn't perfect, but it's real. I have momentum now. I've built a life that feels more like me. I'm learning to process as I go, and I lean into my support network, which has become very important to me. I'm proud of myself for beginning when it was hard.

Reflect

Once you've finished journaling for both sides of the V, take a few minutes to sit with what you wrote.

- What stood out the most?

- Which version felt more familiar? Which felt more inspiring?

- What choices might you make today that could begin shaping the version of you that you want to grow into?

If you'd like to deepen the experience, try reversing roles: Become your future healed self and write a short message or letter to the you of today.

Only You Can Change You

"The tragedy of life is in what dies inside a man while he lives—the death of genuine feeling, the death of inspired response," said the brilliant humanitarian Dr. Albert Schweitzer.[4] As adult children of alcoholics, these words carry a profound resonance for us. Growing up in an atmosphere of addiction or relational trauma can numb our emotional awareness, leaving us disconnected from our vitality. Recovery asks us to reclaim that lost aliveness—to reopen the pathways to feeling, creativity, and connection that were once shut down for survival.

Couples therapist Esther Perel, author of *Mating in Captivity* and the daughter of Holocaust survivors, reflects on the differences between Holocaust survivors who merely "went on living" and those who truly "came back to life." Perel highlights the profound distinction between survival as an act of endurance and the ability to reclaim joy, vitality, and connection after unimaginable trauma. She explains that some survivors carried their pain in ways that limited their capacity to fully engage with life; they were alive but remained emotionally entwined with their suffering. Others, however, found a way to reintegrate into the world with a renewed sense of purpose, often by creating meaning from their experiences, embracing relationships, or reclaiming their ability to experience pleasure and joy. They didn't discount their suffering; they transformed it.[5]

Perel shares that resilience and healing often emerge through the power of reconnection—to others, to oneself, and to life's joys. She aligns this with the belief of psychologist and concentration camp survivor Viktor Frankl, author of *Man's Search for Meaning*, that meaning and connection are not just vital for enduring trauma but also for restoring emotional and spiritual vitality. These shared insights illuminate how love, community, and purpose can transform survival into renewal. *You can change your life.*

When you take the first tentative steps toward resolving and reframing the emotional burdens you've carried, something remarkable happens. You begin to sense inner movement almost immediately. You experience the relief and feeling of empowerment that comes with saying, "I can do something about this." The weight that felt immovable starts to shift, and a sense of hope dawns. You can exhale the breath you hardly knew you'd held.

This process becomes cumulative over time and creates a ripple effect back and forth through the generations. Healing doesn't just stop with you; it moves outward, creating a legacy of change. And the opposite is true as well: Unresolved pain can create a legacy of emotional paralysis. *Don't let this be you.*

Trauma doesn't just wound; it steals. It robs you of your present, tethers you to the worst parts of your past, and buries the good times beneath layers of emotional numbness. But every step you take toward healing, no matter how small, is a quiet rebellion against that theft. It's an act of courage and love, not just for yourself, but for those who come after you. With each step you take, you create space for healing, for connection, and for breaking the cycle. You get closer to remembering the love and connection you also experienced, which is as responsible for having made you as the problematic side of your past.

Trauma can draw a line in the sand—a before and an after. The before can vanish into the fog of forgetting, causing you to lose touch with your happy self, your good memories. Then you circumnavigate around the split-off parts that hold your sense of aliveness. But frozen beneath your pain, your innocence and wonder are still there, so as you bring your wounds back to life and process them, you wake up your capacity for joy and pleasure, too.

I remember many years ago walking down Central Park West with an agent I had at the time and asking him, "Why do self-help books sell?" The truth is I didn't know if what I said in my books would help or not; I just knew I had to say it and hoped it would. He looked down at me with an expression I will never forget, a sort of sensitive acceptance of something sad, and said, "Most people live lives of quiet desperation," paraphrasing Henry David Thoreau. *Don't let this be you.*

Addiction can turn anyone into a monster. As ACAs, we experienced the dark side of life, and we can recreate it. We can model a parent who numbed their inner world and distorted their own reasoning to such an extent that a significant part of them died while they were still living. We carry heavy and disturbing memories of plates and hearts being broken as though they were of equal value. These are the kinds of frozen wounds that can only express themselves through mindless, brainless acting out and transferences, through speaking in an unconscious voice that is filled with finger-pointing and displacement of pain. The cost of addiction is misunderstanding and hurt that ripple through the generations. *Don't let this be you.*

As ACAs, we too experienced the kind of inner death that comes from desperately trying to find a parent we loved inside of their dark and tormented world of pain. Some ACAs leave important parts of themselves forever wandering this ghost world. They're in search of something or someone they can't hope to find, ignoring their own lost inner child. *Don't let this be you.*

Choose Life

In this book, we've spent time exploring grief and loss, untangling the attachment wounds that shaped us. But healing is about more than processing pain. It's also about reclaiming our capacity for pleasure, joy, and awe.

Joseph Campbell wrote in *The Power of Myth*: "People say that what we're all seeking is a meaning for life. I don't think that's what we're really seeking. I think what we're seeking is an experience of being alive—so that our life experiences on the purely physical plane will have resonances within our innermost being and reality; so that we actually feel the rapture of being alive."[6] These words remind us that fulfillment doesn't come from grasping at meaning with our minds, or our hands and fists, but from moments that connect us to our own existence: those times when we feel in harmony with something larger, something wild and alive, something that stirs both awe and belonging.

You are more than this human experience. You are part of the same transcendent energy that gives rise to trees and rivers, to the sky, to warmth, and to life itself.

Remember: We think, feel, and act according to what lives within us. No one else is behind the wheel of your mind but you. How you steer, moment to moment, is your choice. The state of your inner world shapes the quality of your thoughts, which manifest through your words, your actions, your relationships. You attract what resonates with your inner state—whether it's a dark harmony or one that nourishes life.

Choose wisely. Choose optimism over despair, gratitude over cynicism, right action over reactivity. Be a force for good in your own life and in the lives you touch.

Choose life.

You Are What You Do: How Your Lifestyle Shapes Your Health More Than Your Genes Do

We have *way* more control over our physical and mental health than we often realize. Life doesn't just *happen* to us; we actively shape it through the way we live.

Groundbreaking research published in *Nature Medicine* in 2025 sheds light on how our habits impact us. A massive study of over 490,000 people from the UK Biobank found that lifestyle and environment play a *far bigger* role in health outcomes than genetics. In fact, the way we live—our daily habits, choices, and surroundings—account for 17 percent of the risk of developing serious diseases, while genetics contributes only about 2 percent.[7]

Some of the biggest health risks? Smoking tops the list, linked to twenty-one different diseases. Socioeconomic factors—things like income, neighborhood, and job stability—are tied to nineteen diseases, while lack of exercise increases the risk for seventeen diseases. The study also found that our surroundings have the biggest impact on lung, heart, and liver diseases, while genetics plays a stronger role in certain cancers (breast, ovarian, prostate) and dementia. And here's something even more eye-opening: As the ACE Study found, early-life experiences can have a lasting impact on health. A significant body of research indicates that factors such as childhood weight, exposure to maternal smoking, and financial stress can increase health risks later in life. Conversely, job stability, financial security, and strong social connections are associated with longer, healthier lives. These findings underscore the potent impact of both early-life exposures and adult socioeconomic factors on long-term health outcomes.[8]

You *can't* change your genes, but you *can* change your habits. And those choices can add years to your life and life to your years. Small, intentional shifts—like moving more, eating more healthily, and building networks of support and relationships—can have a *huge* impact on your long-term health. Your actions today and for the rest of your life truly matter.

Setting Up Your Recovery Supports: Thriving in Connection and Community

Recovery isn't sustained by willpower alone. It doesn't hinge on a single life-altering decision, but rather on the accumulation of small daily choices, how you live day to day, how you connect with others, how you care for yourself. True recovery is about creating a life that supports your healing from the inside out and the outside in.

Creating your support system is more than self-care—it's soul care. It means surrounding yourself with people, environments, and practices that nurture your mind, body, and spirit. In the pages that follow, you'll find strategies designed to help you stay grounded, connected, and resilient. Because recovery isn't just about what you're healing from—it's about who you're becoming and the life you're building along the way.

The longitudinal *Global Flourishing Study*, currently being conducted by Harvard University and Baylor University, is surveying over 200,000 people across twenty-two countries.[9] It has already uncovered profound drivers of happiness: The most consistent predictors of a flourishing life aren't wealth or material success, but strong relationships, meaningful community, and a clear sense of purpose. In other words, what makes life worth living isn't what you have; human connection, meaning, and purpose are at the heart of it.

Twelve-Step Programs and Support Groups

What has always struck me about twelve-step programs—whether it's ACA, Al-Anon, Codependents Anonymous, Alcoholics Anonymous, or any one of the myriad of others—is the quiet, steady power of human connection they offer. Their rooms, whether you attend in person or virtually, are built on shared understanding. You sit with others who may never have met you, but who know something about you. There's no need to explain the family chaos, the emotional aftershocks, the ache to be seen, nor the longing for peace and healing. In these circles, you *are* seen. And that being seen, that mutual recognition, becomes a healing force.

Twelve-step programs not only offer support and structure, they invite transformation. And they somehow nourish a spiritual awakening, a grounded kind made real and ordinary by the way it is passed hand to hand, heart to heart. The process creates a common pulse, a coregulation. Through shared stories, deep exploration, honesty, and the good, orderly direction of the steps themselves, something inside us begins to shift. We don't just feel less alone; we start to see our life through a more compassionate, purposeful lens. I've always loved that these programs are free, with no barrier to entry, no pressure to perform. You chip in a few dollars, and if you can't, you're still welcomed. They are global, accessible, and quietly revolutionary in how they create a safety net of purpose, meaning, and belonging that we can access anytime, anywhere. While other forms of paid therapy are generally weekly or more depending on resources, twelve-step support can be available throughout the day or week, which is part of the safety net they create.

One-on-One and Group Therapy: Connection and Healing

Therapy offers more than a place to talk—it gives us a space to soften, to feel, and to find ourself again. One-on-one work provides the intimate holding needed to heal attachment wounds, rebuild trust, and slowly re-inhabit the parts of ourself we may have abandoned long ago. Group therapy brings in the healing force of community. Sitting among others who are also learning how to live more fully creates resonance, identification, and mirroring. If one-on-one is a form of reparenting, group is a form of re-familying.

As psychiatrists Irvin Yalom and Molyn Leszcz describe, group therapy offers not only connection but a sense of hope, altruism, and shared meaning—powerful antidotes to the disconnection, loss, and relational rupture that so often come with trauma.[10] These are rooms where stories are honored, silence is respected, and healing unfolds through insight and presence.

These modalities, twelve step, individual and group, can work beautifully in tandem. And when combined with experiential approaches like RTR, recovery deepens. RTR invites you to revisit the hidden corners of your inner world—the parts that went underground to protect you—and gently bring them back into the light. With care, they can be reintegrated into a self that is growing more coherent, more regulated, and more whole with each healing modality.

Move Your Body, Lift Your Mood: Exercise as a Natural Antidepressant

Regular movement isn't just good for your physical health; it's a powerful tool for relational trauma recovery. Because emotions are stored in the body, activities like walking while talking with a friend can help you discharge those feelings, allowing them to flow instead of staying stuck.

Exercise, in whatever way is accessible to your body, also triggers the release of endorphins, the body's natural mood boosters, which ease stress, regulate emotions, and create a sense of well-being. A 2018 meta-analysis published in the *American Journal of Psychiatry* found that regular physical activity significantly reduces symptoms of depression and anxiety.[11] Whether it's yoga, running, dancing, or simply stretching, movement is a way to reconnect with yourself, shift your energy, and support your emotional healing.

Rest, Leisure, and "Sleep That Knits Up the Raveled Sleeve of Care"

Recovery requires rest—not just sleep, but downtime to recharge. Leisure activities, even simple ones like reading or relaxing, activate the brain's default mode network, which is essential for creativity and problem-solving. Sleep is critical, too, improving emotional processing, memory consolidation, and overall recovery.

Insufficient or disrupted sleep can impair the brain's ability to regulate emotions; hence poor sleep can exacerbate emotional dysregulation. Sleep deprivation has been shown to increase amygdala activity, leading to heightened emotional reactivity to negative stimuli. This heightened reactivity can result in increased anxiety, irritability, and difficulty managing stress.

Moreover, lack of sleep can hinder the prefrontal cortex's ability to modulate emotional responses, further contributing to emotional dysregulation. This impairment can make it more challenging to suppress intrusive thoughts and manage emotional reactions effectively.[12] Prioritize your rest like you would any other cornerstone of recovery!

Good Nutrition: You Are What You Eat

Food is more than fuel: It's information for your nervous system. Every bite you take sends signals to your brain, shaping your mood, your energy, your inflammation levels, and your emotional balance. When you're in recovery—especially from trauma, chronic stress, or emotional neglect—your system is hungry for nourishment that soothes and stabilizes.

A diet rich in whole, nutrient-dense foods does more than support your physical health. It supports your brain chemistry, emotional regulation, and capacity to cope with life's stressors. These foods lower inflammation, balance blood sugar, and support neurotransmitter production, functions that are often disrupted in trauma survivors.

Science is catching up with what many of us have sensed intuitively: The gut and brain are in constant communication. A landmark study published in *The Lancet Psychiatry* confirms the powerful link between nutrition and mental health, showing that a healthy, balanced diet can significantly reduce symptoms of anxiety, depression, and fatigue.[13]

You are not being superficial when you tend to your nutrition. You're reclaiming a relationship with your body that trauma may have interrupted. You're saying, *I matter. My needs matter. I deserve to feel well.* Each nourishing choice becomes a quiet but powerful act of self-respect—a way of grounding yourself in safety, stability, and well-being.

Daily Inspiration: Sustenance for Your Mind and Spirit

What you feed your mind is just as important as what you feed your body. Science is now confirming what many spiritual traditions have long known: Exposure to uplifting messages, beauty, and meaning can physically rewire your brain. A 2020 review by neuroscientist Golnaz Tabibnia highlights the finding that positive input—such as inspiring words, hopeful stories, or meaningful reflection—engages the brain's reward system, increasing dopamine and strengthening neural pathways linked to motivation, persistence, and emotional resilience.[14]

In short: The stories you take in, the words you repeat, and the thoughts you dwell on matter. They can literally shape the way you see the world—and yourself. Whether it's a morning mantra, a few pages of a beloved book, a quote that speaks to your soul, or a quiet moment with a guided meditation, find what resonates with your inner world. Let inspiration become a daily ritual, not because you "should," but because it helps you remember who you are and who you're becoming. A little light each day accumulates into lasting strength.

Gratitude: Seeing and Appreciating Life's Abundance

Gratitude is more than a pleasant thought; it's a literal brain changer. Neuroscientist-backed studies show that when you practice gratitude regularly, you're both shifting your mood and rewiring your mind. The prefrontal cortex—the part of your brain responsible for planning, emotional regulation, and meaning making—lights up. Meanwhile, deep in your limbic system, your hypothalamus—the control center for sleep, appetite, and stress—responds with subtle but powerful shifts.

And it gets better. Gratitude can lower cortisol, the stress hormone, by up to 23 percent, and it boosts serotonin and dopamine, the mood-enhancing chemicals that help you feel more hopeful and alive.[15]

Over time, this practice becomes self-reinforcing: The more you look for what's good, the more good you see. Your brain begins to tilt toward abundance, even when life is hard. Gratitude doesn't erase the pain, but it makes room for joy alongside it.

Find Your Flow: Activities That Regulate and Nourish You

Take a moment to consider: What activities make you feel most absorbed, most at ease—where you lose track of time and come fully into the moment? As we discussed in chapter 7, *flow*, a term coined by psychologist Mihaly Csikszentmihalyi, describes this state of deep immersion in an activity for its own sake.

His research showed that flow arises when you're engaged in a task that challenges you just enough—stretching your abilities, but not overwhelming them. In this state, your attention narrows, self-consciousness fades, and the experience becomes its own reward. Whether you're playing music, solving a problem, cleaning, painting, writing, cooking, or gardening, flow experiences tend to share certain qualities: clear goals, immediate feedback, a sense of agency, and a feeling of intrinsic motivation.

Csikszentmihalyi did not frame flow as a therapeutic or regulatory state per se, but his findings have since been taken up in broader fields—including education, creativity studies, and, more recently, wellness and trauma recovery—for their implications in fostering focus, engagement, and psychological well-being.[16] For those healing from complex PTSD, flow can offer a gentle reprieve from the chronic vigilance and inner fragmentation that so often accompany relational trauma. Experiences of deep focus and intrinsic motivation can help shift the body out of protective states and into a felt sense of safety and connection. In moments of flow, the nervous system isn't hijacked by threat; rather, it's engaged, present, and attuned.

Engage in Creative Activities

Creativity offers more than expression—it offers integration. When we create, we give shape to what's unspoken. We turn sensation into symbol and overwhelm into form. Research shows that engaging in creative activities—whether through art, music, writing, or movement—can reduce cortisol levels, improve mood, and activate brain regions associated with reward and emotional regulation. But beyond the science, creativity allows us to meet ourselves differently. It bypasses the rational mind and accesses deeper truths, helping us process experiences that may be too complex or painful for words alone. In recovery, creativity becomes a bridge: between what we feel and what we understand, between our fragmented parts and our emerging wholeness. It doesn't just help us tell our story, it helps us transform it. Weaving us into flow states, it brings us into a quiet passion through purposeful, meaning-filled activities.

Reflective Journaling: Unwinding Your Inner States Through Writing

Putting your thoughts on paper may start as an act of expression, but it can become a powerful tool for healing. Writing helps you make sense of your inner world, reduce stress, and regulate emotions. Social psychologist Dr. James Pennebaker's research shows that writing about emotionally significant experiences for just fifteen to twenty minutes can strengthen your immune system, lower blood pressure, and reduce symptoms of anxiety and depression.[17] A 2005 study also found that expressive writing boosts overall well-being and alleviates depressive symptoms.[18]

Journaling gives you a safe space to externalize pain, process emotions, and reclaim a sense of control. It transforms swirling thoughts into something tangible—you begin to see your inner world more clearly as your feelings and reflections unravel across the page. In doing so, you make room for integration. Writing shifts from offering insight to engaging the nervous system itself, becoming a steady practice of emotional regulation and repair.

Time in Nature: Healing Through Green Spaces

Spending time in nature has profound effects on mental and emotional well-being. Whether you're walking in the woods, sitting by water, or even tending a garden, exposure to green spaces can reduce stress and improve mood. Remember Matthew Lieberman's research on the social brain? Interestingly, this same neural network is quieted during immersive sensory experiences like time in nature. Nature bathing—spending intentional, mindful time outdoors—has been shown to reduce rumination and deactivate the default mode network, giving the nervous system a break from social preoccupation.[19] It soothes the mind by shifting us from mental overdrive to embodied presence.

A 2019 study in *Scientific Reports* found that just 120 minutes a week in nature significantly boosts physical and mental health.[20] In recovery, nature can become a quiet ally, helping to regulate your nervous system and restore balance. When you pause to appreciate a small moment—like the warmth of the sun, the breath you're taking, or even your own perseverance—you're resetting your nervous system, lowering stress hormones, and strengthening the parts of your brain linked to connection and calm.[21]

Step into Sunlight and Wellness: The Transformative Power of Walking

Walking is one of my favorite go-to recommendations for clients. It's simple, accessible for most people, and remarkably powerful for supporting overall well-being—especially when done outdoors in natural light. And when you walk with a friend, there's another layer of connection: In addition to moving your body, you're also moving emotions. Shared movement can create space for meaningful conversation. You're warming up your limbic system, and your thoughts and feelings seem to flow more easily.

Beyond its physical benefits, walking helps clear mental clutter and regulate emotions. Sunlight plays a vital role in this process, helping to recalibrate your circadian rhythms, which are essential for sleep, energy, and emotional stability. A 2019 study in *JAMA Psychiatry* found that moderate daily exercise like walking significantly reduces symptoms of depression and anxiety.[22] And with sunlight exposure comes a natural boost in vitamin D, a nutrient crucial to mood regulation and emotional resilience.

Nature built us to move, to walk, to commune. Whether you're taking a mindful stroll, enjoying a brisk walk, or engaging in a moment of connection with the natural world, walking and nature bathing are among the most accessible ways to help you to bring your inner state into balance.

Focus on What You Have, Not What's Missing

Recovery isn't just about what you leave behind; it's about what you choose to grow toward. Your attention is powerful. Whatever you dwell on, you nourish. Linger on what's missing, and you're essentially rehearsing absence, training your system to expand *that* inner state. But you can shift this. You can train yourself to focus on the *good that is there*.

Learning how to enter and sustain positive inner states, noticing when you fall out of them, and developing the skill to return is one of the most transformative practices in recovery. It's a reset you can learn and practice time and again throughout your day.

According to psychology professor Barbara Fredrickson's work on emotional flourishing, we need a ratio of about three positive emotions for every negative one in order to sustain psychological well-being and resilience and counteract our natural negativity bias. And those emotions don't have to come from grand events; they often grow out of moments of intentional appreciation, gratitude, love, and awe.[23] When you practice these inner states deliberately, you begin to interrupt the old neural grooves of despair or scarcity and create new, life-affirming pathways in your brain.

This part of your happiness is within your control. It's in your mind and in the thoughts you think. Take time every day to connect with your inner being and align yourself with the energy that creates worlds, life, fruit, human beings, animals—everything. This universe is attraction based. If you focus on what is negative, empty, or disappointing in life, the universe will hear that as you inviting more of it. But if you are grateful for the life you have, the universe will hear that as a wish to extend that state, and you will see more beauty manifest in the life you already have.

Exercise

The Resilience Timeline: Claiming Your Strength and Growth

The very fact that you've read this book to the end is proof of your resilience. No matter what has happened in your life, you have kept moving forward and growing. The following exercise will help you consolidate your gains and recognize where you marshaled your own strengths and took hold of your life.

Gather Your Materials

To begin, grab a large sheet of paper or open a blank journal page. Draw a horizontal line across the bottom of the page. This is your resilience timeline. Next, mark points at five-year intervals along this line (birth, age five, ten, fifteen, and so forth) up to your current age. You can even begin your timeline before birth if you feel you brought in ancestral strength.

Enter Periods That Helped to Build Resilience and Strength

Anywhere along your timeline, jot down key moments, mentors, or events that represent your resilience, wisdom, or growth. These could be:

- A great decision you made that led to other good choices

- A mentor, friend, relative, teacher, or pet who helped you in some way

- Something or some time where you felt great about yourself

- A glimpse of the spiritual, beauty, or goodness in life

- Strengths and grit you built by facing certain challenges

Reflect on Your Journey

On your timeline, write down phrases that elaborate on the key moments. Describe what they were, how they felt, what strengths you built, and what gains or insights you had.

Reflect on Your Timeline

As you fill in your timeline, pause at each marker and write down phrases that come up around what you've entered. Let yourself truly take in what that season of life held. On or around each point, you might ask yourself:

- What inner strength emerged in me here—even if I didn't see it then?

- Who or what steadied me, offered kindness, or gave me hope when I needed it most?

- What challenge, though difficult, helped carve depth, wisdom, or resilience into me?

- What choice or turning point am I proud of, no matter how small it seemed at the time?

- Where did I catch a glimpse of light—beauty, love, or possibility—shining through the cracks of difficulty?

Deepen With Journaling

Beneath the timeline entries, let your words spill out—phrases, images, or fuller reflections that bring these moments alive. Ask yourself:

- What did this experience reveal or teach me about who I am?

- How does the strength I found then still live in me today?

- If I could reach back to my younger self at this point, what would I say to them? What would I do with or for them?

- What thread of resilience—subtle or strong—can I trace weaving its way through my life story?

Closing Reflection

Step back and take in the whole line of your life, the mosaic of moments that make you who you are. Allow yourself to see what was always there, even if hidden:

- What recurring patterns of resourcefulness, ingenuity, hard work and creativity, or courage do I notice across the years?

- How does honoring these moments or qualities shift the way I view myself in this present moment?

- As I look forward, how do I want my resilient qualities to guide me—toward what kind of choices, relationships, and ways of living?

Conclusion

My father and I used to sit together before anyone else was awake, talking about the sky, the sun, and the taste of the food he'd prepared as we sipped café au lait in the morning light. In those small interactions was everything: God, connection, love. With him on those early mornings, I learned what it meant to love and be loved and how it felt to share my real thoughts and feelings with another human being. I learned how to be my authentic self in relation to another.

To say that losing my father broke my heart would be an understatement. His loss fragmented something in me that once felt whole. But this passage from Rumi's collection of mystical poetry the *Diwan-e Shams-e Tabrīzī* describes a different kind of wholeness. Here the Sufi poet asks his spiritual teacher Shams for guidance:

> Rumi: "What about my heart?"
> Tabrīzī: "Tell me what you hold inside it."
> Rumi: "Pain and sorrow."
> Tabrīzī: "Stay with it. The wound is the place where the Light enters you."

And it's true. I became as filled with light as I was with pain. The very place that ached the most also became something luminous. It was a mystery I can't explain. The pain of loss both carved and filled what in twelve-step programs we call "the God-shaped hole." The wound became my teacher.

Theologian Pierre Teilhard de Chardin once wrote, "We are not human beings having a spiritual experience; we are spiritual beings having a human experience." Recovery, I've come to see, is not a destination but a sacred unfolding. I have learned to use the moments that activate me, those that sting or stir something unresolved or make me freeze, as portals. They point me toward my unconscious inner states and invite me to become willing to see what wants to come from the background to the foreground, the unconscious material waiting to be felt, unpacked, and integrated.

As Carl Jung reminds us, "One does not become enlightened by imagining figures of light, but by making the darkness conscious." The shadow, that collection of disowned parts of ourselves, holds not only our wounding, but also our buried vitality. In the places we least want to look live our intuition, our creativity, our wildness, and our wisdom. There is treasure in the dark. What we turn toward with tenderness loses its grip. What we integrate becomes ours to use.

To choose life is to choose all of it: the mess and the mystery, the ache and the awe. This is the alchemy of recovery—transforming what once hurt too much to touch into the gold of wholeness. Healing isn't about becoming someone new; it's about becoming more deeply, more honestly yourself. And in that brave act of facing what we once fled, we discover relief, renewal, and a deeper capacity for wonder.

Experiential, relational, embodied therapy is not passive work. It asks you to become an active participant in your own becoming. Each time you choose presence over dissociation, connection over isolation, repair over reenactment, you carve new neural pathways—pathways leading toward a life you've never lived before. It's in these seemingly small choices that lasting change takes root.

Recovery invites you to become an observer of your inner world in all its complexity and beauty. You don't need to escape your life to heal. With the right supports—safe enough people, grounding practices, rituals of repair—even ordinary life becomes a crucible for growth. You can live it more consciously and let your path itself reveal the mysteries of life and healing that unfold for you along the way.

My hope is that through this work, you've begun to recognize and bring into compassionate awareness the unseen forces of your past—the attachment injuries and relational patterns that subtly shaped your nervous system and informed how you move through the world. That you've loosened the grip of these early imprints—those implicit memories and survival strategies that once narrowed your emotional range and kept you caught in cycles of reenactment.

In this process, you've begun cultivating the capacity to observe and regulate your internal states, to feel and integrate rather than suppress or carry unresolved pain in your mind/body. While your past has shaped your development and conditioned your patterns of protection, it does not have to dictate your future. Each moment of awareness is an opportunity to interrupt those patterns and to step more fully into presence, possibility, and choice.

There is more beauty in this world than sorrow. More possibility than despair. You are allowed your grief. You are allowed your anger. But you don't have to live there. They brought you to the threshold, but they don't have to hold you back anymore.

Life, this present moment, is where your aliveness and purpose live. You can join it at any time. The invitation is always open. This healing path isn't a one-time crossing. It's a lifelong devotion. You can walk it awake. You can walk with the intention of letting each challenge show you more of you, so you can become more whole. And you don't have to walk it alone.

If you're looking for more resources and support, you can visit my website, tiandayton.com. See you there.

Exercise

Letter of Gratitude to Yourself

Time to thank yourself. This final exercise is a chance to express gratitude toward yourself and acknowledge the effort you've made, the strength you've shown, and the resilience that you've found and nurtured inside!

Find a quiet space to sit or lie down and take a few grounding breaths. Settle into a sense of presence with the version of you who began this journey and the version of you who's sitting here now. When you feel ready, write a letter from your present self to you along the journey—a love letter, a thank-you, a moment of truth and appreciation for yourself. You might include:

- What you've learned about yourself

- What surprised you

- What you're proud of

- Moments when you kept going, even when it was hard

- The ways your perspective has shifted

- Your hopes for the road ahead

Let this letter be yours. It doesn't need to be polished or perfect. Let it come from your heart. Fold it into a journal, tuck it in a drawer, and reread it whenever you need a reminder of who you are and what you're capable of. Healing is not about perfection; it's about showing up with honesty again and again and partnering with yourself in creating the life you want to live!

Acknowledgments

Where It All Began

The ACA phenomenon grew out of a convergence of chance encounters, visionaries taking action, and the transformative alchemy of people sharing their most heartfelt truths. It was the power of an idea whose time had come.

"In the spring of 1978, I met Janet Woititz completely by chance at the Seattle airport," recalls publisher Gary Seidler. "Our luggage hadn't made the flight. As we stood flipping through laminated photos of missing suitcases, we struck up a conversation and quickly discovered we were heading to the same place—the National Council on Alcoholism's annual meeting. By the time we reached the hotel, we'd already shared stories about our work and our passion for the field of addiction. Janet told me she was writing a book about Adult Children of Alcoholics and looking for a publisher."

At the time, Seidler and his partner, Peter Vegso, had just launched Health Communications Inc. (HCI) As he listened to Janet describe her manuscript, Gary's ears immediately "perked up." He thought of Canadian social worker Margaret Cork, who had weekly brought groups of young children who were growing up with addiction by their Toronto office while researching her groundbreaking book *The Forgotten Children*.

Recognizing the same urgency and truth in Janet's work, HCI published *Adult Children of Alcoholics* in 1979—112 pages, typeset by Seidler himself and printed on their small press. "It didn't take off overnight," Seidler remembers, "but word of mouth spread. By 1982, it had reached the *New York Times* bestseller list, where it stayed for 54 weeks. People would find it in bookstores, open it, and for the first time, see themselves in print."

While that wave was building, another thread of the ACA movement was taking shape—one that would lead directly to the founding of the National Association for Children of Alcoholics (NACoA).

In November 1982, at a Betty Ford Center conference held at the Annenberg Center in California, Medical Director Joe Cruse invited Sharon Wegscheider-Cruse, Claudia Black, Cathleen Brooks, and Stephanie Brown to speak. Among the attendees was philanthropist Joan Kroc, wife of McDonald's founder Ray Kroc. Deeply moved by what she had heard, Joan wrote a note: "I'm inviting you all to the Kroc Ranch. I will cover all your expenses... and all I ask is that at the end you give me a report about what you would say to the nation if you had a forum."

In the early 1980s, Kroc had launched Operation Cork, a public education effort about alcoholism. One of its books, *The Secret Everyone Knows* by Cathleen Brooks Weiss, focused not on the alcoholic, but on the children impacted by parental addiction. This shift in lens was profound. Until this time, it was generally thought that if the addict got sober, the rest of the family would automatically be fine. We knew little about the long-term cost to the lives of children who were growing up with addiction.

Claudia Black recalls, "Cathleen called me in Laguna and said, 'Let's gather the people who've been carrying this message.' So we made lists, we made calls. We invited Robert Ackerman, Sharon Wegscheider-Cruse, Bob Subby, Herb Gravitz, Rockelle Lerner, Tim and Mary Cermak, Julie Bowden, and others. We were each doing this work in our own silos, but this was the first time we sat face to face."

As Sharon Wegscheider tells it, "We spent that whole first weekend crying—telling our stories, hearing each other's truths. It was the first time any of us had been in a room where everyone understood without needing a translation."

At the close of that first gathering, Joan Kroc said something prophetic: "I don't think you've done what I invited you here to do—but I think you have something here worth continuing to explore."

She invited them back for a second meeting. When they reconvened, the vision became clear—a national voice for children of alcoholics, later named NACoA. With no office or budget, Dr. Black and Dr. Ackerman recall those early meetings in Dr. Tim Cermak's San Francisco basement, the humble starting point of a movement that would change lives.

By then, the cultural wave was already rolling. Janet's groundbreaking book—along with those written by these other NACoA founders and given a platform through Health Communications and its partner conference arm, U.S. Journal Training—opened the floodgates, putting "Adult Children of Alcoholics" into the national vocabulary. Soon, people who hadn't grown up directly with alcoholism, but with other forms of family dysfunction, also began to identify with the characteristics of growing up with addictive and dysfunctional behaviors. Out of this awakening, the codependency movement also caught fire.

ACA and CODA (codependents anonymous) support groups began springing up everywhere. For the first time, the public understood that addiction wasn't just an individual problem—it was a family one, whose impact spread like an unbroken chain of wounds, shaping the lives of children who, without healing and recovery, would carry those injuries into the generations that followed. This is how a movement began that has been changing countless lives. And now it gains new momentum, meaning, and purpose with you!

Notes

Introduction
1. A. R. Todd, G. V. Bodenhausen, J. A. Richeson, and A. D. Galinsky, "Perspective Taking Combats Automatic Expressions of Racial Bias," *Journal of Personality and Social Psychology* 100, no. 6 (2011): 1027–42, doi.org/10.1037/a0022308.

Chapter 1: Understanding Your Past, Reclaiming Your Present
1. Gabor Maté, *The Myth of Normal: Trauma, Illness, and Healing in a Toxic Culture* (Avery, 2022).
2. National Association for Children of Addiction, *Impact of Alcohol/Opioid Use Disorder on Children*, 2025.
3. Peter Levine, endorsement for Tian Dayton, *Treating Adult Children of Relational Trauma: 85 Experiential Interventions to Heal the Inner Child and Create Authentic Connection in the Present* (PESI Publishing, 2023).
4. A. N. Schore, "Right-Brain Affect Regulation: An Essential Mechanism of Development, Trauma, Dissociation, and Psychotherapy," in *The Healing Power of Emotion: Affective Neuroscience, Development, and Clinical Practice*, ed. D. Fosha, D. J. Siegel, and M. F. Solomon (W. W. Norton, 2009), 112–44; Stephen Porges, *The Polyvagal Theory: Neurophysiological Foundations of Emotions, Attachment, Communication, and Self-Regulation* (W. W. Norton, 2011); Deb Dana, *The Polyvagal Theory in Therapy: Engaging the Rhythm of Regulation* (W. W. Norton, 2018).
5. Pete Walker, *Complex PTSD: From Surviving to Thriving* (Azure Coyote Publishing, 2013); Bessel van der Kolk, *The Body Keeps the Score: Brain, Mind, and Body in the Healing of Trauma*

(Viking, 2014); Gabor Maté, *In the Realm of Hungry Ghosts: Close Encounters with Addiction* (North Atlantic Books, 2010).

6. Maté, *In the Realm of Hungry Ghosts*; Judith Lewis Herman, *Trauma and Recovery: The Aftermath of Violence—from Domestic Abuse to Political Terror* (Basic Books, 1997).
7. Porges, *The Polyvagal Theory*; Robert Muller, *Trauma and the Struggle to Open Up: From Avoidance to Recovery and Growth* (W. W. Norton, 2018).
8. Van der Kolk, *The Body Keeps the Score*; John Briere and Catherine Scott, *Principles of Trauma Therapy: A Guide to Symptoms, Evaluation, and Treatment*, 2nd ed. (Sage Publications, 2014).
9. Herman, *Trauma and Recovery*; Peter Levine and Pat Ogden, *Trauma and the Body: A Sensorimotor Approach to Psychotherapy* (W. W. Norton, 2006).
10. Daniel Siegel, *The Developing Mind: How Relationships and the Brain Interact to Shape Who We Are*, 2nd ed. (Guilford Press, 2012); John Bowlby, *A Secure Base: Parent-Child Attachment and Healthy Human Development* (Basic Books, 1988); van der Kolk, *The Body Keeps the Score*.
11. Maté, *In the Realm of Hungry Ghosts*; Tian Dayton, *The Soul's Compass: A Guide to Navigating Life's Challenges* (Health Communications, 2021).
12. Sharon Wegscheider-Cruse, *Choice-Making* (Health Communications, 1985); P. L. Ackerman, "Motivation and Cognitive Abilities: An Integrative/Aptitude-Treatment Interaction Approach to Skill Acquisition," *Journal of Applied Psychology* 74, no. 4 (1989): 657–90; J. S. Lerner and J. B. Renshon, "Decision-Making, the Role of Emotions in Foreign Policy," in *The Encyclopedia of Peace Psychology*, ed. D. J. Christie and C. Montiel (Wiley-Blackwell, 2011), 313–17; Tian Dayton, *The Soulful Journey of Recovery: A Guide for Healing from Addiction and Trauma* (Health Communications, 2012); Julian Ford, *Treating Complex Traumatic Stress Disorders in Children and Adolescents: Scientific Foundations and Therapeutic Models* (Guilford Press, 2013).
13. Herman, *Trauma and Recovery*; Dayton, *The Soulful Journey of Recovery*; Walker, *Complex PTSD*.

14. Amir Levine and Rachel Heller, *Attached: The New Science of Adult Attachment and How It Can Help You Find—and Keep—Love* (TarcherPerigee, 2010); Allan Schore, *Affect Dysregulation and Disorders of the Self* (W. W. Norton, 2003).
15. Van der Kolk, *The Body Keeps the Score*; Peter Levine, *Waking the Tiger: Healing Trauma* (North Atlantic Books, 1997); Dayton, *The Soulful Journey of Recovery*; Wegscheider-Cruse, *Choice-Making*; Claudia Black, *It Will Never Happen to Me: Growing Up with Addiction as Youngsters, Adolescents, and Adults* (Ballantine Books, 2001).
16. Briere and Scott, *Principles of Trauma Therapy*; Muller, *Trauma and the Struggle to Open Up*.
17. Porges, *The Polyvagal Theory*; Dana, *The Polyvagal Theory in Therapy*; Herman, *Trauma and Recovery*.
18. Herman, *Trauma and Recovery*; Jerry Moe, *Understanding Addiction and Recovery Through a Child's Eyes: Hope, Help, and Healing for Families* (Health Communications, 2007); Maté, *In the Realm of Hungry Ghosts*.
19. Jerry Moe, *Understanding Addiction and Recovery Through a Child's Eyes: Hope, Help, and Healing for Families* (Health Communications, 2007); Diana Fosha, Daniel Siegel, and Marion Solomon, eds., *The Healing Power of Emotion: Affective Neuroscience, Development, and Clinical Practice* (W. W. Norton, 2009), 112–44.
20. Dayton, *The Soul's Compass*.
21. Maté, *In the Realm of Hungry Ghosts*.
22. R. G. Tedeschi and L. G. Calhoun, "Posttraumatic Growth: Conceptual Foundations and Empirical Evidence," *Psychological Inquiry* 15, no. 1 (2004): 1–18.
23. Siegel, *The Developing Mind*.
24. Dayton, *The Soulful Journey of Recovery*.
25. Sybil Wolin and Steven Wolin, *The Resilient Self: How Survivors of Troubled Families Rise Above Adversity* (Villard Books, 1993).
26. Dayton, *The Soulful Journey of Recovery*; Wolin and Wolin, *The Resilient Self*.
27. Black, *It Will Never Happen to Me*; Pia Mellody, Andrea Wells Miller, and J. Keith Miller, *Facing Codependence: What It Is, Where It Comes from, How It Sabotages Our Lives* (Harper & Row, 1989).

28. Dayton, *The Soul's Compass*; Robert Ackerman, *Children of Alcoholics: A Guidebook for Educators, Therapists, and Parents* (Simon & Schuster, 1986); Sharon Wegscheider-Cruse, *Another Chance: Hope and Health for the Alcoholic Family* (Science and Behavior Books, 1989).
29. Dayton, *The Soul's Compass*; Janet Woititz, *Adult Children of Alcoholics* (Health Communications, 1983).
30. Herman, *Trauma and Recovery*.
31. Dana, *The Polyvagal Theory in Therapy*.
32. R. G. Tedeschi and L. G. Calhoun, "Posttraumatic Growth."
33. Dayton, *The Soul's Compass*; Viktor Frankl, *Man's Search for Meaning: An Introduction to Logotherapy* (Beacon Press, 1959); Porges, *The Polyvagal Theory*.

Chapter 2: What the Body Remembers

1. Ernest Hemingway, *A Farewell to Arms* (Charles Scribner's Sons, 1929).
2. V. J. Felitti et al., "Relationship of Childhood Abuse and Household Dysfunction to Many of the Leading Causes of Death in Adults: The Adverse Childhood Experiences (ACE) Study," *American Journal of Preventive Medicine* 14, no. 4 (1998): 245–58, doi.org/10.1016/S0749-3797(98)00017-8.

Chapter 3: Attachment Patterns

1. Allan Schore, "Minds in the Making: Attachment, the Self-Organizing Brain, and Developmentally Oriented Psychoanalytic Psychotherapy," *British Journal of Psychotherapy* 17, no. 3 (2001): 202.
2. Mary Main and Judith Solomon, "Discovery of a New, Insecure-Disorganized/Disoriented Attachment Pattern," in *Attachment Theory: Social, Developmental, and Clinical Perspectives*, ed. Susan Goldberg, Roy Muir, and John Kerr (Analytic Press, 1995), 95–140.
3. Mary Main, "The Organized Categories of Infant, Child, and Adult Attachment: Flexible vs. Inflexible Attention Under Attachment-Related Stress," *Journal of the American Psychoanalytic Association* 48, no. 4 (2002): 1055–96, doi.org/10.1177/0003065102048004180.
4. Levine and Heller, *Attached*.

Chapter 4: Survival Roles
1. Wegscheider-Cruse, *Another Chance*.

Chapter 6: Triggers as Teachable Moments
1. Deb Dana, personal communication with the author.

Chapter 7: Process Addictions
1. K. C. Berridge and T. E. Robinson, "The Neural Basis of Drug Craving: An Incentive-Sensitization Theory of Addiction." *Brain Research Reviews* 18, no. 3 (1993): 247–291.
2. K. C. Berridge and T. E. Robinson, "Liking, Wanting, and the Incentive-Sensitization Theory of Addiction," *American Psychologist* 71, no. 8 (2016): 670–679.
3. Robert Anda et al., "Relationship of Childhood Abuse and Household Dysfunction to Many of the Leading Causes of Death in Adults: The Adverse Childhood Experiences (ACE) Study," *American Journal of Preventive Medicine* 14, no. 4 (1998): 245–58.
4. Ibid.
5. Aimie Apigian, *The Biology of Trauma: How the Body Holds Fear, Pain, and Overwhelm, and How to Heal It* (BenBella Books, 2025).
6. Peter Levine, *In an Unspoken Voice: How the Body Releases Trauma and Restores Goodness* (North Atlantic Books, 2010).
7. Ibid.
8. Mazen Kheirbek, Mazen Kheirbek, PhD, Professor, Department of Psychiatry and Behavioral Sciences, University of California, San Francisco.
9. K. I. Erickson, C. M. Stillman, and S. D. Donofry, "Physical Activity, Fitness, and the Aging Brain: Structural and Functional Correlates" *Nature Reviews Neuroscience* 25, no. 3 (2024): 129–45.
10. Fernandes de Sousa et al., "Physical Activity and Neuroplasticity in Neurodegenerative Disorders: Mind–Body Practices," *Brain Plasticity* 6, no. 2 (2020): 123–42.
11. M. Wang et al., "Effects of Tai Chi on Anxiety and Theta Oscillation Power in College Students During the COVID-19 Pandemic: A Randomized Controlled Trial," *PLOS One* 19, no. 11 (2024): e0312804, doi.org/10.1371/journal.pone.0312804.

12. Park, B.-J., Tsunetsugu, Y., Kasetani, T., Kagawa, T., & Miyazaki, Y. (2010). The physiological effects of *Shinrin-yoku* (taking in the forest atmosphere or forest bathing): Evidence from field experiments in 24 forests across Japan. Environmental Health and Preventive Medicine, 15(1), 18–26.
13. J. A. Blumenthal et al., "Study: Exercise Has Long-Lasting Effect on Depression," *Duke University Today*, September 24, 2000.
14. F. B. Schuch et al., "Physical Activity and Incident Depression: A Meta-analysis of Prospective Cohort Studies," *American Journal of Psychiatry* 175, no. 7 (2018): 631–48, doi.org/10.1176/appi.ajp.2018.17111194.
15. Blumenthal et al., "Exercise Has Long-Lasting Effect"; ibid.
16. Mihaly Csikszentmihalyi, *Flow: The Psychology of Optimal Experience* (Harper & Row, 1990).

Chapter 8: The Healing Power of Grief
1. J. L. Moreno, *Psychodrama*, vol. 1 (Beacon House, 1946).
2. Woititz, *Adult Children of Alcoholics*.

Chapter 9: A Sanctuary for Self
1. Siegel, D. J. (2020). *The Developing Mind: How Relationships and the Brain Interact to Shape Who We Are* (3rd ed.). Guilford Press.
2. Wolin and Wolin, *The Resilient Self*.

Chapter 10: Spiritual Transformation and Post-Traumatic Growth
1. R. G. Tedeschi and L. G. Calhoun, "Posttraumatic Growth."
2. Wolin and Wolin, *The Resilient Self*.
3. Matthew Lieberman, *Social: Why Our Brains Are Wired to Connect* (Crown Publishers, 2013).
4. Norman Cousins, *Dr. Schweitzer of Lambaréné* (Harper & Brothers, 1960), 221.
5. Esther Perel, *Mating in Captivity: Unlocking Erotic Intelligence* (Harper Perennial, 2006).
6. Joseph Campbell, *The Power of Myth* (Vintage, 1991).

7. M. A. Argentieri et al., "Environmental and Lifestyle Factors Outweigh Genetic Influences on Health Outcomes: A UK Biobank Study," *Nature Medicine* (2025).
8. World Health Organization, *Social Determinants of Mental Health*, 2014, apps.who.int/iris/bitstream/handle/10665/112828/9789241506809_eng.pdf; American Psychological Association Working Group, *Stress and Health Disparities*, 2017, apa.org/pi/health-disparities/resources/stress-report.pdf; Urban Institute, *How Are Income and Wealth Linked to Health and Longevity?*, April 2015, urban.org/sites/default/files/publication/49116/2000178-How-are-Income-and-Wealth-Linked-to-Health-and-Longevity.pdf; Carly Smith, "How Social Connection Supports Longevity," Stanford Center on Longevity, December 18, 2023, longevity.stanford.edu/lifestyle/2023/12/18/how-social-connection-supports-longevity/.
9. Harvard University Human Flourishing Program, "Global Flourishing Study," April 30, 2025, hfh.fas.harvard.edu/global-flourishing-study.
10. Irvin Yalom and Molyn Leszcz, *The Theory and Practice of Group Psychotherapy*, 6th ed. (Basic Books, 2020).
11. F. B. Schuch et al., "Physical Activity and Incident Depression."
12. A. N. Goldstein and M. P. Walker, "The Role of Sleep in Emotional Brain Function," *Annual Review of Clinical Psychology* 10 (2014): 679–708; M. M. Menz et al., "The Role of Sleep and Sleep Deprivation in Consolidating Fear Memories," *NeuroImage* 75 (2013): 87–96; S. S. Yoo et al., "The Human Emotional Brain Without Sleep: A Prefrontal Amygdala Disconnect," *Current Biology* 17, no. 20 (2007): R877–78; M. O. Harrington et al., "Sleep Deprivation Impairs Suppression of Unwanted Memories," *Proceedings of the National Academy of Sciences*, 2025.
13. J. Sarris et al., "Nutritional Medicine as Mainstream in Psychiatry," *The Lancet Psychiatry* 2, no. 3 (2015): 271–74.
14. G. Tabibnia, "The Positive Psychology of Persistence and Flexibility: The Role of Dopamine and Its Implications for Resilience," *Current Opinion in Behavioral Sciences* 35 (2020): 76–82.
15. M. R. Chowdhury, "The Neuroscience of Gratitude and Effects on the Brain," *PositivePsychology*, April 9, 2019, positivepsychology

.com/neuroscience-of-gratitude/; UC Davis Health, "Gratitude and Its Impact on Health," *Wellness News*, issue 49, November 2019, health.ucdavis.edu/nursing/academics/studentwellness/pdfs/BIMSON_Newsletter-November_2019.pdf.

16. Mihaly Csikszentmihalyi, *Flow: The Psychology of Optimal Experience* (Harper & Row, 1990).

17. James Pennebaker, *Opening Up: The Healing Power of Expressing Emotions* (Guilford Press, 1997).

18. K. A. Baikie and K. Wilhelm, "Emotional and Physical Health Benefits of Expressive Writing," *Advances in Psychiatric Treatment 11*, no. 5 (2005): 338–46.

19. G. N. Bratman et al., "Nature Experience Reduces Rumination and Subgenual Prefrontal Cortex Activation," *Proceedings of the National Academy of Sciences* 112, no. 28 (2015): 8567–72, doi.org/10.1073/pnas.1510459112.

20. M. P. White et al., "Spending at Least 120 Minutes a Week in Nature Is Associated with Good Health and Wellbeing," *Scientific Reports* 9 (2019): article 7730, doi.org/10.1038/s41598-019-44097-3.

21. Bratman et al., "Nature Experience Reduces Rumination."

22. K. W. Choi et al., "Assessment of Bidirectional Relationships Between Physical Activity and Depression among Adults: A 2-Sample Mendelian Randomization Study," *JAMA Psychiatry* 76, no. 4 (2019): 399–408, doi.org/10.1001/jamapsychiatry.2018.4175.

23. B. L. Fredrickson and M. F. Losada, "Positive Affect and the Complex Dynamics of Human Flourishing," *American Psychologist* 60, no. 7 (2005): 678–86.

Index

activation (feeling activated), 148–49
addiction, 109, 162–63
    see also process addictions
Adult Children of Alcoholics (Woititz), 36
adult children of an alcoholic or addict (ACAs), 1–3, 10–11
    GCoAs (grandchildren of addicts), 8–9, 172–74
    sexual abuse, 168–72
    shadow boundaries, 204–12
    statistics, 25
Adverse Childhood Experiences (ACE) study, 53–54, 167–68
Ainsworth, Mary, 68
anxiety, 37, 46, 116, 193
    exercise, 238
    reflective journaling, 242
    sleep deprivation, 239
attachment, 58, 64–67
    attachment styles, 68–69; anxious/ambivalent, 68–72, 81; avoidant, 69, 72–73, 75–82; disorganized, 69, 73–74, 82–83; secure, 68, 70
    attachment styles and work, 83–86
    attachment styles and parenting, 74–75
    attachment styles quiz/questionnaire, 69
    attachment theory, 68–69
    earned secure attachment, 70
    projection, 86–88
    Still-Face experiment, 65
    Strange Situation experiment, 68
attunement, 40, 58, 60, 65–66

body memories, 45–47
boundaries, 202–24
    codependency, 205–6
    friendship boundaries, 222
    healthy boundaries, 214–24; inner child safety, 215–17; physical distance (magic two-hundred-mile radius), 215
    integration, 202
    intimate relationship boundaries, 222–23
    learning to set boundaries in five stages, 217–21
    listening to your body, 203–4
    parenting boundaries, 223–24
    shadow boundaries, 204–12; boundary enforcement through fear, punishment, or abuse, 210; boundary evasion through humor, deflection, or shame, 211; emotional blackmail or secrecy, 209; gaslighting, 209; pretend normal boundaries;

proxy boundaries, 207; role-based boundaries: false-self functioning, 211; silent control (withholding), 208–9; weaponized boundaries, 210

workplace boundaries, 221–22

Bowlby, John, 68

brain
- amygdala, 49, 65, 114, 239
- brain functioning during traumatic events, 45–46, 49–50
- constructing reality, 144
- neuroplasticity and creating new patterns, 203
- *Social: Why Our Brains Are Wired to Connect* (Lieberman), 229

Campbell, Joseph, 234

catastrophizing, 116, 129–30, 133, 138

codependency, 30–35, 205–6
- egocentricity of childhood, 31
- traits, 33–35
- *see also* cognitive and somatic distortions and biases

cognitive and somatic distortions and biases, 112–41
- changing cognitive distortions or biases, 124–26
- cognitive distortions or biases at work, 137
- cognitive distortions or biases in daily life, 128
- cognitive distortions or biases in friendship, 138–39
- cognitive distortions or biases in parenting, 132–36; comparing your child to others or yourself, 134; fixing instead of feeling, 133–34; ignoring your own needs, 135–36; living through your child's successes or struggles, 134–35; overexplaining and rationalizing, 135; overprotecting versus underprotecting, 132–33; perfectionism, 133; personalizing your child's pain, 132
- cognitive distortions or biases in romantic relationships, 129–31
- *see also* cognitive distortions

cognitive distortions
- all-or-nothing/black-and-white thinking, 114–15, 129, 132, 137
- catastrophizing, 116, 129–30, 133, 138
- confirmation bias, 122–24
- control fallacy/overresponsibility, 121–22, 138
- discounting the positive, 121, 134
- emotional or intense reasoning, 115–16, 130, 138
- fallacy of fairness, 122
- labeling, 119–20
- mental filtering, 134, 137–38
- mind reading, 120, 138
- minimization, 118
- overgeneralization, 119
- personalization, 117, 130, 132, 134, 138; shifting blame, 116–17
- "should" statements, 118–19
- mental shortcuts, 113
- survival mode, 113

complex post-traumatic stress disorder (cPTSD), 3, 35
- emotional and psychological symptoms, 36–39
- healing, 5–7, 17–20
- making stuff up, 7–8
- myth of thinking yourself better, 50–53

resilience, 5–7, 39–42, 232, 245–47
Trauma and Recovery (Herman), 35–36
see also post-traumatic growth; post-traumatic stress disorder; relational trauma; Relational Trauma Repair

confirmation bias, 122–24

Disenfranchised Grief: Recognizing Hidden Sorrow (Doka)

exercises
- Dialogue with Your Body, 60–62
- Exploring Your Process Addictions, 176–78
- Feeling Floor Check, 42–43
- Frozen in Time, 110–11
- Gathering the Pieces of My Story, 196–97
- How Shadow Boundaries Live On, 212–14
- Listening to the Story in Your Body, 126–28
- Mapping Your Unseen Family Dynamics, 107–9
- Owning Your Side of a Conflict: Giving Voice to Your Activated Self, 157–61
- Recognizing and Voicing Disenfranchised Grief, 192
- Resilience Timeline: Claiming Your Strength and Growth, 245–47
- Role-based Letter Writing, 88–89
- Unpacking Your Childhood Story, 139–41
- Using Triggers as Windows into Your Unconscious, 147–48
- The V of Choice: Play It Through to the End, 229–31
- Walking the V: Writing your Soliloquy for Self-Regulation, 155–57
- What Are Your Roles?, 102–3
- What Is My Behavior Trying to Tell Me?, 194–95
- When Old Wounds Meet New Moments: Separating My Story from Theirs, 199–201

family dynamics
- addiction, 109
- alliances, 105–6
- compartmentalization, 104–5
- disengagement, 104
- divides and factions, 105
- family survival roles, 91–94; the addict, 95–96; the hero, 99; the lost child, 98–99; the mascot, 100; the scapegoat, 97; the symptom bearer, 98; the whistleblower, 100–1
- family sculpting, 12
- triangulation, 106–7
- unconscious family dynamics, 103–4; enmeshment, 103; parentification and spousification, 103

see also attachment; cognitive and somatic distortions and biases

flow state, 180–81, 241

gaslighting, 209, 213
Global Flourishing Study, 236
grandchildren of addicts (GCoAs), 8–9, 172–74
see also adult children of an alcoholic or addict (ACAs)
gratitude, 240–41, 250–51
grief, 184–201
  ACA grief, 188–91, 195–96

grief (*continued*)
  age correspondence grief reaction, 197–201
  disenfranchised grief, 188–91
  Disenfranchised Grief: Recognizing Hidden Sorrow (Doka), 188
  psychodrama, 186–87
  signs and symptoms of unresolved grief, 192–94

health risks, 235–36
Herman, Judith, 35–36
hypervigilance, 4, 6, 22, 32–34, 37, 46, 84

identity protection, 123

Jung, Carl, 145, 249

Levine, Amir, 70
Levine, Peter, 28, 174–75
Lieberman, Matthew, 229
lifestyle choices and health risks, 235

Maté, Gabor, 203
Moreno, J. L. and Zerka, 12–14, 186

nature time, 242–43
neuroception, 10, 58–60, 94
nutrition, 239–40

panic attacks, 47
parenting, distortions and biases, 132–36
  comparing your child to others or yourself, 134
  fixing instead of feeling, 133–34
  ignoring your own needs, 135–36
  living through your child's successes or struggles, 134–35
  overexplaining and rationalizing, 135
  overprotecting versus underprotecting, 132–33
  perfectionism, 133
  personalizing your child's pain, 132
Perel, Esther, 232
perfectionism, 99, 133
polyvagal theory, 10, 64, 144
Porges, Stephen, 10–11
post-traumatic growth, 226–47
  blocks on the path, 228–29
  Challenge Model, 228
  choosing life, 234–35
  creative expression, 241–42
  exercise, 238
  flow state, 180–81, 241
  gratitude, 240–41, 250–51
  Holocaust survivors, 232
  journaling, 242
  lifestyle choices, 235–36
  mind and spirit sustenance, 240
  nature time, 242–43
  nutrition, 239–40
  positive emotions and inner states, 244
  recovery supports (connection and community), 236; therapy, 237–38; twelve-step programs and support groups, 237
  Resilience Timeline: Claiming Your Strength and Growth (exercise), 245–47
  sleep and leisure time, 238–39
  survivor's pride, 228
  The V of Choice: Play It Through to the End (exercise), 229–31
post-traumatic stress disorder, 35

brain functioning during traumatic events, 45–46, 49–50
post-traumatic reaction, 47–50; collapsing of time, 48–50
see also complex post-traumatic stress disorder

process addictions, 162–83
Adverse Childhood Experiences (ACE) Study, 53–54, 167–68
body's role in process addictions (somatic connections), 174–76
common process addictions, 165–67
dopamine, 162–64, 178, 181–82, 240
downregulating, 164
flow state activities, 180–81, 241
incentive salience, 164
intergenerational impact, 172–74
motivational importance, 164
sexual abuse, 168–72
understanding and compassion for yourself, 165
walking and movement as medicine, 178–80

psychodrama, 12–13, 28–30, 53, 55–58, 229
allowing the inner child to show their story, 55–58
grieving, 186–87
role-play, 60, 63
see also Relational Trauma Repair

recovery. *See* post-traumatic growth

relational reliving, 149–50

relational trauma, 21–42, 229
codependency, 30–35
emotional and psychological symptoms, 36–39
see also Relational Trauma Repair

Relational Trauma Repair (RTR), 12–17
embodied healing, 26–28
embodied role-play, 14
floor checks, 15–16, 26; feeling floor check exercise, 42–43
role reversal, 15
sculpting, 17
social atom, 17
timelines, 16; attachment wound timelines, 16; resilience timelines, 16; trauma timelines, 16
see also psychodrama, relational trauma

resilience, 5–7, 39–42, 232, 245–47

role-play, 14, 60, 63

Satir, Virginia, 12
Schweitzer, Albert, 232
sexual abuse, 168–72
shame, 25, 34, 36–37, 120, 194
Siegel, Daniel, 202
sleep and leisure time, 238–39
Social: Why Our Brains Are Wired to Connect (Lieberman), 229
sociometry, 14
Somatic Experiencing work, 28

trauma, 146
unconscious body memories, 45
unresolved trauma, 45–46
act hungers, 47
disassociation, 47
emotional flooding, 47
open tensions, 47
panic attacks, 47
physical manifestations of, 46–47

unresolved trauma (*continued*)
   relational reenactments, 47
   relational reliving, 149–50
   see also cognitive and somatic distortions and biases; complex post-traumatic stress disorder; relational trauma; Relational Trauma Repair

Trauma and Recovery (Herman), 35–36

triggers, 142–61
   brain constructing reality, 144
   owning it, 153–54, 157–61
   past meets present, 145
   perception narrowing, 146
   reacting automatically, 146–47
   relational reliving, 149–50
   "state creates story," 144–45
   trigger versus activation, 148–49
   triggers as chances to heal unresolved wounds, 153–54, 157–61
   window into your unconscious, 147–48

Tronick, Ed, 65

van der Kolk, Bessel, 36, 187

walking and movement as medicine, 178–80, 243–44

Wegscheider-Cruse, Sharon, 12

When the Body Says No (Maté), 204

Woititz, Janet, 36, 195

About the Author

For more than thirty years, Dr. Tian Dayton, MA, PhD, TEP, has been has been a leading voice in the fields of trauma healing, addiction recovery, and experiential, embodied therapy. A clinical psychologist, licensed creative arts therapist, and certified trainer in psychodrama and sociometry, with a master's in educational psychology she is a Senior Fellow at The Meadows and the author of over fifteen acclaimed books including *Growing Up with Addiction*, *Treating Adult Children of Relational Trauma*, *The ACoA Trauma Syndrome*, *Sociometrics*, *Emotional Sobriety*, *Forgiving and Moving On*, and *Trauma and Addiction*.

Her pioneering work integrates psychodrama, sociometry, and nervous system-informed approaches into a cohesive model Relational Trauma Repair (RTR) used by therapists and treatment centers across the world. As a Fellow of the American Society of Psychodrama, Sociometry, and Group Psychotherapy, she has received their highest honors, including the Lifetime Achievement Award, the Scholar's Award, President's Award, and Gratitude Award. She also served for eight years as Editor-in-Chief of the *Journal of Psychodrama, Sociometry, and Group Psychotherapy*. She is on the scientific board of The National Association of Children of Alcoholics, (NACoA). In the addictions field, her contributions have been recognized with The Martie Mann Award, The Mona Mansell Award, and The Ackermann Black Award.

Dr. Dayton's work is widely respected in both academic and clinical settings, as well as in the public sphere. She has been a guest expert on NBC, CNN, MSNBC, and other national platforms, and is a frequent speaker at leading conferences and on podcasts on trauma, ACAs, mental health, and recovery. Her work is the subject of the docudrama *The Process*.

To learn more about her work, visit tiandayton.com.

About Sounds True Books

Sounds True was founded in 1985 by Tami Simon with a clear mandate: to disseminate spiritual wisdom. Since starting out as a project with one woman and her tape recorder, Sounds True has grown into a mission-driven learning and media company, partnering with many of the leading wisdom teachers and visionaries of our time.

Every Sounds True Book is designed to not only provide information to a reader but to also to embody the quality of a wisdom transmission, unlocking our greatest capacities to love, serve, and uplift others.

Sounds True Books are part of St. Martin's Essentials, an imprint of Macmillan Publishers.